In Uncle Sam's Service

In Uncle Sam's Service

WOMEN WORKERS WITH THE

AMERICAN EXPEDITIONARY FORCE,

1917–1919

SUSAN ZEIGER

Cornell University Press

ITHACA AND LONDON

First published 1999 by Cornell University Press

Printed in the United States of America

Library of Congress Cataloging-in-Publication Data

Zeiger, Susan, 1959–
   In Uncle Sam's service : women workers with the American Expeditionary Force, 1917–1919 / Susan Zeiger.
      p. cm.
   Originally presented as the author's thesis (Ph. D.)—New York University, 1991.
   Includes bibliographical references (p.) and index.
   ISBN 0-8014-3166-2
   1. World War, 1939–1945—Women—United States.   2. United States—Armed Forces—History—World War, 1939–1945.   3. World War, 1939–1945—United States. I. Title.
   D810.W7Z36 1999
   940.4′0082—dc21   99-41300
                                             CIP

Cloth printing   10 9 8 7 6 5 4 3 2 1

For Jeffrey,
And for our sons,
Daniel and Micah.

Contents

[vii]

Acknowledgments

Many wonderful and knowledgeable archivists helped me to make my way through the vast records of the American war effort. Michael Knapp and William Lind were my untiring and good-humored guides at the National Archives, Military Research Division. Early in my research, Andrea Hinding made accessible the crucial collections of the Y.M.C.A. of the U.S.A. Archives in Minnesota, with the assistance of David Carmichael; Andrea also graciously answered a series of questions in the final stages of the project. An Advanced Research Fellowship award from the U.S. Army Military History Institute enabled me to use the unique resources of their World War I survey and their photographic archives. Elizabeth Norris of the YWCA National Board Archives introduced me to numerous valuable sources. Thanks also to the staffs of the Salvation Army Archives and Research Center, the American Jewish Historical Society, the Nursing Archives of Boston University, the Arthur and Elizabeth Schlesinger Library on the History of Women in America, the Illinois State Historical Society, the Minnesota State Historical Society, the Maine State Library, the Massachusetts Historical Society, the Cornell University Library, the Countway Library Rare Book Collection at Harvard University, the Boston Public Library Rare Book Collection, the New York Public Library Research Branch, the Princeton University Archives, and the Petersham (Massachusetts) Historical Society.

It was my privilege to interview three extraordinary women, veterans of the Great War: Alma Bloom, Ethel Pierce, and Josephine Davis Gray. These conversations were the highlight of my research experience and deepened my understanding of women's war experience in many ways. The network of women veterans in the Women's Overseas Service League helped me to locate people and resources. Mark Hough, an attorney who assisted female Signal Corps veterans in their campaign for military status, also generously shared his experiences and records.

My warm gratitude also to the teachers and friends who trained me and sustained me at New York University. Susan Ware was in every way an ideal mentor; I am more grateful than I can say for her friendship, for her meticulous comments, and for her sustained interest in this work. This book began as a history dissertation at New York University; the Graduate School of Arts and Sciences was generous in its support, including a crucial dissertation research grant. Daniel Walkowitz, Paul Mattingly, Marilyn Young, and Thomas Bender read the dissertation in its entirety, and their comments, suggestions, and occasional objections were invaluable. An exceptional group of graduate school colleagues listened to and helped me clarify my ideas, notably Annelise Orleck, Adina Back, Patrick Kelly, Barbara Balliet, Susan Yohn, and Jean Houck. Patrick Kelly and Adina Back read and critiqued substantial portions of the book and helped to keep me focused on the big ideas.

The book is far better for the incisive comments of three anonymous readers from Cornell University Press. Many thanks to the patient and agreeable Peter Agree, acquisitions editor at Cornell University Press, and his accommodating staff. Special thanks also to the staff of Textbook Writers Associates, especially to my excellent project manager, Betty Barrer. The ever-brilliant Sonya Michel helped me to work through a number of key ideas along the way. Susan Reverby, Nancy Tomes, and Karla Goldman rendered valuable advice at important moments. Administration and faculty colleagues at Regis College provided support and encouragement, most notably S. Leila Hogan, academic dean, and S. Catherine Meade, history chair. My student, Genevieve Dybka Longtin, was a tenacious and intelligent research assistant. Holly Fossel provided flawless and friendly computer programming. I owe a special thanks to Grey Osterud, friend, colleague, and editor; no word properly describes her role in this book, so, by analogy, I thank her for being its midwife.

My final and deepest gratitude is to the friends and family who continued to be encouraging as the years turned into a decade; a collective hug to all, with my beloved parents, Herbert and Hanna Zeiger, at the center. The wonderful people who helped to teach and care for my children were essential; special thanks to Mary Ann Ohlbash and Paula Langley and to the teachers of the Arlington Children's Center and A Place to Grow. My husband Jeffrey Katz has shared everything about my life, including this book, for many years. To him, and to our beautiful sons, it is most humbly and lovingly dedicated.

In Uncle Sam's Service

Introduction

On a spring Sunday, May 6, 1917, a crowd was gathered at Saint Paul's Cathedral in Boston to honor the commonwealth's first soldiers. The Harvard Unit, Base Hospital No. 5, had been called into service in France just a week before. Public excitement was heightened by news that either Harvard or Cleveland (home to the Secretary of War) would be the first American unit to plant its flag on French soil. All the seats in Saint Paul's, one of the city's leading churches, had been taken early that morning, and spectators spilled down the steps and onto Tremont Street. Newspaper accounts pointed out the distinguished guests who filled the pews inside, including Governor McCall, Mayor Curley, President Lowell of Harvard, and the Reverend Endicott Peabody.

The ceremony to dedicate the unit was impressive and solemn, a ritual of war and nation with the parts distributed according to an ancient script of power and masculinity. The climax came with a tableau lighted from behind by the towering stained glass window: three young men in olive drab uniforms stood with the flag to receive the blessing of the bishop, dressed in scarlet and white. "Teach our hands to war and our fingers to fight against all who would take from us our fathers' heritage of freedom," Bishop Lawrence intoned. At the conclusion of the invocation, the choir burst forth with the national anthem, and the audience rose to its feet. Upstairs in the balcony, the women were crying, noted the reporter for the *Boston Herald*.[1]

Strikingly absent from all newspaper accounts of this event was the information that one-third or more of the "departing soldiers" seated in the church that morning were women.[2] Dressed in uniform and drilled for marching, sixty-five nurses and three clerical workers were bound for the front as members of U.S. Army Base Hospital No. 5. "Doctors, Nurses and Enlisted Men Bidden Godspeed at the Catholic Church of St. Paul," read the sub-headline in the *Boston Daily Globe*, but the text made no mention of the nurses. The *Boston Herald* referred to nurses only in passing.

Yet, the presence of the women, although unacknowledged, marked an irrevocable shift in the meaning and practice of war in the United States.

World War I was the first U.S. war in which women were mobilized on a large scale by the armed services.[3] At least sixteen thousand five hundred women served overseas under the auspices of the American Expeditionary Force (AEF) as members of the army, as civilian employees of the army, or as employees of the official welfare agencies working with the army in France.[4] Stateside, more than twelve thousand women enlisted in the Navy and the Marine Corps, and tens of thousands of civilian women were employed in army offices and hospitals. Overseas, women worked for the AEF in a wide range of occupations, including automobile and ambulance drivers, bacteriologists, dietitians, and librarians. But most served the AEF as nurses, canteen workers, clerical workers, and telephone operators.

If some aspects of women's service in World War I have been rendered invisible, others are thoroughly familiar. Images of female ambulance drivers, hospital volunteers, and canteen workers are part of the collective Anglo-American memory of the Great War. *Red Triangle Girl in France, Canteening Overseas,* and dozens of other memoirs by upper-class women who volunteered at the front were published during the war years, sometimes with private funds; such accounts were intended to promote a patriotic, nationalist view of the war.[5] In popular culture, too, the wealthy American girl who finds her democratic identity through wartime service was a stock character of magazines, fiction, and film.[6] Women's daily work at the front was presented in these accounts as glamorous but essentially frivolous. Their real contribution to the war was understood to be ideological: to strengthen the nation's patriotic resolve, to serve as a role model for other women, and even to symbolize the generosity and idealism of America's errand to Europe. This view of women's wartime service, constructed quite purposefully during the war to serve American nationalist interests, has been adopted by historians essentially without examination in most studies of the First World War.[7]

My purpose here is not to uncover a previously unknown aspect of women's history but rather to reinterpret a familiar story. By examining new sources—personnel records and army files, oral histories, and veterans' questionnaires—I shift the focus of investigations of women's service in the First World War. Wealthy women volunteers are certainly part of this story, not least because the glamorized popular image that elite women helped to define was a powerful force, shaping and influencing the context of all women's wartime service. Yet, the vast majority of AEF servicewomen were wage earners, white, literate, lower-middle-class, and often self-supporting. These women's experiences belong at the center, not the margins, of the examination of women's service overseas in the First World War.

Starting from this new vantage point, one crucial context for understanding women's service in World War I is the history of women's employment in the early twentieth century. Economic growth and corporate expansion during this period profoundly altered the structure of the U.S. economy. New fields of skilled employment were opened up, and native-born, educated women found their labor in demand. Expanded job opportunities for women went hand-in-hand with increased sex segregation in employment and with the maintenance of sex-linked wage differentials. Female wage earners began to dominate such emerging service occupations as telephone operation, typing, and stenography, as well as the "female professions" of teaching and nursing. It was this pool of "white-collar" (or "pink-collar") women, employed primarily in sex-segregated occupations and paid about one-half of the average male wage, that supplied tens of thousands of female workers for the armed services.

These economic developments had a similarly profound impact on the conduct of war during the early twentieth century. Corporate and managerial innovations in communication, finance, personnel, health care, social service, research, and technology revolutionized the organization of armies. New occupations—such as typing and telephone operation—became part of the fabric of the modernized military beginning with the First World War, and emerging professions—such as nursing—gained new prestige within the armed services. "Women's work," far from being frivolous, was now defined as essential to the war effort, and the U.S. military found itself in the uncomfortable position of being dependent on female labor to meet the structural needs of the war economy. Ironically, then, it was the logic of sex segregation in the civilian economy that compelled the U.S. government to grant women entry into the armed services, the ultimate masculine preserve.

Yet, women's work at the front was much more than a simple extension of their participation in the civilian labor force. It was also military or quasi-military service and therefore had profound implications for a society grappling with questions about the nature of women and their place in the public life of the nation, in wartime and peacetime. The idea of military service for women was at least potentially disruptive, for it went against the grain of deeply held beliefs about gender difference and proper gender roles, which rested on the assumption of female subservience and dependency on one hand and male "protection" on the other. The government needed women to fight the war, just as it needed men, undermining female dependency and holding out the possibility of emancipation for women. Furthermore, women's military service posed a challenge to the gender status quo at the very moment at which it was under intense assault by the woman suffrage movement. The army, like the voting booth, was a preserve of male power, autonomy, and control: both were masculine institutions, carefully protected by law and tradition, based on male camaraderie and the exclusion of women; both were defining features of citizenship, representing the privileges and the burdens of civic participation.[8]

These issues point to a second crucial context for interpreting women's service in World War I: new understandings of the role played by war in the social construction of gender. In recent years a rich literature on gender and war has emerged in a wide variety of disciplines, most notably in literary theory, philosophy, history, sociology, and political science.[9] One critical insight emerging from this body of work is that "war must be understood as a *gendering* activity," in other words, that war marks and defines gender identity, creating dichotomies of masculine/feminine, soldier/mother, home front/war front that give shape to relationships of power.[10] The images with which this book began—women weeping on the balcony, uniformed men marching off to fight for them—are much more than a snapshot from U.S. history in 1917; such images, according to many feminist theorists, constitute the "ancient essentialist war myth," the paradigmatic formulation of war and gender in Western culture.[11] Yet, although their work highlights the power and resilience of the essentialist construction of gender in wartime, these scholars have generally critiqued the notion of inherent sex differences or standpoints in relation to war. At its most nuanced, this scholarship has looked closely at particular constructions of gender in their historical context and has stressed the unstable and mutable quality of gender systems.

In the setting of World War I, such theoretical concerns take on special significance, for Americans of the Progressive Era were themselves preoccupied by the problem of gender and war. Their formulation of the issue differed considerably from our own, however. Before the Great War, thinkers from a wide spectrum of political persuasions shared the assumption that there were innate sex differences in relation to war; their debates centered on the political ramifications of these innate differences as they applied to war and peace. Conservative gender ideologists believed that the United States was undergoing a "crisis of masculinity," caused in large part by feminists and by the erosion of women's traditional ties to home and family. Proponents of a revitalized American manhood, most volubly and prominently Teddy Roosevelt, preached that war and military training could renew the virility and fiber of a nation in decline and restore men to a position of leadership and women to their proper role of subservience.[12] "Natural" gender differences, in other words, were called on to reinforce the social and political status quo. On the other end of the spectrum were prominent women leaders and writers, such as Jane Addams and Carrie Chapman Catt, and their influential European counterparts, Emmeline Pethick-Lawrence and Rosika Schwimmer. These founders and theorists of the women's peace movement insisted that innate mother-love was a force against militarism and war, a feminine power that had the potential to lead men out of the darkness and chaos of their current condition and onto a higher plane of civilization based on peace and mutual respect across lines of sex and nation. Like the proponents of militarized masculinity, feminist pacifists before the Great War promoted the idea that men and women have fundamentally different views of war, although clearly they did so for different purposes. Even after 1917, when Catt and Addams had pledged their support to the war effort, they continued to stress the distinctly feminine role that women could and should play through their wartime and postwar service: maternal care and amelioration of the damage caused by masculine militarism.[13]

The specter of female military enlistment and the deployment of women workers in the war zone overseas seemed to pose a threat to the widespread view of war and essential gender differences in the World War I era. But this view, although strong, was not monolithic in the period leading up to the war. The mass mobilization of women for war service occurred at a crucial moment of flux in gender relations, and this instability created a space for women who saw a liberatory potential in nontraditional wartime service. As Nancy Cott and others have shown, notions of gender neutrality and sex-blind "human" rights began to compete for the attention of feminists in the 1910s, particularly among younger women. The idea of women's military service flowed into other tendencies within the women's movement: the "new woman," bohemianism, professionalism, higher education and coeducation, female trade unionism, and the new suffrage militancy. The prospect of women traveling to France to serve their country, alongside men, as professionals and wage earners was aligned with the vision of gender equality championed by a growing number of self-described "feminists."[14] Although American feminists remained deeply divided even after 1917 over the wisdom and necessity of the war, some women were clearly drawn to a new idea evoked by women's military service: that equality in national service could enable women to claim equal citizenship.

As women ventured into the male-dominated terrain of the front, many resources were brought to bear to counteract, or at least contain, the disruptions expected to follow from their participation. This process of managing the gender realignments of the war era—"the deconstruction and reconstruction of gender"—has been aptly described by one group of scholars as a second "battlefront" in both world wars.[15] War opens up to women opportunities previously reserved for men, Margaret Randolph Higonnet and Patrice L.-R. Higonnet theorize, but when this happens, the system of gender relationships shifts, assimilating change and positioning women once again in a subordinate status.[16] In the First World War, this stabilization was sometimes accomplished through official silence, the selective erasure or elision of women's presence. Army nurses in particular, and working women in general, were frequently the object of "silencing" in official or unofficial wartime propaganda. In such venues, the sanctioned vision of "feminine patriotism" was home front voluntarism, and women's military service was simply erased, as in the opening anecdote about the nurses of Base Hospital No. 5. A more complex strategy that I call "domestication"—which was dominant during World War I—involved the reframing of women's military roles in feminized, familial terms. Servicewomen were told that they had a crucial but distinctive role to play, bringing to the hideous chaos of the war zone the moral and comforting influence of the American home and family. By "domesticating" the war and reinscribing women war workers within a family scenario—female kin of a kindly Uncle Sam—the state attempted to make the war more palatable to the American public and to undermine the transformative potential of women's new patriotic and civic participation.

The formulation of the American woman as wartime mother or sweetheart pervaded virtually every role that American women played in the AEF, shaping the work experiences and daily lives of all servicewomen. The argument that American women could and should play a part in protecting young servicemen from moral harm led most directly to the employment of nearly six thousand women overseas as auxiliary, or canteen, workers. Auxiliary women were brought to France explicitly to lend a "homelike" flavor to army life, serving as stand-ins for the female kin left behind while they served coffee and donuts. But the canteen was only the most obvious place in which dominant gender ideology structured women's war front work experience. Although enlisted as skilled workers, army nurses were expected to be charming to their patients and male co-workers alike, and those who deviated faced criticism and hostility. Even telephone operators were persistently told that their presence and their girlish American voices would benefit the war effort by comforting homesick soldiers and lifting their morale. Army policies frequently blurred the lines between women's official work responsibilities for the AEF and their informal, "womanly duties"; for example, it was understood that women workers would attend army dances at night after putting in a full day on the job. Ultimately, describing and analyzing the ways in which the state contained the challenge of women's enlistment in World War I by reinscribing it in a subordinate status is one of the major tasks of this book.

ALTHOUGH IT IS essential to understand the institutions and structures of power that gave rise to women's war service and assigned it a set of meanings within the larger schema of the war, it is equally crucial to understand what their war experience meant for servicewomen themselves. These two tasks are emblematic of two major currents in the study of women's past, frequently contrasted as "gender studies" and "women's history." Women's history, as its central concern, focuses on the individual and collective experiences, consciousness, and actions of women. Gender studies is concerned with relationships of power as they are played out through gender symbols and discourses, often in a realm seemingly removed from human choice or agency.[17] Yet, despite their apparent divergence, these two approaches are complementary, especially in the study of war. Examining the operations of power is especially tempting when considering so powerful and distant an institution as war, one that is seemingly impervious to control by ordinary people. But such an approach presents the very real danger of naturalizing, and perhaps ultimately legitimizing, war itself. It is for this reason that the careful historical and material analysis of human behavior in wartime is so important.

One of the central concerns of this book is the process of resistance and negotiation by which women and men in the AEF struggled over the meaning and implications of women's military service. Working with the methodologies and theories of a social historian, while being attentive to the approaches of gender studies, I have posed a set of related questions. What motivations and aspirations prompted working women to volunteer for military service? What meanings did they ascribe to their wartime roles? What aspects of the dominant discourse of womanhood did they embrace, assimilate, and absorb, and at what points did they resist? What bearing, if any, did they think their service had on the struggle for women's rights and on redefining public and civic opportunities for women?

The answers to these questions emerge through a detailed study of working women's experiences in the AEF and their reflections on that experience. From the outset, American servicewomen were eager to participate in the Great War, for both altruistic and self-interested reasons. Women saw the war as an opportunity for economic and social advancement, a way to legitimate their aspirations for careers and personal independence. Frequently, too, they saw war service as a chance to experiment with new social freedoms. If women's own voices are taken seriously, then their work at the front cannot be interpreted simply as reinforcing traditional feminine roles, as some scholars have asserted.[18] On the contrary, servicewomen perceived many dimensions of their war front experience—military enlistment, exposure to danger, and unconventional work and leisure activities—as a potential challenge to the restrictive gender roles at home.

Most important, American servicewomen viewed themselves as taking part in a great national venture in partnership with men. They believed that they could contribute essential services and skilled labor toward an Allied victory. Indeed, the conviction that their nation required the help of women workers was one of the strongest motivations for enlistment. "I am more than willing to live as a soldier and know of the hardships I would have to undergo," one canteen worker wrote fervently when applying for a position overseas, "but I want to help my country . . . I want . . . to do the *real* work."[19] Most women who traveled to France with the AEF embraced the idea of military-related service as a privileged form of work, which they believed should confer on women the status formerly reserved for male citizen-soldiers. Like the British military nurses whose experiences are so powerfully evoked in Anne Summers's *Angels and Citizens,* U.S. servicewomen welcomed the war as an opportunity and accepted the military values that upheld it.

Yet, at the same time, servicewomen can hardly be regarded as central to the political and military system that perpetrated the war. On the contrary, the contributions of nurses and of clerical, telephone, and canteen workers were consistently marginalized and trivialized by military and civilian leaders, even as they conceded their dependence on female labor. Army policy, as it was constructed by the military and political leadership, was highly gendered, and military leaders were staunchly committed to relegating women to a separate and subordinate sphere at the war front.

The words and actions of AEF women reveal that they recognized and resisted this process. Women and enlisted men in the armed services shared many experiences: subordination within a rigid hierarchy; the fear, boredom, and deprivation of life at the front; and a lively, sometimes humorous war front culture constructed as a counterbalance to the grim horror around them. But women's experience of the war nonetheless differed markedly from that of men. Many women found themselves battling the military: for example, canteen workers who resisted control over their social lives and nurses who struggled for military rank and compensation. Servicewomen did not usually question the idea of war or the legitimacy of the U.S. cause, at least during the war itself. But they did challenge the gender division of war, which excluded them from participation in the war effort on an equal basis with men.

[8]

Most crucially, servicewomen's bid for equality was manifest as a struggle for autonomy and respect in the military workplace. This struggle did not take the form of the open strife that characterized wartime labor relations at home. But in more subtle ways, men and women at the front came into repeated conflict over matters of power. Although historians of work and the labor movement have turned their attention to the experiences of working people in wartime, they have neglected the armed services as a locus of workplace struggle.[20] Understanding women's "work culture" and uncovering the class and gender dynamics of the war front workplace are essential to interpreting servicewomen's experience in the First World War and to understanding the wider history of war and militarism in the twentieth century.[21]

Women's struggles for equality within the military point the way to a final issue: the relationship of AEF servicewomen to the contemporaneous women's movement. The connections are both stronger and more tenuous than might at first seem apparent. Women who volunteered for war service were certainly well aware of the cresting campaign for woman suffrage, and many watched its progress closely. Molly Dewson, a social worker and Red Cross volunteer who later became prominent in Democratic Party politics, noted that news of the New York state suffrage victory reached her aboard a transport train en route to Paris in November 1917; the women on board, social workers and relief volunteers like herself, burst into celebration, she reported in a letter home.[22] Elite women professionals, such as Dewson, were one of the core constituencies of the mainstream suffrage movement; their jubilation is no surprise, and neither is the coverage that their war work received in the suffrage press. But what of the ordinary working women who filled the ranks of the AEF? To the extent that they recorded their views, their sympathies are also clear. One army nurse veteran I had the opportunity to interview, 99-year-old Alma Bloom, greeted my question, "What did you and your friends think about votes for women?" with genuine amusement. "We all thought that was a good idea," she remarked matter-of-factly, and then deadpanned after a pause, "Why, don't you?"[23]

Yet, it would be an overstatement to call Bloom and others like her feminists, even accounting for a diversity of classes, styles, and perspectives in the early twentieth-century women's movement.[24] The working women who served overseas were concerned in their own way with equality for women, and they laid claim to rights and entitlements based on their contribution of skilled labor during the nation's moment of crisis. In this sense, their political views most closely resembled those of Harriot Stanton Blatch, the daughter of Elizabeth Cady Stanton and an important feminist activist in her own right. Blatch founded the Equality League of Self-Supporting Women to highlight the social value of women's productive labor and to unite wage-earning women of the professional and industrial classes to work for the suffrage cause.[25] Not coincidentally, Blatch also played a role in the story of women's overseas service during the First World War. Champion of army nurses in their struggle for military rank and author of a prominent study of women's wartime employment, Harriot Stanton Blatch was one of the small handful of feminists who drew attention to women's military service and argued for its importance for all women's political and economic advancement.[26]

The analogy between Blatch and the AEF servicewomen has serious limitations, however. Servicewomen's politics were not overt; they generally adopted symbolic and individual rather than collective forms of resistance to their subordination. Nurses came closest to organized political action during the war, although even their efforts were a far cry from the mass rallies and parades of the suffragists or the militant tactics of female trade unionists during the same period. Women in the AEF occasionally represented themselves as a vanguard of change for all women, but more often they figured themselves a unique group whose experience had little applicability to the situation of their sisters at home. For its part, the mainstream suffrage movement failed to see the political potential of women war workers. Suffrage leaders, viewing women's military service through a lens of class bias and political self-interest, were unable to articulate or even acknowledge the concerns of AEF servicewomen. In the end, the relationship of women's military service and women's political emancipation was raised during the war but received little sustained attention. The sympathies and tensions between servicewomen and suffragists, their points of interaction and, more often, their points of disconnection, are all part of the story of women's service with the AEF.

Focusing on women's service with the AEF, it is my hope that the chapters that follow will shed light on wider questions about the lives and aspirations of working women during the early twentieth century, the evolution of women's military service and its origins in the female service sector, and the relationship of women as workers, citizens, and soldiers to the twentieth-century U.S. state.

Mobilizing Women for War

More than a decade after the Great War, Julia Stimson, who had worked as chief nurse of a base hospital in France before becoming superintendent of the Army Nurse Corps, served on a committee to review proposed designs for a war memorial honoring women. Drawing on her personal experience, Stimson suggested an image that she believed captured the essence of women's wartime service: "a glimpse inside the screens surrounding a bed on which lay a man dying of burns . . . [a] revolting sight. . . . Beside the bed holding the man's hand sat a nurse, young, dainty, fresh as a flower, smiling at the glazing eyes which were turned towards her."[1] This image of nurturance, passivity, and selflessness is based on Victorian ideals of womanhood; in suggesting it, Stimson invoked a conception of women's wartime role with a long history.[2] The civilian organizations and military services responsible for mobilizing women for war, including Stimson's own Army Nurse Corps, appealed to such sentimental images of femininity in their public justifications of women's war work. But the reality of women's service in World War I was markedly different. American women served the war effort in diverse and unprecedented capacities, on the home front and overseas. The armed services and auxiliary agencies enlisted and employed women as part of a rational plan to recruit the massive, skilled, and reliable labor force required by the war effort.

Early in the war, civilian and military leaders came to view American women as a unique and critical constituency to mobilize. The Wilson administration planned policies designed to win the favor and support of "American womanhood" and to convince them to serve their country. But the administration's plan was not the sharp departure from the gender status quo that some people feared, and others hoped, it might be. The administration had no interest in designing programs that might concede power to women in government or open military service to them on an equal basis with men. Mobilization policy was intended to bring women into the war effort while minimizing the structural and ideological changes that enlisting women in the military would entail. Nonetheless, special mobilization programs called women to serve their nation's cause and constituted an open admission that the government was dependent on women's loyalty and labor. Although images of maternal nurturance and self-sacrifice might contain the disruptive implications of women's commitment to the war effort at the level of public discourse, the meanings that women themselves brought to and found in their unconventional experiences in the war could not be so easily controlled.

THE WILSON ADMINISTRATION began with a conventional view of women's role in wartime. The administration recognized that it had to convince women to relinquish their husbands, sons, and brothers to the armed forces, not reluctantly but seemingly voluntarily. Paradoxically, this imperative became only more pressing after the draft was instituted. President Wilson and Secretary of War Newton Baker were persuaded to support conscription by military planners, who argued that the draft was the only rational and efficient method of raising the mass army required by modern warfare without disrupting agricultural and industrial production, which were equally essential to the war effort.[3] Traditional gender ideologies that prescribed a clear distinction between the positions of women and men in relation to the state shaped public debates about conscription. Compulsory military service was controversial because it overturned a long-standing tradition of local, voluntary enlistment, the "free army of free men" that dated back to the American Revolution. The draft also triggered anxiety about militarism and the subversion of democracy, an issue raised frequently by feminist pacifists before 1917.

With legislative approval of the new selective service system in April, opposition intensified. Large working-class and socialist audiences gathered to hear Emma Goldman denounce the draft; Goldman made her appeal not only to draft-aged men but to their mothers as well. Facing a barrage of criticism, the Provost Marshal-General asked prominent women leaders to lend their voices in support of the draft. Dr. Anna Howard Shaw of the National American Woman's Suffrage Association did so with a ringing call to America's mothers. Acknowledging that this was the one duty from which women might naturally be inclined to "shrink," Shaw declared that "every woman is equally in honor bound to inspire, encourage and urge the men of her family to perform their patriotic duty. This is the service of sacrifice and loyalty which the Government asks of the women of the nation at the present critical hour."[4]

Shaw's statement typifies the gendered rhetoric surrounding the draft in particular and military service in general. "Manliness" was associated with patriotism and democracy. In wartime popular culture, for example, army life turned the effete intellectual, the aristocratic snob, the immigrant, and the shirker into red-blooded American men.[5] The idea of military service as a school of democracy and manhood was articulated most fully by Secretary of War Baker, who held up a vision of the "new army" as "a great educational institution into which mothers and fathers of the country will be glad to see their boys go, because first of the patriotic spirit which service will engender; second, because of the educational opportunities it will offer; and third, because of the democratic fellowship which association in it will entail." Baker concluded, "our purpose is to turn them out trained soldiers, but, in addition to that, trained citizens."[6] Although the war emergency offered an opportunity for the making of real American men, it also held possibilities for the regeneration of American womanhood. The counterpart of the boy transformed into a citizen-soldier by military service was the young woman who enlisted in war service at home. She too underwent a transformation, from a selfish, vain social butterfly concerned only with her own comfort to a patriotic American woman. "You and I have been bequeathed our share of this our Country with our brothers," an "American Girl" reminded her sisters in the *Ladies Home Journal;* "it is not a responsibility we can evade."[7] In presenting women as girlfriends, sisters, and mothers of soldiers, wartime media created the impression that strong family ties, unquestioning female loyalty, and clearly differentiated gender roles were the underpinnings of a successful war effort.

The Wilson administration's emphasis on mass voluntarism for the war effort, coupled with the exigencies of total war, also expanded wartime responsibilities for women. Policymakers anticipated the profound demands that the war would make on civilians, a lesson made apparent in the European experience. For Herbert Hoover, director of the Food Administration, Treasury Secretary McAdoo, and others, the success of wartime mobilization depended on influencing what millions of Americans ate, where and how they worked, and how they spent their money.[8] Hoover summarized the rationale for civilian mobilization programs before a Senate committee, contrasting the U.S. approach with that of the Europeans: "Our conception of the problem in the United States is that we should assemble the voluntary efforts of the people. . . . We propose to mobilize the spirit of self-denial and self-sacrifice in this country."[9] Women were to be a vital component of this home front army.

The government's primary instrument for mobilizing women was the Committee on Women's Defense Work of the Council of National Defense, known as the Woman's Committee. The official purpose of the Woman's Committee was to coordinate and channel the voluntary contributions of U.S. women in directions deemed useful by the government: gardening, conserving food, knitting and sewing, selling war bonds, and bolstering morale. Chaired by Dr. Anna Howard Shaw, the committee comprised eleven women, all leaders of national women's organizations. Although the Council of National Defense apparently tried to strike a balance between pro-suffrage and moderately anti-suffrage representatives, in other ways the committee was homogeneous. No Catholic, black, or Jewish women's groups were represented, revealing the narrow, elite conception of "American womanhood" around which the government's mobilization program was built. Agnes Nestor, vice president of the International Glove Workers' Union and the sole representative of women in industry and the labor movement, was added later at the urging of Dr. Shaw. The Woman's Committee was designed to appeal to white, middle-class, predominantly Protestant women in their capacity as homemakers.

Ironically, although wartime propaganda stressed the private and domestic nature of women's contribution to the war effort, the Woman's Committee itself was set up to take advantage of women's extensive organizational experience in the public realm. The advent of modern "total war" amplified the need for widespread participation in such activities as food and energy conservation, fund raising, home production, social service, and transportation. In many of these capacities, the expertise of women volunteers was considered invaluable. Both President Wilson and Secretary of War Baker had strong ties to the reform community and considerable respect for what women's organizations could accomplish. The Woman's Committee and women's programs within other federal agencies were designed to harness the energy and experience of organized, middle-class women while channeling their energy in safely patriotic directions.

Yet, the administration's reliance on middle-class women's groups never translated into autonomy for their organizing efforts, let alone a policymaking role. Members of the Woman's Committee initially hoped that they could organize and direct women's war work on a national level. But Secretary of War Baker quashed these hopes right away, making it clear that their position was entirely subordinate to the Council of National Defense and federal agencies, their purpose solely to provide advice and support. The Committee received notoriously poor treatment at the hands of wartime bureaucrats. When Herbert Hoover, for example, asked the Woman's Committee to carry out the first food conservation pledge campaign, he contacted the women only 8 days before the date scheduled for door-to-door canvassing of homemakers. Treasury Secretary McAdoo sidestepped the Woman's Committee altogether and established a separate Woman's Liberty Loan Committee headed by his wife, throwing the work of the Woman's Committee into confusion. Other volunteers were victims of political and bureaucratic squabbling among men: literally tens of thousands of knitters for the Woman's Section of the

Navy League, a booster organization, were stranded with their yarn and knitting needles as a result of a conflict between the male leadership of the Navy League and Navy Secretary Josephus Daniels.[10] Civilian women received elaborate rhetorical tributes to their wartime contributions, but little else.

A handful of American women were openly critical of the role that the administration had devised for women in wartime as domestic, poorly respected volunteers. Crystal Eastman and her colleagues on *Four Lights,* the outspoken newsletter of the New York Woman's Peace Party, wrote scathingly of women who assisted a government that treated them as unthinking subordinates. For example, she characterized women participants in the food conservation program as "Hoover Helpers" or "plate-lickers" who "accept their position beside the garbage cans as they have always accepted what God and man has put upon them to endure." *Four Lights* warned that the government's massive use of voluntary female labor could potentially undermine the position of wage-earning women, as in the case of knitting-mill and garment workers who might be forced to compete with the knitting "militias of mercy."[11]

In private, the national leaders on the Woman's Committee would have conceded many of Eastman's points. "Oh my Heaven, deliver me from the pettiness of public officials," Anna Shaw wrote to a friend in the wake of the food conservation pledge campaign. She was highly critical of male officials, who "do not think of approaching [women] in an intelligent way, as they do men, but they use a sort of kindergarten method in which they tell them to do something without telling them any reason for it . . . and think that women, like little children, ought to obey. . . ."[12] Committee members were discouraged by the fact that federal departments and agencies took over work that the women had proposed and initiated, by confusion over their jurisdiction at the state level, and by the lack of authority that prevented them from insisting on the cooperation of national women's organizations. At an executive meeting in January 1918, the committee discussed the idea of disbanding, and even considered the possibility of resigning en masse.[13]

Yet, in public, very few women leaders expressed any criticism of the government's mobilization plan for women. The public face of the Woman's Committee was one of unanimous cooperation and enthusiasm. The reasons for this outward show of good feeling were numerous. Every women's organization represented on the committee hoped to enhance its own status and legitimacy—and by extension, the standing of its women constituents—by a strong, patriotic performance. In the repressive wartime atmosphere, dutifully conceding to administration demands and policies was far easier than trying to alter them. Critics endangered themselves and their reputations, as one woman official of a service organization learned when she spoke out against Herbert Hoover's tendency to blame homemakers, rather than agricultural producers and distributors, for food shortages; Hoover castigated her for her "pro-German" sympathies.[14] Finally, many women leaders anticipated that their work for the war effort would bring them unprecedented access to the federal bureaucracy and an opportunity to carry through their own, long-standing reform agendas.[15] Despite their frustration with many aspects of the administration's mobilization plan for women, therefore, mainstream women leaders decided to keep their criticisms and differences to themselves and offer a public view of American women united to win the war. Emily Newell Blair, a publicist for the Woman's Committee, signaled this resignation to the government's vision of female service when she wrote in the official committee history: "It is generally recognized that the greatest duty of women in war times is to keep social conditions as normal as possible." The Woman's Committee, she concluded, would sound its bugle to remind women of their central responsibility: "to keep the home fires going, while the men fight for the country's defense."[16]

The most visible and familiar of the wartime programs for women, the Woman's Committee made its appeal primarily to white, middle-class women in their role as homemakers. In terms of numbers alone, the primary role of American women during the First World War was indeed "to keep the home fires burning." High-profile programs aimed at middle-class housewives reflected the government's priorities and concerns, and homemakers responded with enthusiasm and energy to this call for their assistance. But women were needed for a much broader range of responsibilities. During the war, traditional forms of female patriotism, such as knitting socks and rolling bandages, existed alongside strikingly new female roles. Although the Woman's Committee focused on women at home, other government agencies were authorized to recruit women for civilian employment on military bases and in war industries and for military service with the American Expeditionary Force (AEF). Specific labor shortages in the civilian labor force and the armed services brought an entirely different female constituency—self-supporting, single women workers—into the war effort. Military concerns about army morale overseas also presented women with new opportunities at the front. The government's mobilization plan for working women, although more modest and more internally conflicted than its plans for homemakers, was ultimately more important, for it anticipated the direction in which women's wartime roles would evolve over the course of the twentieth century. Women went to work in the factories of the U.S. military-industrial complex, performed clerical and communications work in military offices, nursed soldiers wounded in battle, and lifted the morale of Allied troops. Service with the AEF posed the greatest challenges to conventional views of women's place in wartime; bureaucrats, military officials, and the public grappled with the implications of women's service at the front and in the armed services.

SWEEPING STRUCTURAL CHANGES in U.S. economic life during the early twentieth century ensured that the Wilson administration would turn to women as workers, both in the civilian economy and for the armed services. The U.S. entered the war at a time of rapid social transformation, which was both highlighted and accelerated by the First World War. The wartime labor needs of the military were closely linked to those of the civilian economy, and the pattern of sex segregation that developed in the military resembled that in the civilian labor force. As historians have pointed out, the military's reliance on female labor was not an entirely new phenomenon in 1917.[17] By the early twentieth century, however, changes in American society had created the material preconditions for a much broader and more formalized mobilization of working women into wartime service. Warfare had also changed dramatically, and the military had taken on entirely new functions, including health care, sanitation, communications, publicity, and recreation. Army and navy offices needed typists; army training camps and military bases needed cooks and laundry workers; and military hospitals needed nurses and nurses' aids. All these jobs fell to women in a sex-segregated economy.

Although there was no fundamental transformation of the female labor force during the war, Maurine Weiner Greenwald has shown that subtle but important shifts did in fact take place. A wartime labor shortage offered limited opportunities for working women, both black and white, to change jobs and to seek economic advantages for themselves. The public and the media were intrigued by the novelty of women working in "men's jobs," as thousands of women took visible positions as streetcar conductors, elevator operators, and railroad workers. Many more white women obtained employment in offices and as semiskilled factory operatives during the war, moving from lower-paid to better-paid jobs; for example, women left the garment industry to work in steel, chemical, and munitions plants. African-American women took the jobs vacated by white working-class women, turning their backs on domestic service in favor of industrial employment.[18]

Women workers were also required for service with the AEF. But here, necessity collided with deeply rooted gender expectations rather than paralleling and reinforcing them. Civilian and military leaders were divided on the issue of sending American women to France, and they were even more divided on women's proper place on the war front once they had arrived. One risk of admitting women to military service was obvious: it might open the door to women's equality. News of the navy's anticipated enlistment of women was enough to sweep an anonymous suffragist into a wave of equal rights enthusiasm. "I am sure your proposal to recruit women in the U.S. Navy will meet with great success," she assured Navy Secretary Daniels; "The women in this country are eager to do everything they can to help the government—and they are also anxious to become citizens of the U.S.A. I hope you will help women to get the vote and women will show what they can do. 'Women are people.'"[19] Wartime propagandists drowned out such voices, insisting that changes in the material position of women, including military service, need not necessarily lead to changes in the underlying gender system. As if to allay fears of the "masculinization" of women entering the armed services, for example, one male writer reduced and contained the significance of the change by interpreting uniformed military service for women as a new female fashion statement: "A woman responds to costume—at least so I am told— . . . the trig coat and short skirt, the military boots and puttees . . . are apt to bring an enthusiasm in the heart of their wearer that can be translated into actual endeavor."[20]

Interestingly, public controversy over women in the armed services was more muted than the administration's own internal debate. The reaction of the U.S. public can be explained in part by the administration's low-profile recruitment of women into specific occupations and in part by civilian deference to military leadership in wartime. Yet, other contemporary developments helped to prepare the public for the specter of American women in uniform. Women first enlisted in the military at a moment of transition in American gender relations, when many elements of the status quo were being challenged. The suffrage campaign, with its motor brigades and its quasi-martial parades, had accustomed the public to forceful and militant images of women. The late entry of the U.S. into the war also meant that Americans had grown accustomed to reading about European women who were engaged in the war effort, a favorite topic of pro-war propagandists in the preparedness era. In particular, the British experience with women's military service may have eased public acceptance of women in uniform. In Great Britain, a protracted debate over the proper role and organization of women to serve the army as noncombatants resulted in the establishment of the British Women's Army Auxiliary Corps (WAAC) in February 1917, despite continued and vigorous opposition. The creation of the WAAC was followed by the Women's Royal Naval Service at the end of 1917 and the Women's Royal Air Force in April 1918.[21] But U.S. policymakers eschewed the British model of uniformed women's services, opting for a far less ambitious plan and therefore avoiding the full-scale national debate over women in the military that had erupted in Great Britain.

In striking contrast to their British counterparts, American suffrage leaders evinced little interest in the issue of women's military service; indeed, their lack of interest may have been an additional factor in the low-profile public reaction to women in the AEF. Carrie Chapman Catt and other leaders of the National American Woman Suffrage Association (NAWSA), in their official capacity as representatives of the Woman's Committee, dutifully joined with anti-suffragists to focus their full attention on mobilizing women homemakers. Suffrage leaders certainly recognized the ideological and practical gains that wartime service outside the home could bring to women, especially to women workers. "Many doors hitherto closed to women will swing wide to admit them as a result of this world war," was the hopeful assessment of *The Woman Citizen*, NAWSA's official newspaper, in August 1917.[22] Suffrage publications applauded the achievements of women venturing into new occupations during the war; the pages of *The Woman Citizen* were crowded with tales of women breaking down gender barriers to become everything from riflewomen to undertakers.

Yet, the peculiar class myopia of mainstream, middle-class suffragists led them to look for progress in a certain direction. When the AEF floated a plan to address the army's shortage of clerical labor by organizing a Women's Overseas Corps of skilled office workers, the suffragist press remained silent. Similarly, the campaign of army nurses to gain equal military rank was barely acknowledged by most suffragists. Instead, NAWSA leaders and other elite feminists fixed their attention on the Vassar Training Camp for Nurses, an experimental wartime program for nonnurse college graduates designed "to fit educated women as quickly as possible to officer the nursing profession," according to the Barnard College Bulletin.[23] Leaders of NAWSA focused on neither nurses nor telephone operators, who were primarily working-class women in female-dominated occupations, but above all on women physicians, educated women seeking entry into a powerful, male-dominated profession. The cause célèbre of American suffragists during the war was the struggle of women physicians to gain admittance to the Army Medical Corps and Medical Corps Reserve. When the War Department remained utterly opposed, American suffragists teamed up with a group of women doctors and funded an entire hospital staffed solely by women, from surgeons and nurses to ambulance drivers and electricians. The Women's Overseas Hospital, headed by Dr. Caroline Finley, was gratefully accepted for service by the French government and served as a brilliant and dramatic demonstration of the suffragist proposition that talented, educated women were too valuable a resource to waste.[24] However, the suffragists' concentration on women physicians represented a significant missed opportunity for the women's movement, for far from opening gender employment barriers, service at the front during the First World War reinforced the centrality of female-dominated occupations for working women. The suffragists' lack of interest in nurses and office workers presaged the problematic relationship between working women and the women's movement in the twentieth century. Without feminist groups to advocate for working women at the front or to fight for clarification of their status, the War Department was not under pressure to create a British-style women's military corps or even to construct a consistent policy on women's service.

Ultimately, despite internal divisions and public ambivalence, the administration approved and assembled a substantial force of women workers for overseas service. But the War Department formulated no rational, comprehensive view of women's service with the AEF. Some women were full members of the armed services, others were civilian employees of the army, and still others were employed by private agencies affiliated with the armed services, a piecemeal plan that reflected the underlying conservatism of civilian and military leaders on the question of gender roles. Indeed, disagreement and debate over the use of women workers continued within the military establishment for the duration of the war, surrounding servicewomen's status with confusion and ambiguity.

As U.S. military planners surveyed their manpower needs in 1917, it became apparent to many that womanpower was also a necessity. This imperative was most readily apparent in the field of military nursing. Not only was civilian nursing entirely feminized by the early twentieth century, but military nursing had also been established as a female professional domain. The U.S. Army Nurse Corps, created by the Army Reorganization Act of 1901, was firmly in place by 1917 and had gained the respect of military leaders under the able command of a series of strong women superintendents.[25] The Army Nurse Corps had even been tested in battle during the Mexican border war of 1916. Army nurses had a number of clear advantages over other World War I servicewomen: there was precedent for their military service and generally high public acceptance of their role at the front, and they had strong female leadership both inside the Corps and from professional nursing organizations. In the case of nurses, the administration generally set aside concerns about the morality or legitimacy of female military service and focused instead on intensive recruitment. At the start of U.S. involvement in the war, the Army Nurse Corps was a force of only four hundred, and by armistice day, more than twenty thousand nurses were in uniform. The closest thing to a national celebration of military nursing was the striking and successful Red Cross parade held in New York City on October 10, 1917. Uniformed women of the Army and Navy Nurse Corps led twenty thousand Red Cross volunteers, the majority of them women, in the parade. This event, which was well covered by media, was a rare moment during the war when the working women of the military were in the national spotlight.[26]

Clerical and communications work was the second major category of military employment for women in World War I. The situation of clerical workers and telephone operators stood in marked contrast to that of army nurses. A lack of precedent, an absence of civilian support, and, above all, divisions of opinion within the military leadership led to a recruitment policy that was inconsistent and disadvantageous for the women clerks and operators of the AEF. The impulse behind the employment of women in army offices and telephone exchanges lay in the sex segregation of the civilian labor force and the changing nature of work within the armed services. Between 1890 and 1917, women had begun to fill many of the new service jobs in the civilian economy, monopolizing occupations such as telephone operator and typist. As these occupations were absorbed by the military, wartime leaders were presented with a dilemma: how to obtain a sufficient supply of women workers and place them under a level of military control sufficient for the effective management of the war without violating the deep and powerful male prerogative of military service.

In the tug-of-war over women workers, military officers in the AEF, who were directly affected by labor shortages in these occupations, generally pushed for female enlistment, aided by a few supporters in Congress. Civilian leaders in Washington, DC, displayed more caution about disturbing gender roles in regard to war. But the policy was also shaped by competition between the branches of the armed services and by the personal inclinations of individual leaders. Two quite different policy approaches illustrate the controversy surrounding the enlistment of working women and the range of views on women's proper place in the military: the Navy Department's enlistment of women as yeomen and marines and the War Department's refusal to create a women's corps for clerical service in France.

The Navy, under Secretary Daniels, was the first and only branch of the armed services to enlist women on an equal footing with men during the First World War.[27] Having secured a permissive legal opinion on the language of the Naval Reserve Act ("persons" did not mean exclusively male persons, his legal counsel advised him), Daniels opened the U.S. Naval Reserve to women in March 1917; the Marine Corps Reserve enlisted women beginning in August 1918. Women were selected on the basis of office skills and experience. The Marine Corps, in keeping with its elite image, reputedly devised such a rigorous shorthand test that most aspirants were eliminated early in the application process. Called yeoman(F)s and marine(F)s to designate their sex, these women served in uniform. They were enrolled as privates, received the same pay as regular Navy yeomen, and were eligible for promotion to noncommissioned officer status and full veteran's benefits.[28] Secretary Daniels was more inclined to take this action than were other Cabinet members: the son of an employed widow, himself an active pro-suffragist, Daniels relished the role of Washington outsider and "small-d democrat," stepping on the toes of Navy tradition.[29] Competition between the Navy and War Departments for scarce goods and services may also have spurred the decision. At least certain army planners viewed it that way, as one memo makes clear: "the Navy Department . . . satisfied its needs regardless of the needs of others. They wanted clerks and they got them."[30] By the end of the war, the Navy and the Marine Corps had enlisted more than twelve thousand women, dubbed "yeomanettes" and "marinettes" by sailors and the press. Virtually all served stateside, in offices on bases in the United States or in Washington, DC, headquarters.

Secretary Daniels's pivotal role is particularly clear when his policy on female enlistment for the Navy is compared with the stance of Secretary of War Baker. Baker adamantly resisted pressure to create an army corps of women, an American counterpart to the British Women's Army Auxiliary Corps. The pressure came from within army ranks, as base commanders were plagued by chronic understaffing of offices and laundries. In addition to the inadequate supply of workers, a major complaint of department chiefs was that women civilians hired for posts in the U.S. could not be compelled to stay on the job; the chief of ordnance found a yearly turnover among women of almost eighty-four percent. Consequently, plans and proposals for female army enlistment were formulated at various points by the chief of ordnance, the chief of engineers, the quartermaster general, the inspector general, and the operations branch of the general staff. Within the AEF, plans to create a women's overseas corps of five thousand American women advanced even further.

But Baker's opposition to female enlistment was unyielding. It echoed resoundingly in a War Department memorandum on a bill under consideration by the House Military Affairs Committee in the winter of 1918: "The enlistment of women in the military forces of the United States has never been seriously contemplated and . . . is considered unwise and highly undesirable. . . . the action provided for in this bill is . . . exceedingly ill-advised." In May 1918, the War Plans Division reiterated official army opposition, noting that "industrial conditions in the United States are not yet in such shape that it is necessary to undertake a line of action that would be fraught with so many difficulties." Baker's antagonism to female enlistment seemed to stem in part from "moral" concerns about the mingling of sexes in the military. In December 1917, when the War

Department was forced to authorize the employment of female civilians on stateside army bases, it took the opportunity to issue a warning: "With careful supervision, women employees may be permitted in camps without moral injury either to themselves or to the soldiers," but only women of "high moral character" might be employed.[31] In the face of War Department opposition, the AEF was able to recruit only a small token force of American women for overseas service as clerks and telephone operators, and they were hired under circumstances that remain confusing to this day. Officers of the AEF scrambled to fill the gap by hiring English-speaking French and Belgian women, but the supply of office workers and telephone operators available to the AEF was never adequate for the demand. It was not until World War II that the U.S. army formally recognized its dependence on female labor, especially in the clerical occupations, by creating the Women's Army Auxiliary Corps.

But the labor needs of the AEF were not the only factor that shaped and legitimated women's role at the front. The influence of progressive reformers, inside and outside the Wilson administration, was also crucial. So, too, were administration and military concerns about safeguarding the health, morals, and morality of American troops. Two Wilson war cabinet policies in particular imposed a Progressive reform agenda on the conduct of the war and opened an extensive overseas role to women. The first was a major, federally sponsored program to assist French and Belgian refugees, intended both to demonstrate the enlightenment and compassion of the American system and to teach modern, scientific social work techniques to the French. The second was a social service program for the American soldiers themselves, which was carried out under the aegis of the Committee on Training Camp Activities (CTCA). Under the leadership of Raymond Fosdick, a progressive reformer and attorney, the CTCA instituted a sweeping program of education, recreation, and wholesome entertainment on stateside military bases and, ultimately, overseas for the AEF.[32]

These two programs were a highly significant factor in promoting and defining women's participation at the front. They drew heavily on women's voluntary and professional experience, bringing social workers; librarians; settlement house workers; dietitians; recreation, rehabilitation, and public health personnel; and other female "experts" to France to work with the U.S. army and in relief efforts for the European allies. Fosdick's vision of a positive program to safeguard the morals and meet the emotional needs of American soldiers, coupled with army concerns about venereal disease, led to the second-largest occupation for American women within the AEF. Nearly six thousand American women eventually found positions with the official auxiliary agencies affiliated with the U.S. armed services in France, working with American troops. The extensive use of women in welfare work at the front was a tribute to their years of experience in reform and social service on the municipal, state, and national levels. But the programs could point in a different direction as well, toward the engagement of women for their "innate" qualities of nurturance and virtue, comfort, and diversion. Fosdick, the architect of the AEF's social welfare program, was also the most eloquent and prominent spokesman for an exceedingly sentimental view of women's war front role. As he expressed it in one speech: "a woman worker Over There . . . is worth three or four men workers (applause), because . . . those men Over There are homesick, and the thing they want more than anything else is the touch of a woman's hand and the sound of a woman's voice. . . . Oh, you women of America! I do not believe that any women in the history of the civilized world have ever been as idealized as you are idealized by the American Expeditionary Force." Fosdick's pronouncements on women's service were echoed in countless letters, reports, and memoirs, which portrayed women workers overseas as surrogate mothers and sweethearts and stressed the power of women to bring a homelike, pleasing, or "rational" influence into the "hideously irrational environment" of the front.[33] This final point leads us full circle. Women's canteen work overseas in many ways resembled the domestic roles of women in wartime; home front and war front were intricately connected, sometimes in unexpected ways.

Woman's proper place in the war effort was a matter of considerable discussion during U.S. mobilization for World War I. On the home front, women were called on by the government to serve primarily as homemakers, aiding in fund raising, conservation, and the preservation of home front morale. Inherent in these programs was a particular vision of women's role: white, middle-class, native-born women serving as patriotic volunteers, mothers, and wives, private individuals who could best aid the war effort in their private and domestic capacities. Despite the exclusive and elitist nature of its appeal to women and the circumscribed role that it offered, the Wilson administration put out a powerful and compelling message: women's service was desired, even required, to win the war, and American women had a "big job" to do. It is a message that a vast number of American women heeded.

Although the dominant wartime role for women was a highly traditional one, it coexisted, often in tension, with very different claims and imperatives. Women were needed in many capacities in industry and public-sector employment as well as in the military. The leaders of the war effort were forced to rely on female skills and resources in the pursuit of modern, total war. There was little disagreement, as military leaders prepared for war in Europe, that women's service would be required at the front. Ultimately, women were used extensively by the military in three different capacities overseas: as civilian volunteers affiliated with the army (canteen workers), as civilian employees of the military (clerks and telephone operators), and as army servicewomen (army and navy nurses). Yet, disagreement surrounded the nature of women's relationship to the armed forces and the character of their wartime role. A contradiction lay at the core of women's service as it was formulated by government and military officials: Were American women in France to "domesticate" the war, to mitigate its effects? Or were they "soldiers," skilled workers essential to military victory? These competing visions and contradictory messages composed the context in which working women volunteered to serve overseas with the AEF.

[2]

Getting Over There: A Social
Analysis of Women's Enlistment

The application letter of a clerical worker seeking an overseas appointment exemplifies the situation and background of many women who served with the American Expeditionary Force (AEF). After introducing herself and describing her years of clerical employment, Anna Snyder wrote: "In case the question might occur to your mind, if called on I could start right over without any fuss so far as I personally am concerned. I have no dependents, nor any relatives who are near enough to interpose any objections and, needless to say, I have arrived at an age when one is supposed to have some 'horse sense' and fairly good judgment."[1] This letter highlights many of the most important patterns in the lives of servicewomen: women who enlisted were, by and large, mature, single, working women who had already achieved a significant degree of autonomy in their work and personal lives. Woman made the choice to enlist with careful deliberation. Altruism and patriotic self-sacrifice were, for most women, part of the equation, but so was an assessment of the benefits and opportunities presented by the war. During the decade or more before 1917, these women made a series of choices in education, work, and family and living arrangements that reflected their concerns with achievement and mobility. In this sense they were typical of urban wage-earning women whose lives were shaped by economic and social change at the turn of the century. Yet, servicewomen were also an exceptional group: ambitious, unconventional, and eager for an experience previously closed to women. Drawing on data gleaned from personnel records, application files, and base hospital histories, as well as letters, memoirs, and oral histories, this chapter examines the backgrounds and motivations of the nurses, auxiliary workers, telephone operators, and office workers who served with the AEF in the context of the larger transformations in women's lives between 1890 and 1920.[2]

The chapter also examines the organizational structures and procedures that brought women into the AEF and the methods by which they were recruited. In keeping with the overall mobilization strategy of the Wilson administration, the agencies assigned to recruit women for the AEF were, by and large, private rather than governmental organizations. The Red Cross Nursing Service, the Young Men's Christian Association (YMCA), the Young Women's Christian Association (YWCA), and other national service organizations, as well as large corporations, such as American Telephone and Telegraph Company (AT&T), worked in close cooperation with the armed services to supply the AEF with women workers. These organizations and businesses played an important role in shaping the female labor force at the front. Within these organizations, the task of recruiting and training women for war work was often assigned to female managers; thus, the story of women's enlistment with the AEF is also a story of women's interactions across lines of social class, education, and professional training.

ONE OF THE MOST notable features of women's recruitment was its exclusivity. The portrait of the woman war worker created by poster artists, such as Howard Chandler Christy, was quite accurate: with few exceptions, she was native born and white. The recruiting agencies and the government erected policies that effectively excluded many women from service, in particular African-Americans and Jews. The highly limited participation of African-American and Jewish women in work at the front was the direct result of agency and government preferences and restrictions intended to protect the status and prestige of others in the AEF; it by no means reflected a lack of interest on the part of women who belonged to these socially stigmatized groups.

Throughout the war, women leaders and professionals from the growing "black bourgeoisie," along with their male counterparts, agitated for inclusion in the women's services, overseas and at home. Loyalty to country, Christian duty, and the educated black woman's "refining influence" on black soldiers were all put forth as arguments for black women's service. The subtext of these efforts was the perennial debate within the movement for black equality over competing strategies of accommodation and resistance, cooperation and separatism. During World War I, a consensus developed within the black community in support of the "war for democracy." Black women participated actively in home front campaigns, knitting, selling war bonds, and providing social services for black enlisted men and their families. When black nurses received no call from the Red Cross, Adah Thoms, an African-American nurse leader who had helped to found the National Association of Colored Graduate

Nurses, established a separate corps for black nurses under the auspices of the newly formed Circle for Negro War Relief. These "Blue Circle" nurses met an essential need during and after the war in black communities, which were neglected by other public health organizations. At the same time, black leaders, including Emmett J. Scott, the special assistant for Negro Affairs in the War Department, and Robert Moton, president of Tuskegee, lobbied the War Department and the Red Cross for the enlistment of black nurses.[3]

Yet, all these organizing efforts elicited the merest token response. Only three black women served in France as YMCA secretaries with segregated military units up until April 1919, when they were joined by a dozen or so others. Black leaders were reluctant to criticize the YMCA, which was the only auxiliary agency that employed black men and women in France. Kathryn M. Johnson, one of the black secretaries, commented with gentle irony that the YMCA had left "three colored women to spread their influence as best they could among 150,000 men." The situation with nursing was much the same. Not a single African-American nurse was accepted for service in France. During the final months of the war, as the influenza epidemic swamped medical resources in the U.S., two dozen black nurses were assigned to military installations in Ohio, Illinois, and South Carolina, where they lived in racially segregated quarters but cared for white and black influenza patients alongside white nurses.

The policy of segregation and exclusion of black women was a deliberate one. In comparison to the segregation of black male soldiers in the First World War, however, discrimination against black women was more subtle and indirect.[4] Emmett J. Scott, after repeated attempts to clarify the War Department's position on black nurses, declared it a policy of "passing the buck." The Army Nurse Corps itself could not accept black nurses, the Surgeon General explained to Scott, because it lacked "separate quarters" for them, but they would "in all probability" use black nurses in the army reserve if they were properly enrolled in the Red Cross Nursing Service. The Red Cross was "entirely willing to enroll colored nurses," according to Jane Delano, head of the Red Cross Nursing Bureau, but black nurses could not be enrolled until the Surgeon General assigned them.[5] By "passing the buck," the government and the Red Cross denied responsibility for barring black nurses from overseas service but effectively excluded them nonetheless. The enlistment of black nurses and other black medical personnel was perhaps a threatening prospect for white health care leaders, for it might well have opened to scrutiny the entire structure of racial segregation in the U.S. health care system. During the war, African-American women were actively and successfully excluded from service with the military and its cooperating agencies at the front, although they organized a flourishing network of mutual aid within their communities at home.

Jewish women encountered similar barriers to their participation in auxiliary work overseas. Early in the war, under pressure from the YMCA, the major auxiliary organizations involved in war service devised a plan whereby soldiers from the three major faiths would be ministered to separately: Protestants by the YMCA, Catholics by the Knights of Columbus, and Jews by the Jewish Welfare Board (JWB). Not surprisingly, this division of labor led to discrimination; the YMCA, the largest of the three by far, employed few non-Protestant women for canteen work. The JWB, established to support Jewish servicemen socially and to advocate for them in matters of military policy, did send almost two hundred welfare workers overseas, more than half of them women. But Jewish workers encountered numerous barriers to their enlistment.[6]

In the era of the Great War, "hyphenated Americans" were regarded with tremendous suspicion, and Jewish-Americans faced anti-Semitic prejudice in education, housing, and certain occupations and professions. The World War I era was characterized by frenzied activity on the part of nativists, nationalists, and negrophobes: within the political system, deportation, repression, and the first literacy restriction on immigration; outside it, lynchings and mob violence. According to John Higham, the war "called forth the most strenuous nationalism *and* the most pervasive nativism the United States had ever known."[7] These attitudes and practices influenced War Department policy. Clearance by the War Department, an apparently routine process for civilian workers from other organizations, was an elaborate and time-consuming process for JWB applicants, ostensibly because Jews were likely to be of "enemy" German or "Bolshevik" Russian ancestry. Applications from the JWB were routed to Military Intelligence and delayed indefinitely. The Military Intelligence branch asked to review the JWB's application form in June 1918; Jewish men and women were required to provide information on immigration, naturalization, and nativity, both for themselves and for their parents, as well as three letters of recommendation vouching for "the candidate's loyalty and attitude towards the war in general, and towards all or any one of our Allies."[8] When a JWB applicant was finally cleared by the U.S. government and received her passport, she encountered a second barrier in attempting to obtain a visa. The French and British embassies routinely turned down JWB applicants on the basis of their "nativity." As late as June 20, 1918, not a single JWB applicant had been successfully processed, according to an exasperated official of the organization. Inquiring about the source of the delay, he reported the following conversation with an official from the British consulate: "The officer stated that there was considerable objection to Russians on the part of

1. Auxiliary workers of the JWB on duty in France, 1919 in one of the few Jewish units approved for service. U.S. Army Signal Corps photograph (U.S. Army Military History Institute, Carlisle Barracks, Pa.)

the British authorities, and suggested that since there were one hundred million Americans, we might well afford to leave Russians out of consideration. I explained that we were dealing not with one hundred million Americans, but with three million Jews, most of whom were of German, Austrian or of Russian antecedents. . . . I was informed that the matter would have to be taken up with the home office."[9]

As a result of these obstructions, Jewish women auxiliary workers were in service overseas only during demobilization.[10] Yet, despite the barriers, their enthusiasm ran high. As one Jewish woman put it in her letter of application, "I am more than willing to live as a soldier and know of the hardships I would have to undergo—and the possible and probable dangers—but I want to help my country and my people."[11] The Jewish-American women who participated in war work had, like other women, black and white, a complex set of motivations for seeking an assignment at the front. They shared with African-American women a desire to affirm their identity as equal citizens and to advance the status of their community by displaying loyalty in the face of prejudice. Yet, the white, Christian-American majority resisted more strenuously than ever the inclusion of African-Americans, Asians, and European immigrants in the American polity in the World War I era.[12] Thus, women's wartime service was connected, through questions of race, religion, and ethnicity, as well as through the matter of sex, to the evolving debate over U.S. citizenship in the early twentieth century.

RESTRICTIONS ON JEWISH and African-American women were only the most obvious way in which auxiliary agencies and government policies structured the female work force overseas. Agency requirements and expectations about age, training, and previous experience were also brought to bear in the recruitment process. At the same time, the work force was shaped just as definitively by the inclinations and choices of the women who served. Who were the women who volunteered and were accepted for service at the front?

Anna Snyder's letter of application for the AEF offers a telling portrait of one woman's life, which outlines the biographical features of the group as a whole. As a working woman, Snyder represents the class background typical of AEF servicewomen. Despite the popular image of women at the front as "heiresses" using their wealth and influence to aid the cause, the majority of women who served with the AEF were in fact from the lower middle class.[13] The family of Florence Goodenough, who became an AEF nurse, illustrates the economic aspirations and practices that were typical of this group. Lower middle-class families often depended on multiple wage earners, including mature daughters who continued to live at home. In 1913, Florence and her sister Nettie both worked as nurses, supporting their mother and a brother, Swain, who was a student; by 1916, Swain was a high school teacher and another sister, Bessie, had joined Florence and Nettie in nursing. Households that lacked male breadwinners were able to manage financially as young women entered the expanding white-collar occupations, such as office work.[14] Marion Price, a nurse, lived with her father, who listed no occupation, and four female relatives, presumably sisters; Barbara and Mabel worked as clerks, while Ethel and Katherine were stenographers. Occupational data on the fathers of servicewomen, where available, reveal a range of middling occupations, including small retailers, professional and white-collar workers, craftsmen, and unskilled laborers.[15]

Class was inextricably intertwined with ethnicity. Servicewomen in the AEF and their families were primarily Protestant and seemed to be of "old stock," northern and western European descent. Native-born (and nativist) Americans deemed these well-assimilated groups far less objectionable than the southern, central, and eastern European immigrants who were arriving at the turn of the twentieth century. In this respect, AEF servicewomen resembled the pool of white, native-born, educated workers that monopolized skilled and white-collar positions in the urban labor force.[16] Some servicewomen were the daughters or granddaughters of immigrants, as such names as Tekla Lyndberg, Melda MacDonald, and Ingrid Petersen suggest, and a few were immigrants themselves, listing such countries of origin as England, Norway, and Sweden. Only a small number of canteen workers, clerks, and nurses were Irish Catholic or Jewish, however. The only significant exception, the concentration of Catholic French and French-Canadian immigrants among telephone workers and, to a lesser extent, nurses and canteen workers, resulted from recruiting agencies' preference for women who spoke French fluently. But the vast majority of servicewomen were white, Protestant, and native born.

To understand the life situations that led individual women to enlist in the military, it is necessary to examine the choices they had made prior to 1917 in their household arrangements, education, marital status, and work history. The economic and personal independence that Anna Snyder asserted in her letter is a common theme in the lives of women war workers. Although servicewomen's prewar living situations varied widely, many apparently lived outside of their fathers' control and without their fathers' economic support. In a contingent of fifteen clerical workers sent to France in August 1918, for example, only three listed a father or husband as their emergency contact; mothers, sisters, brothers, nephews, and, in one case, a female attorney, were designated as next of kin.[17]

Substantial, although fragmentary, evidence suggests that many servicewomen came from households that did not resemble the patriarchal families then considered to be the norm. Sisters living and working together in an independent household, a working daughter supporting a widowed mother, brothers and sisters supporting a disabled or unemployed father—all these are represented in the prewar experiences of nurses, auxiliary workers, and office workers. Lettie Oliver, who joined the Army Nurse Corps, shared a household in Rochester, N.Y., with her sister, a telephone operator. Miriam Clarke of Medford, Mass., was living with her mother when she enlisted as a canteen worker; both women were employed as teachers. Among a group of eleven Rochester, N.Y., nurses who lived with their families before the war, six lived in households headed by a mother or female relative with the same surname, and two others boarded with a sister or female relative; only three lived in a household headed by a male relative.[18] Such family arrangements no doubt entailed extensive responsibilities for women. Indeed, the only common reasons for women to resign from AEF service were a family illness or an acute need in their family for financial support.[19] Although the absence of male breadwinners placed an economic burden on women, it offered them a certain amount of power within the family as well.

Furthermore, many women who entered the service in 1917 were, either by choice or by necessity, already living independently from their families. Like Anna Snyder, they had "no dependents, nor any relatives . . . near enough to interpose any objections." During the early twentieth century, self-supporting women who lived outside traditional families formed a growing proportion of urban working women. According to Lynn Weiner, "these self-supporting women were a third of the urban female labor force, and they were also at the heart of a widespread public controversy over the morality of women's work." The contemporary term for such independent women, "women adrift," suggests the anxieties that this phenomenon aroused.[20] Servicewomen from suburban areas or small towns more often lived with their families than women from cities did, but a substantial minority lived alone. Nurses often resided in residences attached to hospitals and training schools or in boarding houses near their places of work. Two-thirds of the nurses with Base Hospital No. 19, from Rochester, N.Y., were living apart from close relatives five years before enlistment; by comparison, at the turn of the century only one-fifth of all working women in the city lived independently.[21] For example, in 1913 Mary McGrath was living at the Rochester Homeopathic Hospital and Clinic; three years later she was renting a room at another address in town. During the same period, Mary Harriman boarded at the Homeopathic Hospital, which later supplied the core of the nursing unit for Base Hospital No. 19.

Urbanization was another force that shaped the lives of servicewomen and their peers before 1917. These women had taken advantage of the narrow space created by urban life for single women in white-collar and professional fields to support themselves in their own households. As the U.S. economy shifted toward consumption, the service sector expanded, and new communications technologies were adopted, the metropolis became a center of opportunity for women, not only in work but also in education and social life. The women who served overseas in World War I were part of this new, urban world. Of women workers for the YMCA, almost one-third lived in the eight largest cities in the country, and nearly half lived in cities with more than one hundred thousand inhabitants.[22] Four industrialized states—New York, Massachusetts, Illinois, and Pennsylvania—together accounted for half of the YMCA workers despite the fact that recruitment was organized through local offices distributed across the country. The YMCA women were thus a far more urbanized group than most Americans: in 1910, only one-eighth of the U.S. population lived in cities of a half-million or more, and less than one-

Table 1 Percentage of YMCA Auxiliary Workers and of the General
Population Living in Cities of Specified Size

Size of City	YMCA Workers		General Population
	N	(%)	(%)
500,000+	122	30	12
100,000–500,000	78	19	10
25,000–100,000	61	15	9
<25,000	147	36	69
Total	408	100	100

Sources: YMCA keypunch card sample; *Thirteenth Census of the United States*, vol. 1, "Population, General Report and Analysis" (Washington, D.C.: U.S. Government Printing Office, 1913).

fourth of Americans lived in places whose population exceeded one hundred thousand (Table 1).

Some servicewomen had moved to urban centers in search of opportunity. A majority of women employed by the JWB and the YWCA reported having moved to a different city or state at least once before enlistment, often to improve their employment opportunities.[23] Mary Anderson, a YWCA worker, exemplified this process; born in Hudson, Wisc., she earned a B.A. at Lake Forest College in Illinois and a master's degree at Columbia University. From New York City, she took a position as an assistant high school principal in Indiana, served as assistant principal again in Wisconsin, and finally became principal of a high school in Minnesota.[24] Many women had to relocate to attend college or nursing school. Susan Reverby found that only 5 percent of nursing students who entered three Boston training schools between 1900 and 1919 were born in Boston, and she posited that for many rural, small-town, and suburban women, nursing training was "the portal to the freedom of the urban working world."[25] Among the minority of auxiliary and office workers who were educated beyond the local high school or seminary, "going away to college" had prompted many to leave home. But women from rural areas often needed to relocate simply to attend high school. The story of two sisters from rural Maine who entered army nursing, Jane and Alma Gray, is illustrative. Jane moved to Augusta and lived with a married sister to enroll in the town high school; later she moved to a suburb of Boston to train as a nurse. Her younger sister, who had decided to follow her into nursing, left their country home to train at Mount Sinai Hospital in New York City.[26] The experiences of the Gray sisters and many other women like them suggest that servicewomen had a prewar history of moving in pursuit of education and job advancement, goals

Table 2 Age of YMCA Auxiliary Workers at Enlistment

Age at Enlistment	YMCA Workers	
	N	(%)
<24	13	3.2
24–27	90	22.1
28–31	118	28.9
32–35	76	18.6
36–39	48	11.8
40–43	26	6.4
44–47	21	5.1
48+	16	3.9
Total	408	100.0

Source: YMCA keypunch card sample.

that their families and peers seemed in most cases to consider legitimate, if somewhat uncommon, for young women of their social class.

Servicewomen's decisions to delay or forgo marriage also point to a deliberate strategy of planning for personal independence and professional careers. Like Anna Snyder, the women who enlisted were overwhelmingly mature and single. Women workers with the YMCA were nine times more likely to be single than married, and married women were barred from the Army Nurse Corps and Army Nurse Corps Reserves.[27] Certainly, it is not surprising that the majority of women in overseas service were single. Although the absence of their soldier-husbands may have freed a small number of wives to take a wartime job or volunteer for service overseas, responsibility for children or the household tied most American wives to the home during World War I.[28] Although some married women entered the labor force during the war, few white married women held paid employment during the early twentieth century.[29] What is most striking is the combination of singlehood[30] and age among servicewomen. Women in the United States typically wed just under the age of 22 years, but the majority of servicewomen had remained single well past that age.[31] The average age at enlistment for YMCA workers was 32.8 years, and only one-fourth were younger than 28 years. The average age of JWB workers at enlistment was 31 years (Table 2).[32] The AEF nurses in a typical state contingent also averaged 31 years of age at enlistment; although the Army Nurse Corps' age limits were lowered to 21 years in the spring of 1918, more mature women still predominated among overseas nurses.[33]

The recruitment and personnel policies of the auxiliary agencies were particularly influential in shaping the age structure of the work force at the front. Anna Snyder was well aware that "horse sense" and "good judgment" were necessary qualifications for overseas service, and that both were assumed to be acquired over time. Numerous younger women who applied for canteen positions were turned away in disappointment by the YMCA and Red Cross, especially before the armistice. "I can't get over how lucky I am . . . for I realize how few girls of my age are getting across," wrote a youthful canteen worker of her own acceptance by the "Y."[34] According to the assessment of the YMCA staff, a young girl was apt to lack the "steadying influence" and unsentimentality of the mature woman, whereas a woman who was "too old" might be unequal to the physical rigors of war service; their decisive conclusion was that "women in the thirties" were at their "zenith" and "were best equipped for service with the army."[35] In their initial bias toward mature workers, however, the auxiliary agencies were at odds with the desires and plans of military commanders. As a result, minimum age limits were lowered later in the war by both the auxiliary agencies and the Army Nurse Corps. Still, the agencies' initial preference for single women in their early to mid-thirties was an important factor in the recruitment process.

The policies and preferences of recruiters coincided with the life choices of the women workers who went to France. For women like Anna Snyder, single life was not a momentary hiatus between adolescence and marriage but rather a prolonged and sometimes permanent period of independence. Servicewomen participated in a significant demographic trend during the early twentieth century: the postponement or avoidance of marriage among a substantial proportion of women. Ideologically conservative white critics defined the phenomenon as a "problem," warning against "race suicide" and deploring the ruinous effect of higher education on women, and it is likely that in the process they exaggerated the extent of spinsterhood. Nonetheless, at the turn of the twentieth century, more American women than ever before did postpone marriage or choose not to marry at all.[36] For this cohort of women, the decision to remain single opened a wide range of possibilities for voluntary and paid work, including wartime service in France.

College education for women has been closely linked to the phenomenon of rising rates of singlehood, and this pattern appeared among the significant minority of war workers who had attended college before the war. Beginning in the 1870s and 1880s and accelerating after the turn of the century, women from prosperous families enrolled in colleges and universities in ever-growing numbers, although higher education continued to be accessible to only a fraction of women. The vast majority of early graduates chose to pursue careers, and many found a rich and satisfying life with other women, in exclusive relationships or "Boston marriages," or in the supportive female networks of settlement houses

Table 3 Level of Education among YMCA Auxiliary Workers

	YMCA Workers	
Level of Education	N	(%)
Below college	143	41
Partial college*	90	26
College	107	31
None given	8	2
Total	348	100

Source: YMCA keypunch card sample.
*"Partial college," the category used by the YMCA, included any education beyond public high school, including business college, normal school, nursing school, summer college courses, and seminaries.

and college communities. Single female college graduates filled the ranks of civilian relief agencies in France during the war, as Smith, Wellesley, Vassar, and other women's colleges organized their alumnae—social workers, physicians, and dietitians—to assist in refugee and reconstruction efforts. A sizable number of AEF servicewomen fit this profile of college graduates who had postponed marriage. Nearly one-third of the YMCA auxiliary workers were college graduates (Table 3). Typical of college-educated canteen workers was Elizabeth Abbe of Windham, Conn.; after graduating from Smith, she taught high school for a number of years before enlisting. The early telephone units were also filled out with French-speaking college graduates. Some, such as Barnard alumna Grace Banker, had already been employed in the telephone industry; others, such as Berkeley student Louise Le Breton Maxell, enlisted straight out of college and received telephone training in the service.[37]

The overwhelming majority of nurses and most canteen, office, and telephone workers who served in World War I were not college graduates, suggesting that the single life appealed to a broad spectrum of women. Agnes Von Kurowsky, the nurse who was the inspiration for Catherine Barkley in Ernest Hemingway's *A Farewell to Arms*, led a remarkable life. Trained at Bellevue Hospital, Von Kurowsky went to Italy as a Red Cross nurse in June 1918, at the age of 26 years. After the war she served first in Rumania and then in public health in Haiti under the U.S. occupation. Von Kurowsky did not wed until the age of 36 years. Oleda Joure, a telephone worker, followed a similar course during her twenties. Unable to attend college because her family could not afford it, she completed high school and went to work for Michigan Bell Telephone. Although she enjoyed the work, her personal aspirations made her look for further challenges: "I wanted to travel, see some of the world and experience new adventures."[38] Women like Agnes Von Kurowsky and Oleda

Joure delayed or avoided marriage for a variety of reasons: commitment to a profession or a job, a primary attachment to a woman partner, the desire to seek adventure before settling down.

Women's personal independence was made possible by expanded employment opportunities. Changes in work transformed the lives of many American women between 1890 and 1920. With the consolidation of corporate capitalism and the rationalization of the work place, ever greater numbers of women were drawn into the paid labor force to toil at typewriters and adding machines, to sell, file, and keep records. Most of the new jobs in offices, stores, and businesses went to white, native-born women who, like Anna Snyder, possessed both the basic education and the "character" that employers in these occupations considered desirable and who could be hired at considerably lower wages than men. Other women from similar social backgrounds prepared for work in the nurse training schools that multiplied during this period. Simultaneous changes in the structure of affluent households freed women from elite families to engage in activities outside the home: social reform, politics, paid and volunteer work, and education. After 1900, such women increasingly pursued careers in the female-dominated "semiprofessions": the traditional occupation of teaching and the new fields of social work and librarianship. The women who enlisted in the military during World War I were part of this employment boom in the service sector. Army nurses, telephone operators, and office workers, by the very nature of their assignments, almost universally had prewar work experience. But canteen workers as well were far more likely than their single female peers in the U.S. to be gainfully employed during the years before World War I; fully two-thirds of the YMCA women had worked for pay outside of the home before the war, compared with less than half of all single women. For the YWCA, the employment figure was even higher, more than 90 percent.[39]

Canteen workers' prewar employment histories reveal the options that had been available to women who enlisted with the AEF and highlight the relationship among employment choices, social class, and military service for women (Table 4). The application records of the YMCA allow us to identify the occupations of a significant portion of auxiliary workers. By far, the two largest categories of employment for canteen workers before enlistment were teaching and office work, including typing and stenography; together, these two categories accounted for well over one-third of the workers. In contrast to the employment patterns of servicewomen, American women in general continued to work primarily in agriculture, manufacturing, and domestic service; none of the YMCA women had worked in these fields right before the war. Similarly, the traditional, "genteel" forms of employment—boardinghouse

Table 4 Prewar Occupations of Servicewomen in Three Auxiliary Organizations

Occupations	YMCA		YWCA		JWB	
	N	(%)	N	(%)	N	(%)
Clerical/stenographer/typist	92	23	5	10	5	21
Teacher	65	16	15	30	6	25
Religious/welfare worker	18	4	11	22	1	4
Principal/school administrator	11	3	2	4	1	4
Librarian	9	2	—	—	1	4
Bookkeeper/accountant	8	2	—	—	3	13
College professor	8	2	5	10	—	—
Social worker	6	1	2	4	4	17
Other	66	16	7	14	1	4
No occupation	125	31	3	6	2	8
Total	408	100	50	100	24	100

Sources: YMCA keypunch card sample; Jewish Welfare Board passport applications, JWB Papers, American Jewish Historical Society, Waltham, Mass.; YWCA personnel file sample, National Board of the YWCA Archives, New York City.

keeper, tutor and governess, housekeeper, companion, untrained nurse, and seamstress—were largely absent among auxiliary workers, while new business fields—real estate, hotel and restaurant management, insurance, and bookkeeping—were modestly represented. A mere handful of the YMCA's female recruits had entered traditional male professions, such as architecture, law, and academics.[40] Three times as many canteen workers held positions in the female semiprofessions of social work, nursing, librarianship, and school administration.

As a group, auxiliary workers pursued employment in female-dominated occupations that required training or education, primarily in the new white-collar sector. Within this broad pattern, however, some important differences existed, especially between lower white-collar and semiprofessional women. The substantial representation of teachers and other educators in the auxiliary work force was linked to the continued dominance of teaching as *the* professional career option for women and to the substantial proportion of college-educated women among auxiliary workers. The recruitment techniques and policies of auxiliary agencies were a factor in the composition of the work force: the Women's Division of the YMCA consistently promoted its work on college campuses, and in April 1918 it initiated a cooperative arrangement through which Barnard, Wells, Newcomb, Vassar, Wellesley, and Bryn Mawr recruited and financed canteen "units."[41] The difference between "college girls" or professionals and those who were not was a major source of division among women workers in France.

Auxiliary workers from smaller organizations, such as the JWB and the

YWCA, had comparable work histories (Table 4). Teaching and clerical work were the predominant occupations for Jewish women in war service, although bookkeeping and social work were also well represented. Women in the YWCA had the highest professional and educational status of any group, with teachers topping the list and with as many college professors as clerical workers. The YWCA was also the only organization that had its own female professional staff before the war; almost one-fifth of the YWCA workers overseas was hired from within. Most African-American women in auxiliary work also seem to have been teachers, welfare workers, or reformers.[42]

The outline of previous employment for auxiliary workers is highly suggestive of the class and social status of the group. On the one hand, canteen workers were generally not drawn from elite families, despite the well-publicized cases of "society women" who paid their own way to France (often usefully bringing their automobiles with them).[43] Administrators for the auxiliary organizations, who were professionals or reformers themselves, had a strong preference for working women. Members of a YMCA regional committee in Pittsburgh described their recruitment procedure to journalists: "One of the first questions asked the candidates is: 'Have you ever worked before?'" As the writer explained, "snobs . . . are simply not tolerated" in the army. She reported that the committee immediately rejected one "immaculately-gowned young woman" when she voiced her disdain for paid employment.[44] On the other hand, factory operatives and domestic servants were also absent from the ranks of women auxiliary workers. In contrast to the more numerous elite applicants, there is no evidence that industrial workers applied for service in large numbers. Early recruitment publicity, which stressed the desirability of women paying their own expenses, undoubtedly discouraged poor and working-class applicants. Even after these policies were changed, families that lacked the minimal resources to educate daughters for teaching, nursing, or office work may well have balked at giving up a daughter's wages. Both employment opportunities and wages in industry were increasing significantly during the war years. The story of one factory worker who attempted to enlist in the navy stands out by virtue of its uniqueness. A worker at the Weber Candy Company in Milwaukee, Wisc., a daughter of Syrian immigrants, volunteered in the spring of 1917; predictably, she was rejected.[45] Without nurse training, clerical skills, or other white-collar work experience, a working-class woman who wished to enlist had little chance of acceptance.

The nurses, canteen workers, office workers, and telephone operators who went to France with the AEF had more economic security than most female factory workers, yet as working women who supported themselves or who contributed to a family income, they took financial considerations into account in their decisions. This impression is borne out by an examination of women's concerns related to enlistment. Money certainly mattered to most servicewomen, as the government and the auxiliary agencies discovered when recruitment got under way. The YMCA women's division was unable to recruit a sufficient number of volunteers on an unpaid basis, so it soon offered, "where necessary," to pay all or part of a woman's expenses.[46] By March 1918, the head of the women's division in France, Gertrude Ely, recommended that all YMCA secretaries, male and female, be paid employees. Later, the Executive Committee in Paris unanimously urged the New York office that "women workers be recruited on the same financial basis as men." The Executive Committee agreed to establish a uniform salary arrangement for all workers; the standard fee was $100 per month, or $1200 per year in living expenses. Full uniforms were also provided to women workers free of cost. Perhaps most telling of all, the YMCA agreed in October to offer a cash advance to "any Y.M.C.A. worker, man or woman," who arrived in France "without sufficient funds of their own to tide over until they receive their first month's allowance."[47] These policy changes were surely a matter of necessity rather than principle. Women auxiliary workers in France, most of whom were either self-supporting or contributing to a family income, did not have the resources to forego wages for the duration of service.

For army nurses, the issue was not whether they would be paid, but how much. From the inception of the Army Nurse Corps in 1901, nurses were paid monthly while on active duty. Between 1910 and 1918, Army Nurse Corps pay was $50 per month. In July 1918, the base pay was increased by federal legislation to $60 per month and to $70 per month for foreign service. Even with the increase, critics pointed out, army pay was still substantially below what nurses could earn in civilian jobs.[48] It is interesting that top nursing leaders and their reform allies, many of whom were part of the elite cadre of unpaid administrators brought to Washington, D.C., during the war, argued before a House committee in spring 1918 that the pay increase provision of the nursing legislation was not important to army nurses; only the provision granting military rank was essential, they incorrectly insisted. As one nonnurse leader testified, "I have just one interest in the world, and that is the soldiers in our army— to help see that they get the best possible care. And that is why I am interested in this bill. . . . There is not another thing we want at this time." Their strategy in dealing with Congress, it seems, was to portray nurses as holding only the purest of disinterested motives.[49] Then too, they may have feared that the image of women agitating for more money might strike the public as ungenteel.

But the opinions of women workers diverged from those of women leaders on the question of financial sacrifice in wartime. Values surrounding money and ladylike behavior were certainly rooted in social class. Conflicting values became visible in an incident at Red Cross head-quarters. An army nurse on sick leave reported to the nursing bureau "looking most untidy," according to the Red Cross staff member who interviewed her. "She wore white shoes, white silk waist and hat that was nondescript, and her uniform was shabby and spotted." The staff member suggested that the nurse outfit herself with a new suit, new shoes, and the regulation hat and shirtwaist, an ensemble that she estimated would cost no more than $50; but the nurse replied "that she did not intend to spend any money on her equipment, and that she expected to get these in Paris without cost." Sensibly, this woman felt no compulsion to sink a month's pay into her uniform if she could obtain one for free. But Clara D. Noyes, secretary of the Red Cross Nursing Service, disapproved of this attitude, warning that "there is a feeling on the part of many people that some of the nurses are accepting the generosity of the Red Cross too freely and allowing themselves to become pauperized."[50]

Although their publicists might wish to present them as pure and ethereal beings, servicewomen were well-versed in managing their pocketbooks. Women's letters home offer a rare glimpse of how a group of working women handled financial matters. Carrie Hall, who went to France as chief nurse for Base Hospital No. 5, wrote her brother George long directives about her bonds and investments and about the care of her automobile.[51] Bank accounts and money juggling were equally familiar to a nurse from Waco, Tex., but hers was the uncomfortable familiarity of someone scraping to get by, as her anxious letters to her mother and "Pops" suggest.[52] Some women had gained financial experience through managing inherited wealth or negotiating a professional salary; for others, it came simply from keeping a household afloat. Servicewomen's letters reveal a high degree of familiarity with and sophistication about money, garnered through their prewar engagement in the marketplace.

WHEN THE UNITED STATES entered the war, recruitment posters and advertisements stressed the idealistic contributions that women could make to their country through wartime service, and recruitment pamphlets emphasized the skills and competence they sought in women workers. This mixed but potent message proved appealing to the numerous women who quickly presented themselves as volunteers. The highly publicized efforts of wealthy American women on behalf of the French and Belgian people also spurred interest in war work and loaned it an air of prestige and glamour. To many, the most exciting news of all was that women would be recruited for the AEF in France. As recruitment began, first for nurses and canteen workers and then for telephone operators and office workers, many American women were both qualified and eager to serve their country at the front.

The recruitment campaigns for nurses and canteen workers, the two largest categories of servicewomen in the AEF, were carried out by nongovernmental groups designated by the war administration in Washington, D.C., and spearheaded by women at the national level, who in turn relied on vast, local networks of female support. Yet, these two efforts also differed: most strikingly, nursing leaders struggled against a shortage of qualified candidates, whereas auxiliary agency officials were forced to fend off a flood of volunteers.

The Red Cross Nursing Service, a civilian organization, held primary responsibility for the enlistment of military nurses, for it was designated as the official reserve for the Army Nurse Corps. The decision to put all nurse recruitment in the hands of one body was ultimately a wise one, for it allowed for the coordination of civilian and military needs. Although many trained nurses failed to meet the strict criteria of the American Red Cross regarding age, training, and physical health, almost all were needed for wartime work. During the first National Nurse Drive, from June 3 to July 17, 1917, thousands of local branches of the National American Red Cross cooperated to register nurses for service. Despite the urgent need to attract nurses to the military, national nursing leaders kept recruitment publicity carefully in hand, in part to avoid stimulating the interest of well-meaning amateurs. In advance of the major registration drives, advertisement was done almost exclusively through professional organizations, such as the American Nurses' Association, and through the professional nurse training schools. Most army reserve nurses accepted by the Red Cross were subsequently assigned through base hospital units organized by major teaching hospitals and nurse training schools. Others were assigned to replacement units and sent to France to augment the staff of existing hospitals. The army's demand for nurses was tremendous, climbing steeply throughout the war and ultimately taxing the trained nursing resources of the United States to a critical degree. Army Nurse Corps requirements were loosened several times during the war, and few graduate nurses failed to take part in public service of some sort during the war years.[53]

The key organizations for the recruitment of auxiliary workers for overseas service were the official auxiliary agencies. Although many service organizations vied for recognition by the AEF, only a handful was selected as official "army welfare" agencies, providing services to U.S. troops at the front. In the summer and fall of 1917, the YMCA, JWB, Knights of Columbus, and Salvation Army initiated recruitment at the invitation of Raymond Fosdick and the Committee on Training Camp Activities. The National American Red Cross later gained permission to

2. Clara D. Noyes, first director of the Bureau of Nursing Service of the American Red Cross (1916–1919). Noyes oversaw the recruitment of more than twenty thousand nurses for the military effort. (Source: National American Red Cross, *History of American Red Cross Nursing* [New York: Macmillan Co., 1922].)

join the inner circle of official army welfare agencies. Challenging the YMCA's dominance in canteen work overseas and insisting that hospital canteens were within its jurisdiction, the Red Cross eventually developed a large and diversified program that included work with French, British, and American soldiers as well as civilians. Finally, the YWCA had a unique role among the official auxiliary agencies, selected by Fosdick to cater to the needs of the small army of women war workers in France.

In contrast with nurse recruitment, the number of applicants for army auxiliary work greatly exceeded the number of positions. By May 1918, the YMCA was receiving twelve hundred applications each week for a few thousand positions overseas.[54] Difficult tests were employed and bureaucratic barriers erected to sift through the candidates, intensifying the competition among them. Anna Snyder, an Ordnance Department clerk in Washington, D.C., admitted candidly that she planned to "pull any strings" she could think of to get to France. It is not clear what kinds of connections helped in maneuvering through the process. The YMCA and the Red Cross used local interviews, conducted by representatives of the state committees, to screen applicants. In Pittsburgh, Pa., the local chairwoman of the YMCA Overseas Committee interviewed hopeful applicants from all over western Pennsylvania. Mary Josephine Booth traveled to Chicago from Charleston, Ill., for her interview. Not only was she fortunate enough to gain approval, but she was also proffered some candid advice: the interviewer "told me to go ahead and not be 'so doggone frank about saying I did not speak French.' She is going . . . herself and she said her own French is rotten." A month later, Booth was dismayed to learn that the Red Cross had instituted a French language test, a change of policy that prompted her to submit an application to the YMCA.[55]

For telephone operators' positions with the Army Signal Corps, enlistment procedures and policies were also designed to sort through a high volume of applicants. The Bell System was intimately involved in the recruitment process, just as it was involved in the establishment of a communications system for the AEF. The AEF put out its first call for female telephone operators on November 8, 1917; seven thousand six hundred Bell telephone workers responded, yet all but a handful were excluded by the requirement that operators be fluent in French. Soon the army altered the criteria to include bilingual women who lacked telephone experience, but it added a series of tests administered through the Engineering Department of AT&T. The tests were apparently difficult: of a group of ninety-three women examined from the northwest region, only five were sent to New York City for final approval.[56] Later in the war, the Signal Corps shifted policy again and made telephone expertise the primary consideration, prompting another wave of applicants from inside the industry.

"Zigzagging" was the army's term for the route that U.S. military transports took across the Atlantic, making oblique turns to elude German submarines. "Zigzagging," as one auxiliary worker pointed out, could also describe the route that brought sixteen thousand women first to New York City, then to the ports of embarkation in New Jersey or New York, and finally onto steamers headed for Europe. Although some enlisted women were sent off directly to the front, many endured long delays or went through training programs at stateside hospitals and camps. Entering overseas service often involved a period of preparatory service in the United States. Clerical workers flocked to Washington, D.C., to fill positions in army headquarters; the first female stenographers brought to France were drawn from this group. When Josephine Gray learned that women operators would be accepted for overseas service, she quickly applied for a position with the Cumberland Telephone Company in New Orleans, La., to get some experience and, she hoped, improve her chance of acceptance by the Signal Corps. Auxiliary agencies also offered coveted overseas positions to women who had put in their time in stateside war work. "Of course those already in canteen service were preferred," Isabel Anderson noted in discussing her enlistment; head of a Red Cross soldiers' canteen in Washington, D.C., Anderson was selected early for service in France, although her wealth and connections certainly helped. Young women rejected by auxiliary agencies as too immature for overseas service would sometimes sign up for domestic war work to prove their worth. The popular Ruth Fielding books, a series for girls published during the war years, followed Ruth's progress from hometown knitting circle (in *Ruth Fielding in the Red Cross, or Doing Her Best for Uncle Sam*) to canteen and hospital at the front (*Ruth Fielding at the War Front* and *Ruth Fielding Homeward Bound*). The practice of rewarding welfare workers with overseas positions backfired in some cases: the YWCA had so many of its own secretaries apply for overseas service that its domestic programs were depleted.[57]

Women generally underwent a period of training after being selected. "We had received preliminary . . . experience at various army hospitals across the country," one nurse wrote, "and now we were to be outfitted and whipped into shape for overseas duty. We were drilled in the old 71st armory—squads right-about face-march. . . . Given what information and advice we would need . . . Always wear your uniforms and dog-tags, never drink water unless you know it is safe." The Signal Corps established telephone training centers in seven cities; the curriculum included telephone fundamentals as well as army etiquette and daily drill. In New York City, telephone operators were taught to march by eager Signal Corps lieutenants on the roof of AT&T headquarters in Manhattan. Workers from the YMCA and JWB, who came to New York City by rail from all over the country, took a week of training at Barnard College, including French lessons, calisthenics, and lectures on doughboy psychology and the goals of army welfare work. One participant summed up the program in verse: "In a week/ We've learned to speak/ The language of the French./ We know what is expected/ Both outside and in a trench." The program was also the final hurdle for auxiliary workers: the faculty meticulously observed each participant, and a woman could be rejected at this late stage if found deficient.[58]

Once approved, women made final arrangements and waited for ship assignment. Uniforms were fitted and ordered. Recommended items, such as matches, sugar, candles, soap, and warm underwear, were purchased and packed. Auxiliary workers were allowed one steamer trunk; "it was a masterpiece of packing that stowed away all the necessary articles in so small a space," wrote Isabel Anderson. All women received smallpox, typhoid, and paratyphoid vaccinations. Civilian workers obtained passports. In New York City, women war workers were honored at society luncheons and elegant receptions. Uniformed women took part in 5th Avenue parades, where they were praised by politicians and applauded by bystanders. Waiting in Hoboken, N.J., women wrote letters.[59]

Inoculated, outfitted, photographed, and feted, many women found time amid this whirl of preparation to send home first impressions and final good-byes. Women from small towns in the West and South were dazzled by the vast commercial mecca of New York. "It sure is a wonderful city! I will never get to see it all. For miles and miles and miles you see nothing but tall buildings," reported Grace Williams, a Texan; "I certainly notice the difference from Waco with its three blocks of business district." It was equally dazzling to be feted as heroines bound for the front. A telephone operator marveled at how warmly New Yorkers had received them, years later recalling the free rides to which she and her companions had been treated at Coney Island. Each base hospital unit was dedicated shortly before its departure in a ceremony at Saint Paul's Cathedral, the nurse wrote home to Waco, and presented with a unit flag.[60]

For some, the days of preparation were also an opportunity to reflect on the process and the events that had brought them to New York, bound for the war in Europe. Some women had arrived through elaborate planning, utterly certain of their decision and reasons. In other cases the sense of urgency is palpable but the reasons are obscure: "I would like to go to France as a nurse real—real son [sic]. the sooner the better—feel as if it is my duty to go help our soldiers and country— . . . do not know where to write . . .—want to go so badly," one woman wrote to the Secretary of War. Still others continued to find the prospect of going to war amazing. "Even now . . . it seems incredible to me that a young woman from a small city in Montana could rate an assignment that would involve telephone service not only to the outstanding men of our own country, but of the world," said one operator.[61]

How did women on the eve of departure frame or justify their decision to volunteer for war front service, an unconventional choice for the time? Some, at the time or in retrospect, presented themselves principally as sisters and daughters, citing an array of highly individualistic motivations for enlistment grounded in family and private life. Many women claimed they were prompted by a family tradition of military service. Alma Gray, when asked why she signed up with the Army Nurse Corps, placed herself in a long line of male soldiers, including a grandfather, father, and brother. The union cause specifically was a vital family tradition for many women. "My grandfather lost a leg in the Civil War," explained a Red Cross auxiliary worker, and "Clara Barton, . . . took him from the battlefield in a dumpcart and saved his life. Small wonder, then that I was brought up on grandfather's wooden leg, and tales of Clara Barton, and that I just naturally gravitated to the Red Cross service." Indeed, both principal leaders of the American Red Cross Nursing Service in World War I, Clara D. Noyes and Jane Delano, were daughters of Union soldiers, and Delano's father was killed in the Civil War. Numerous younger nurses had brothers in the service in World War I. Ethel Pierce, an army nurse, insists that she enlisted to watch over and protect her younger brother. Josephine Davis, a telephone operator, claims that she was compelled to take the place in the army of her brother, who had died shortly before the war. Whether women enlisted for the sake of sweethearts is less openly discussed, although Vera Brittain, the most famous female memoirist of the Great War in England, portrayed her own war service as closely linked to the fate of both her brother and her lover.[62]

Yet, families were more likely to discourage or prevent a woman from enlistment than they were to support her. One nurse had to fight for her father's consent for 6 months; she felt her father was influenced to discourage her by his second wife, a woman of German descent. Many families believed a daughter's primary responsibility was to home, not country. Ethel Pierce's mother, a lifelong invalid who made numerous demands on her daughter, forbid her to join the Army Nurse Corps. When Ethel did so anyway, her mother cabled the authorities demanding that she be released to care for a gravely ill parent. Interestingly, the army was willing to comply with this family request, according to her account. Ethel's insistence alone kept her in the service. One woman recalls that her mother left a disordered family in Virginia and came north at the age of 15 years to become a nurse; she found in nursing school, and then later in the army, the kind of security and order that her family had lacked.

Examples such as these left even contemporary commentators skeptical of the claim that family duty was the basis for women's service. Journalist Margaret Deland, a war correspondent, astutely observed that the parents of servicewomen actually held little direct authority over their daughters: "They may stand on the dock and squeeze the wet ball of a handkerchief against quivering lips, and they may run halfway down the gang-plank . . .—but they cannot hold their girls back from the gray sea."[63]

Parental resistance to enlistment suggests that for most women, military service meant not the fulfillment of familial roles and responsibilities, as some historians have suggested, but a certain kind of liberation: personal freedom, release from social constraints, a unique opportunity to seek new experiences, and even adventure. The cliché about military service offering a "chance to see the world" certainly has some truth in World War I, for women as well as for men. Foreign travel as recreation was not a possibility for working-class or most middle-class Americans. For the women who volunteered for service, the experience of going to the war *as* an experience was certainly a consideration. One woman explained her mother's decision to enlist in the Signal Corps in 1918: "My mother was an adventuress; she wanted to travel, to see a lot of life."[64]

The kinds of adventures and experiences that the war offered women were perhaps less important in themselves than were their social meanings. Ultimately, enlistment was for women a highly visible and public act, the construction of a public identity. Personal motives—a death in the family, the conscription of a loved one—might provide a trigger for enlistment, but in women's own accounts, private circumstances are subsumed by wider concerns. American women who enlisted in overseas service were generally experienced and independent working women. Sometimes with and sometimes without the support of their families, they had pursued opportunities before the war in work and education that held out the promise of social and economic mobility. Enlistment was in many ways an extension of the same strategy; yet it went further, in seeming to offer legitimacy to women as civic participants, as recognized members of the national state. In the decision to volunteer for war front service, altruism and self-interest were clearly intertwined.

Looking back years later, the servicewomen who responded to an army-sponsored questionnaire virtually all offered impersonal, public explanations for why they chose to enlist: "to serve my country by nursing ill soldiers," "to be of service to my country and our boys," "because the need was great." Although it is easy to dismiss such pat, patriotic responses, especially when summoned up in hindsight, these answers remain significant. Enlistment for women workers was adventure, opportunity, and service on a wider stage. Above all, women's military service was work, and the public and civic identities women created at the front were work identities. The chapters that follow explore the meaning of service to country, and the clash between expectations and war work itself, for three different groups of women with the AEF: auxiliary workers, telephone operators and office workers, and nurses.

[3]

Serving Doughnuts to the Doughboys: Auxiliary Workers in France

"Do you know I have wanted to write to you often, but I just hated to make you feel badly about not being over here," Bertha Laurie wrote from France to a friend back home. "It certainly is the most worth-while work a woman can do." A single woman from Harrisburg, Pennsylvania, Bertha Laurie had worked before the war as a stenographer and bank clerk. Written after her first full day of canteen work, her letter reveals her pride and excitement. Like many women in her position, she regarded enlistment as an adventure and a challenge, a chance to increase her opportunities in life and to participate in what she saw as a momentous national event.[1]

Women workers such as Bertha Laurie hoped to carve out a path of war service roughly equivalent to the war service of young men, but that goal proved elusive. Military officials and civilian administrators defined women's service with welfare organizations in a way that most women found confining or inadequate. First, officials regarded women's auxiliary work as akin to domestic service or the unpaid services women performed at home, work that was necessary but unskilled and little respected. Although auxiliary workers served with pay, and although many brought relevant occupational experience to their jobs, auxiliary women still had difficulty escaping the aura of volunteerism that surrounded their work. At the same time, officials conceptualized women's role in canteens as essentially social, fulfilling soldiers' recreational and emotional needs. The role of canteen workers took shape in the embattled war front arena of sexual and gender politics. As Cynthia Enloe writes, "the military relies on particular ideas of sexuality to mould women and men into the kind of organisation it needs, and military elites have been as self-conscious as any factory manager about designing and

[51]

redesigning sexual divisions of labour."² Both the control and the deployment of female sexuality in wartime are clearly demonstrated in the army's structuring of female auxiliary service with the American Expeditionary Force (AEF).

Most auxiliary workers did gain a sense of satisfaction from their work with soldiers. But women who toiled at menial kitchen tasks in canteens or served as dance or tennis partners in leave areas found a gulf between their prewar expectations and daily life in the AEF. The social nature of the work, the sexual and moral requirements of the job, the gender and class division of labor in the canteens, and the implication that women were enlisted for what they *were* rather than what they could *contribute*— all these factors led auxiliary workers to question whether the work was indeed the most worthwhile they were capable of offering their country.

WOMEN WHO WORKED with voluntary agencies in France were referred to by a slew of titles. In ubiquitous army slang, they were "doughnut girls" or simply "American girls." The women themselves generally preferred "war worker." United States officials called them secretaries, canteeners, field representatives, welfare workers, and women war workers. The French provided the useful and succinct title "auxilaires," or auxiliary workers, to inscribe their relationship to their sponsoring agencies, the civilian welfare organizations.

This semantic confusion reflected the undifferentiated and ambiguous character of their position. Female auxiliary workers performed a range of tasks and were often moved from one job to another. Canteen work was the most common assignment for an auxiliary worker. But a woman might find herself assigned to a hospital, taking surgical notes in the operating room, recording medical histories, writing letters, serving food, running a recreation room for staff, reading to the patients, and, during a crisis, even performing the work of a nurses' aid. In a base canteen she might be expected to cook, serve food at the counter, make change, organize linen, sew buttons, entertain, write letters, run a small library, and plan social events. The nature of an auxiliary's work depended on her specific placement. Women were assigned to base camps, training camps, corps schools, combat divisions, leave areas, dock and supply areas, and headquarters. At a major base she would usually find herself part of a large staff, taking orders from a male secretary or canteen director; but in a mobile hut attached to a combat division she might work alone, establishing a canteen, building rough furniture, and commandeering supplies.

The number of female auxiliary workers who served in France with the official welfare organizations was approximately six thousand: 3,198 with the Young Men's Christian Association (YMCA), 2,503 with the

American Red Cross, 260 with the Young Women's Christian Association (YWCA), 104 with the Salvation Army, and 76 with the Jewish Welfare Board.[3] A group of YMCA women set up the first canteens for the AEF in August 1917, but American women did not arrive in large numbers until the spring of 1918, when transportation improved and the auxiliary organizations had their recruitment systems in place.[4] For the Red Cross, for example, the months that the largest number of women arrived in France were August, September, October, and November 1918. Women's participation in auxiliary service overseas actually peaked well after the armistice, in the demobilization period that extended into the summer of 1919. General Pershing and Army Headquarters Staff regarded the morale and welfare services provided by women workers as absolutely crucial in the difficult months after the fighting was over, when men waited for transportation home. When women themselves were finally demobilized, a number chose to stay on in France, Belgium, and Germany, working for the Peace Commission, in relief work, or with the Army of Occupation in Coblenz, Germany.

The background to women's auxiliary service overseas was the program of army "welfare work" at domestic military training bases, sponsored by Raymond Fosdick's Commission on Training Camp Activities (CTCA). Just weeks after the U.S. declaration of war, Secretary of War Newton Baker created the CTCA to control immorality on and around military training camps in the United States. The impetus behind Baker's action was the highly publicized "vice problem" of U.S. troops in the Mexican conflict of 1916. At that time Baker had sent a young acquaintance from progressive political circles, Fosdick, to investigate the Mexican border situation.[5] Fosdick's hair-raising report on drunkenness, rowdyism, and "crib prostitution" (named for the cagelike "cribs" where prostitutes practiced their trade), and his thoughtful suggestions for amelioration, earned him the chairmanship of the CTCA in April 1917. The commission's first task was to establish "sanitary zones" around the stateside training camps, cleared of bars and brothels and thereby free of moral temptations for the young draftees. With support from the powerful Anti-Saloon League, as well as from local women's clubs, temperance societies, suffrage groups, and some town councils near military bases, the "sanitary zones" were authorized on April 28 through sections 12 and 13 of the Selective Service Act.[6] The CTCA's plan for securing the zones had two components: police and Justice Department personnel conducted intensive surveillance and detention of prostitutes and "charity girls," while the commission, with War Department backing, directed economic threats against noncompliant municipalities. The plan was immediately successful in curbing prostitution and drinking.

Under the vigorous leadership of Fosdick, the CTCA went much further, aiming through morale and "uplift" programs to prevent immorality in the armed services rather than simply to regulate it. The CTCA was deeply tied to the spirit and the goals of progressive reform. The idea that misbehavior could be prevented and human character trained in desirable directions was a basic tenet of those progressive reformers whom Paul Boyer called "positive environmentalists."[7] Through several decades of work with immigrants, young people, and the poor, these reformers had developed such "constructive" techniques as settlement houses, parks, playgrounds, clubs, and recreational programs. Fosdick himself had first-hand experience with this type of reform work; after his graduation from Princeton, Fosdick had spent a year in residence at Lillian Wald's Henry Street Settlement, running a boys' club for Russian Jews while putting himself through law school. In his Mexican border investigation, he had taken special note of a fledgling program of physical recreation undertaken by the YMCA's Army-Navy Department.[8] In the first months of the war, Fosdick began to experiment with a variety of programs at the training camps, including circulating libraries, theatrical performances, recreational huts, and the employment of athletic directors and song leaders. Fosdick believed the work could be carried out most efficiently through existing organizations; the initial group, composed of the American Library Association, the Playground and Recreation Association (renamed War Camp Community Service), and the YMCA, was soon expanded to include the Jewish Welfare Board, the Knights of Columbus, and the National YWCA. The training camp programs initiated by these groups through the commission reflected a unique, progressive-era view of governmental responsibility: on the one hand, the government was charged with the stewardship and protection of the enlisted man; at the same time, this responsibility was to be carried out not by the government but by voluntary agencies overseen by the government.

Women's work in stateside military camps began when the National Board of the YWCA approached Fosdick with a plan to establish "hostess houses" in several training camps, facilities that provided a comfortable, chaperoned setting for enlisted men to entertain female visitors or, in the words of one observer, a place where "the sweetheart came to say goodbye to her loved one, the wife to see her husband for the last time, and the mother to bid her son farewell."[9] Fosdick recalled that the Army General Staff "hooted" when he presented the hostess house concept to them. Many commanding officers and military officials found such programs unnecessary and distracting, particularly when they brought women onto the bases. Congress also resisted funding measures such as the Liberty Theater, which were regarded as "frills."[10] In fact, Fosdick's ambitious program of progressive reform for the military might well have foundered but for the high-level support it received from the executive branch. Wilson and his cabinet, especially Secretary of War Baker and Secretary of the Navy Daniels, enthusiastically supported the CTCA's work throughout the war.

Fosdick's welfare program for domestic army bases was transported to Europe along with the first American troops. Objections to the stateside program evaporated in the case of the AEF. American troops had never before been so far from home in such large numbers (with the exception of the Philippine Conflict). The view of the army as moral steward of American youth loomed especially large in France, which figured in the American imagination as a place of special dangers, Catholic, foreign, and sophisticated, a land of wine and "fast" women. And if boredom was thought to lead to mischief at statewide bases, how much more threatening was actual combat, thought by many progressive and religious thinkers to release the worst of masculine urges.[11]

Military and civilian officials immediately gave American women a much larger and more vital role in welfare work in France than they ever achieved in stateside camps. In part, the choice was practical: women were an eager work force, and by employing them, the auxiliary agencies did not have to compete with the army. The Jewish Welfare Board, for example, turned to women workers when recruitment advertisements failed to turn up a sufficient supply of suitable Jewish men.[12] The availability of men for army welfare work also declined significantly, and the value of women rose, when the adjutant general ruled that no draft-eligible men would be allowed to serve as auxiliary workers. But availability and convenience were not the primary explanations, for auxiliary agencies employed very few women in stateside training camps, even though it was far easier to obtain and transport women workers within the United States than it was to bring them to France. Furthermore, the decision to use women auxiliary workers was made by the YMCA, the Salvation Army, the Red Cross, and others long before draft-eligible men were barred from auxiliary positions.

Three powerful constituencies were behind the decision to employ women overseas in army welfare work. First, a group of wealthy and influential women had been aiding the Allies since the outbreak of the European war in 1914. Women such as Alva Belmont, Edith Wharton, Anne Morgan, and Martha McCook (the sister-in-law of Teddy Roosevelt, Jr.) had taken up canteen, ambulance, and hospital work through high-profile organizations such as the American Fund for French Wounded (whose motor service was sometimes called the "heiress corps") and the American Ambulance Hospital at Neuilly. When the United States entered the war, such women had connections, reputations, and organizational structures in place and held an impassioned belief that women belonged at the front. Their determination to create an official role for American women was difficult to oppose or ignore, although ironically many of these women were "demoted" after 1917 when the U.S. army set up its own operations in France.

Joining these women leaders, although for different reasons, was the AEF command in Paris. Venereal disease in the army was a matter of tremendous anxiety and concern at AEF headquarters, and military health officials held the belief that the presence of American women in France could be an important tool in the fight against sexual diseases. The movement for "social hygiene" in the United States reached a peak during World War I. Within the AEF, high-ranking medical officers were assigned to investigate the problem of venereal disease; they issued numerous memos, bulletins, and reports on its dangers to the fighting effectiveness of the U.S. forces and practical advice on "combating" such diseases. The ideological connection between venereal disease and prostitution in military life had been codified as early as the 1860s, with the first Contagious Diseases Act in Great Britain; U.S. military officials followed the British in blaming disease in the armed services primarily on prostitution, and in France of course, on foreign prostitutes. Women were viewed not only as cause but also as cure for this problem. In the summer of 1917, for example, the AEF General Staff sponsored a "conference on prostitution" with the heads of welfare agencies in France; military officials at the conference connected the fight against venereal disease with the importation of American women, who were expected to provide the troops with a wholesome but winning distraction from French prostitutes or lovers. Following the advice of his health officials, General Pershing signed on to a policy of sexual continence for the AEF, and, as a result, gave strong support to the recruitment of American women as auxiliary workers.[13]

Equally important was the influence of Raymond Fosdick, himself. Fosdick held a different view of the ideal welfare worker than did Secretary Baker. Baker envisaged the army welfare worker as a virile college professor, coach, and teacher, a pal who built the bodies, minds, and spirits of his young charges. Fosdick, on the other hand, considered women vital to the morale program: "a woman worker Over There . . . is worth three or four men workers . . . because . . . those men Over There are homesick, and the thing they want more than anything else is the touch of a woman's hand and the sound of a woman's voice." Fosdick argued that only women workers could create the homelike atmosphere that would bolster the morals and spirits of soldiers.[14]

Within the auxiliary agencies, similar factors led to the recruitment of women for overseas service. Prominent women reformers worked behind the scenes to persuade male leaders to recruit women. Colonel

Harry Cutler, chairman of the Jewish Welfare Board, was confronted by leaders of the Council of Jewish Women and the National Federation of Temple Sisterhoods with an ambitious proposal for an autonomous Women's Division; Cutler was able to quash the plan only by opening overseas welfare work to women and initiating his own recruitment program with the assistance of the YMCA.[15] The desire to advance individual organizational interests was also an important impulse. As the auxiliary organizations vied with one another for contributions, prestige, and positive publicity, leaders found the employment of women auxiliary workers to be the key to bolstering their popularity with the troops.[16] Finally, like Fosdick, the leaders of the auxiliary agencies emphasized the special contribution that women could make at the front by bringing moral influence and a bit of homelike cheer to the soldiers. Making the case with unintended humor, one leader insisted that an American soldier would see his mother's face through the hole of each doughnut that a canteen worker fried.[17]

This point is central to understanding the decision to employ women overseas. By the fall of 1917, an official view of women's auxiliary service had crystallized and was promoted by civilian leaders, the military, and the press: women in France were envoys of the American home front, representatives of the mothers, wives, and sisters left behind. This imagery appeared incessantly in magazines and newspapers, exuding sentimentality or homey comfort. "These women . . . are the 'little mothers of the battlefields' whom you read about as cooking, mending, singing, praying . . . serving hot coffee to sentinels in the dead of night, and doing what you mothers of fighters would do for your boys if YOU were over there!" read subscribers to the *Ladies Home Journal*.[18] In military publications the language was sometimes gruffer but the sentiments the same: *Stars and Stripes* pronounced having "real American women" in France "a mighty fine thing for this man's army."[19] Much as a shared heritage of chivalry, as Paul Fussell famously observed, was the cultural underpinning of the British war effort, a discourse, quite literally, of apple pie and motherhood was a foundation of patriotic obligation for Americans in the Great War.[20]

How should such domesticated sentiments be viewed? To some extent they could be accepted at face value. Many early twentieth-century Americans regarded middle-class home and family life as the preserve of their nation's finest values. One thread of progressive-era social policy was an attempt to bring domestic values to bear on social and political relationships.[21] The domesticating impulse was manifested in the army, not only in the creation of "homey" canteens but also in such efforts as the armywide "write-to-mother" day sponsored by AEF headquarters and the postmaster general and in an orphan-sponsorship program widely promoted in the AEF. But sentimental rhetoric was a cloak for other concerns and purposes as well. Americans were deeply divided in 1917 over the wisdom or necessity of sending American boys to fight the "European war"; mass conscription heightened soldiers' sense of anonymity and alienation. The official view of women's work was an assurance to parents that their sons were being well cared for. Selling the war to an uneasy American public was also a major concern of the Wilson administration, and a sanitized, safe, and homelike war was far easier to sell.[22] Feminist theorists have made a similar point, asserting that the "patriarchal, militarist" notion that "Mother" or the "Motherland" wants men to fight has been used to legitimate war. By casting women in two roles, mother and nurse, the state "depicts death and destruction as protected and perpetrated by the maternal life force," argues Jane Marcus. The language of domesticity, when applied to war, implies that men fight and die for their womenfolk, thus deflecting attention from war's economic and political causes.[23]

Policymakers were concerned as well by the age-old association of women at the warfront with "camp followers" or prostitutes, a potential impediment to women's enlistment for overseas service. Women's labor was essential to the war effort; yet, fear of moral corruption awaiting young women in the war zone could hamper recruitment, not just for canteen work but in the crucial field of nursing as well. The creation of the mother-sister image, a safe and sanctioned role for women overseas, broke the association with camp followers and allayed anxieties about what might happen to women alone with fighting men.[24] That the army was involved in myth-making is made clear when one considers that real families were not at all welcome at the front; until the final months of the war, female relatives of servicemen were technically barred from enlistment through what was popularly called "the brother/sister rule" or the "sister exclusion." While military and civilian officials considered real sisters and wives a disruptive force, they believed that surrogate families or pseudofamilies could have a salutary effect on soldiers by reminding men of their responsibilities to the women they left behind.

But military and civilian officials walked a fine line: if American women were needed as a diversion from French prostitutes, they could not be exclusively the chaste, desexualized angels, or even the kid sisters, projected in the official view. A striking letter from Fosdick to the YMCA Department on Women's Work disingenuously revealed the military's other agenda for female auxiliary workers. Fosdick wrote to Elsie Mead in Paris: "The girls recently coming over under your auspices are splendid. . . . Bishop Brent . . . told me that on his boat were 90 new Y.M.C.A. girls. . . . He spoke of them as being 'dangerously attractive' which is just the way the A.E.F. likes to have them. Pulchritude helps."[25]

3. Auxiliary workers of the YMCA preparing a fire and heating coffee in back of a mobile canteen. Physical working conditions were often rudimentary. U.S. Army Signal Corps photograph (U.S. Army Military History Institute, Carlisle Barracks, Pa.)

Fosdick's use of the word "danger" is particularly interesting, for it conflicts with the image of woman as "safety," a haven from the danger of war. Yet the roles of mother and seductress were clearly linked on one level, reflecting the dialectical construction of female sexuality that has figured prominently in the rhetoric of modern warfare.[26] The complexity of this view of women left open a set of significant questions about female auxiliary workers and their place in the army. Were these women employed for their strengths and skills as workers, for their inherent moral influence, or for their dangerous attractions?

In the official view of women's auxiliary service promoted by military and civilian leaders, women canteen workers went to France as dutiful daughters and sisters to safeguard the morals and morale of their male compatriots. Given the prevalence of this view and the powerful rationalization it offered for women's service overseas, it is not surprising that some women represented their canteen work as an effort to domesticate the war. But many female journalists, who were insightful observers of gender relations in the AEF, sensed that something quite different was going on. Margaret Deland, sent to France by the *Woman's Home Companion*, noted that women enlisted for auxiliary service in France out of a "desire to stand up beside the boys and say, 'Here! Look at me! I'm just as good a soldier in my way as you are in yours!'"[27] Altruism, adventure, and ambition were all factors in auxiliary women's enlistment. Some women were driven by a desire for social and sexual freedom, and some by a craving for equality and public recognition. Above all, most women were motivated by an ideal of patriotic service. The working women who volunteered for overseas service considered their work both an important source of identity and a form of engagement in the social contract, a vital connection to the public realm. Auxiliary workers felt that they could be useful, despite their frequent uncertainty about their role, by offering their labor at the front. Yet in the end, they were disappointed: their work was more closely tied to voluntary domestic work in the home than to public service or paid employment; and they were generally isolated from the military aspects of the war. The sentimentalized and domesticated rhetoric permeated all of their tasks for the AEF. These definitions and limitations frustrated auxiliary workers' aspirations and reinforced their doubts about the usefulness of their contribution.

For the majority of auxiliary workers, the workplace was a canteen, which served as the social center for the enlisted men in the camp, base, or village to which she had been assigned. Workdays were long and shifts were hectic. Typically, canteens were open from mid-morning until nine or ten at night, and with preparation and clean-up time, women worked for twelve hours at a stretch. In many places, the day was even longer. On an aviation base where men arrived cold and hungry on early morning flights, Lucy Lester began making a fire for cocoa at 6:00 A.M. "We are supposed to have aff [sic] a day every week, several hours every day, but I can truthfully say that neither I nor my co-worker has had more than an hour free any day since we went to work." "Had a miserable night at the canteen," wrote Margaret Hall, who worked in a Red Cross facility that served both French and American troops. "Couldn't sleep much. Thought I'd die between 4 and 7. No time to drink a cup of coffee before I began, so I got almost to a state of fainting from exhaustion . . . lifting those heavy pitchers and rushing madly about to keep all the poilus [French soldiers] satisfied and not let any feel neglected . . . eight hours without one second off!" Marian Watts concurred: "Our days are hectic, 5000 things to do all at once."

In large canteens, the sheer volume of work was overwhelming. "Spent this afternoon making caramels and fudge," wrote Bertha Laurie, "but we shall not waste time on it again. . . . It would take days and a long kitchen range to feed 300 boys." The infamous Salvation Army doughnut, a concoction primarily of flour and lard, was one solution to the problem of mass-producing treats with limited supplies and minimal staff. Margaret Hall found work under these conditions impersonal: "There are such mobs at the canteen all the time that I could give my best friend coffee with my own hands and never know it. My eyes never get above the pitcher I am holding, or the cups I am filling. Hour after hour I do that, coffee in one hand, chocolate in the other, often trying to make change in between."[28]

Finding herself too busy for personal interaction was especially trying for an auxiliary worker, since her relationships with the men in her canteen were the very heart of her job. Indeed, socializing was a primary part of a canteen woman's work, which enormously complicated social relations for canteen workers at the front. There was little differentiation between work and leisure for auxiliary workers; not only was their job performance measured in terms of how well they got along with men, but their leisure activities were also subject to scrutiny. Canteen women were asked to meet the social demands of their "customers" while striving to conduct a social life of their own in a novel and often discomfiting setting. Most difficult of all, canteen workers were expected to walk a tightrope in their relations with men, on the one hand upholding the norms of decent, respectable behavior suitable to the envoys of middle-class American womanhood and, on the other hand, offering diversion or distraction to the soldiers through just the right amount of humor, high spirits, and flirtation. Negotiating her way between these conflicting demands surely tested a canteen worker's flexibility and social ingenuity.

Winning over her "customers" was the canteen worker's first and most essential task. A popular, crowded canteen was the clearest measure of a woman's success, according to canteen workers and their supervisors. "When I appear in the morning with my mammoth key, there is always a long line of boys waiting for me to open up shop," Marian Baldwin wrote happily. If a canteen worker was not a "good mixer" or was too stiff or reserved, it was a cause for concern among her supervisors. Yet, gaining the friendship of the men was sometimes a challenge, as one woman found: "The first night after the Chief had taken me over . . . and I had had one cursory glance at them [the soldiers], I came back feeling that my hut contained the roughest, toughest set of young ruffians that I had ever laid eyes on." The rougher and tougher the group, the greater the woman's sense of accomplishment when she won their trust. Class and ethnic differences frequently added layers of complexity to the process. Many women, particularly those from elite families, were exhilarated by the chance to "mingle" with men of different backgrounds. "You know I have only known one sort of people all my life. Now I am becoming acquainted with a good many sorts and am liking them all," wrote a YMCA worker from a well-to-do family, who had befriended a former pugilist and a man with tattoos. "Two or three Irish lads with merry blue eyes and the most alluring brogues are generally hanging over the end of the counter and are very much my friends," wrote another, who described her division as "fascinating," a "cross section of the Lower East Side."[29] Yet this sort of democratic romanticism or patriotic "slumming" easily edged into condescension, or worse. "Absurd, snobbish little Jew," "ridiculous niggers," and similar phrases pepper the writings of some women workers. While many women were challenged by the diversity of the AEF, others harbored typical racist, anti-Semitic, and other prejudices that were expressed in an acute unease with the heterogeneity of army life.[30]

Relationships between canteen women and soldiers depended on the attitudes and behaviors of enlisted men as well. On the surface, soldiers seemed to adopt the sentimental view of women auxiliary workers. Agency reports and canteen workers' memoirs record numerous comments like this one, in which a soldier compared canteen women with angels: "The first day you came here? I looked up and saw two American ladies standing there and I felt you had come right from heaven." Charles Williams of the Hampton Institute, who toured France for a report on African-American servicemen, found a similar attitude among black soldiers: "To the Negro soldier no thought was dearer or more inspiring than that of these women at home. . . . Only such feeling explains the tenderness, even the tears, with which the men in uniform greeted the women of their race who in one way or another strove to help them." Homesickness, fear of dying, and the horror of combat might well have prompted American soldiers to turn to female auxiliary workers for the homey comforts of hot chocolate and conversation. Canteen workers made constant reference to the soldiers' desire to "hear an American woman talk English."[31] Men in a foreign country where their language was not widely understood undoubtedly experienced a sense of alienation and loss of control, and familiar-sounding female voices may well have been a reassuring reminder of home.

At the same time, chaplains, auxiliary workers, and the military all had their own reasons for presenting the doughboy in this sentimental light. Soldiers' letters to women workers, informal camp magazines "published" by soldiers, disciplinary proceedings, and stories, poems, and sayings that were passed around by the troops, materials that might be termed war front folklore, show a very different picture. Together with auxiliary women's writings, they offer a more ambiguous and multifaceted portrait of relations between men and women in the canteens.

On the most elemental level, soldiers regarded female auxiliary workers as providing a practical, useful service. In Washington, D.C., Paris,

4. Salvation Army canteen workers serve black and white soldiers together at a field canteen. U.S. Army Signal Corps photograph (U.S. Army Military History Institute, Carlisle Barracks, Pa.)

and New York, officials might expound on the elevating, civilizing effect of the canteen, but soldiers themselves were genuinely appreciative of something hot to drink and a dry, well-lighted place to play cards or write letters. Furthermore, canteen relations were in many instances commercial relations, as canteens operating in the rear sector often charged a nominal fee for their "treats." Doughboy poems and letters assessed the quality of the services they received; women were commended if they made change properly, baked special treats such as pies and cakes, and greeted the men cheerfully at all times. Fairness and impartiality were also a great concern. Some organizations, especially the YMCA, were criticized by enlisted men for favoring officers or "gouging" them for donated goods. African-American soldiers complained of discriminatory treatment by auxiliary workers. In one incident, a soldier complained that a young Southern white woman closed her canteen rather than serve a black man; black soldiers praised the Knights of Columbus for its explicit refusal to "maintain the color line" in its own huts.[32]

What mattered most to soldiers, however, was that auxiliary workers were women. Marguerite Cockett, a YMCA recruiter who had run one of the first AEF canteens, told her female audiences not to be flattered by soldiers' attentions along these lines: "They look straight in our eyes but they don't see us. They see mother, wife, or the girl back home." Yet, the sources suggest that women often mattered for themselves, not as a symbol of or substitute for women "back home." Some enlisted men found in their interactions with women auxiliary workers a type of intimate contact that they had not previously enjoyed. A soldier named Buddie wrote a poignant note to the YMCA: "I was in the army for twenty-six months, joining in May 1917, and when leaving France it made me sad to think that all the pleasant associations of "Y" girls would be ended. . . . Have been without home or any family for eight years and sometimes the monotony of living in one room is overpowering."[33]

The awestruck reverence that soldiers sometimes expressed toward American auxiliary women, documented thoroughly by the agencies, was just as frequently balanced by a tone of teasing, jocularity, and flirtation. One Salvation Army worker carefully preserved the tokens of friendship given to her by soldiers, many of them as fond and teasing as this one: "There aint [sic] a thing here, nothin! Not so much as a cough-drop. We haven't seen a dough nut for days and our digestions are all in perfect condition. John is desolate as usual, and still mopes in a very unmanly fashion. Very seriously we all miss you very much. Everyone sends their best regards—Italians, Chinese, Hebrews, Hard-shell Baptists and the Captain. You have our cosmopolitan compliments." Soldiers preferred women workers who could dish out army lingo, jokes, and sassy answers along with the cocoa and coffee, and who were familiar with the individuals who frequented their hut.[34] For some of the American men and women who encountered one another in the canteens, such open and unsupervised interaction was itself a new and exhilarating experience, an initiation into the high-spirited, heterosocial forms of leisure forged by urban, working-class youth.[35]

Interaction with women overseas could be transforming for men in complex and contradictory ways. In August 1918, a YWCA hostess in Paris received a special request from an officer, who had signed up to use the Y's shopping service. The woman reported that the officer "wanted to spend 75 dollars for lingerie for his wife. He showed me her picture and told me something of her life so that it was a real pleasure to feel that you were buying something beautiful for a woman who had live [sic] a rather uneventful life in a Wisconsin lumber town whose husband . . . wanted to bring back something from Paris that she would never think of buying for herself."[36] Whether one interprets the officer's request as representing newfound sensitivity and tenderness or as indicating increased sexual sophistication and new demands, wartime experiences in France had clearly taught him something that would alter his relationship with his wife back home. It is clear from army disciplinary proceedings too that despite all of the efforts expended on their morals, some American soldiers did engage in sexual experimentation in France, and some committed acts of sexual violence, although against French rather than American women, the pattern of disciplinary cases indicates.[37]

Doughboy customers and canteen supervisors expected women workers to provide a charming and ready diversion from the monotony, fear, and loneliness of army life. Canteen workers responded to these expectations in a wide variety of ways. Elizabeth Putnam felt confused by the pressure from supervisors and coworkers to be pleasing to the men; "I understand that men *en permission* should have anything they want," she wrote, apparently including herself among those things, as she debated whether to accept an unwelcome theater invitation from two soldiers. A woman who resisted such demands could be made to feel uncomfortable or inadequate. Katharine Prest, who was enlisted by the YMCA soon after the armistice, never seemed to get over her discomfort and reticence around enlisted men; her relationship with the men in her canteen was often cool and sometimes antagonistic, as when soldiers destroyed her garden or "borrowed" her uniforms one night and greeted her in the morning in mocking imitation of herself. Grinnell's account suggests that soldiers may have penalized or harassed women who failed to meet their standards of accessibility and charm, as well as rewarding those who did.[38]

Some auxiliary workers experienced war front social relations between men and women as threatening or dangerous. Geneva Ladd, a Salvation Army worker from Portland, Maine, was induced by her mother to wear a pair of horn-rimmed glasses around the troops to "disguise her looks" and protect her from unwanted male attention. "I tell you seriously," Marian Watts wrote half-jestingly of her canteen work with the men, "it is no place for a young girl!"; but, in all seriousness, Marian and her female coworker would not walk home to their billet at night, fearful not of German air raids but of the American doughboys coming back from town. Still other women were assertive in upholding an older, alternative set of social norms, which was made plausible by the age gap between most canteen workers and soldiers. On their own initiative, for example, women workers for the YMCA established a "women's street patrol" in Paris and London, with the goal of policing American soldiers' behavior.[39]

Many women took no interest in new forms of social relations with men, preferring the familiar comfort of female companionship. Some auxiliary workers enlisted as friend, sister, or partner couples. Bertha Laurie wrote that the proximity of her hometown companion Marian Watts kept her from homesickness and that without her at the canteen she would have "succumbed" to despair.[40] New female friendships were also forged overseas, although such relationships seldom received explicit attention in women's accounts. In keeping with the conventions of the period, the intimate details of these relationships are never discussed in the sources, by the partners, or by other observers. Yet, some women clearly sought the company of other women. In their letters, some wrote touchingly of female friendships, at times suffused with romance. Rather than attending an army dance, which was "quite against [her] inclination," Elizabeth Putnam spent a "much pleasanter" evening in the company of a female coworker, strolling in the country for hours and watching the sun set over a quiet garden supper. The popularity of the YWCA's network of woman-only clubs, restrooms, and leave areas for overseas war workers suggests that many women wished to spend their leisure time with other women, reproducing overseas the patterns established at home in women's colleges or in predominantly female social or occupational settings, or among circles of lesbian couples.[41] It seems likely that the army and auxiliary agencies' insistence on heterosexual sociability and careful control of women's leisure time reflected in part anxiety over the possibility of lesbian liaisons in the AEF. Ironically, the canteen women who focused their social lives around other women may have had the most satisfying auxiliary experience, for they managed to carve out a social space distinct from their daily work responsibilities.

Still other auxiliary women found the new, more open forms of social interaction with men liberatory and highly desirable. One young canteen worker for the YMCA, for example, took delight in such exploits as an unchaperoned motorcycle outing with an officer and a series of private flying trips. Her letters home, surely meant to shock her elite and rather straight-laced parents, contained descriptions like this one: "My other adventure was a delightful moonlight ride in a motorcycle side-car, with an ex-national racer driving. Maybe that wasn't fun, too! . . . He has raced under an assumed name. His family have never known about it." Some women engaged in the racier amusements of urban social life, prompting a warning from YMCA headquarters: "We ask that no Y.M.C.A. woman worker should smoke or drink wine in public places and that in the field no one should lunch or dine with an officer . . . [or] accept an invitation to use an Army car except on Y.M.C.A. business."[42] Motoring, smoking, and dining in public, activities that came to be associated with a flapper lifestyle in the 1920s, had their proponents among American women at the front.

Some women experimented with more open expressions of sexuality. A few canteen workers, despite rather severe uniform regulations, wore clothing that auxiliary managers found shocking or overly revealing; a bookkeeper from South Dakota, for example, was criticized and labeled "ordinary" by her YMCA supervisors for her low-necked shirtwaists. Women from the YMCA's entertainment division were apparently the trendsetters in forging this new liberated style. The celebrated vaudeville performer Elsie Janis, on tour for the AEF, reported that one female entertainer for the YMCA wore strikingly short skirts on stage; Janis herself was known for telling off-color stories to the troops and dancing on tabletops.[43] On the far end of the spectrum, a few women initiated sexual relationships with men or engaged in ongoing love affairs and defended their right to do so. One Red Cross worker overheard another American woman invite a soldier to "pet her": "He had no idea of 'petting' before, but accepted the invitation, and they went away from the station in Coblenz arm in arm." Accounts of camp love affairs were recorded in diaries and letters, and rumors of scandal surfaced occasionally. Of course, it is impossible to know how prevalent such relationships were. Two anonymous and ostensibly autobiographical novels published a decade after the war portrayed nonmarital sexual relations, or "living together," as a pattern among war-weary Red Cross and YMCA workers in France. A sophisticated modernist literary style may account for the open depiction of female sexuality in these works. Yet, at least some women in France seized the opportunity to explore sexual relationships that were not acceptable among the "respectable" working and middle classes in the United States.[44]

Canteen women were faced with a contradictory set of expectations in regard to their conduct. They were encouraged and even enjoined by their supervisors to be pleasing to the men, as long as their interest appeared impersonal. But auxiliary agencies were quick to condemn their female employees for behavior that crossed into "indiscretion." Supervisors' evaluations for the YMCA demonstrate just how subtle the limits were; in a typical critique, for example, a female supervisor described one canteen woman as "not perhaps so in earnest as she should be and rather flashy."[45] Canteen workers' behavior was examined, not only by supervisory personnel, but also by casual observers of all sorts. The YMCA received numerous letters such as this: "I saw some rather disgusting conduct on the train among the women workers. . . . In January, while on my way to Nice, there were three Y.M.C.A. girls in the compartment with myself and three other officers, and two of these girls were lying up in the arms of two of the officers. . . . I happened to know that they were canteen workers and not entertainers."[46]

Reports of misbehavior among canteen workers were in part responsible for a large-scale investigation of the auxiliary agencies by military intelligence during the early spring of 1919. The report ultimately exonerated canteen women, concluding that, with the exception of singers and entertainers with the YMCA's entertainment division, indiscretion had amounted to no more than a few isolated, minor incidents.[47] Yet the fact that the investigation was done was more significant than its conclusions, for its focus on female morality and comportment suggests the extent to which canteen work was inextricably tied to notions of "womanliness" rather than to "rational" judgments of specific skills or accomplishments.

WOMEN FOUND CANTEEN work satisfying when they established a successful, popular canteen and developed good relationships with the soldiers. Planning and carrying out holiday celebrations—Christmas holidays with trees and carols, Jewish High Holy Day meals—also held special significance. Most women workers assured their family and friends that their work made a difference. But when the excitement of settling into a canteen had worn off, women began to wonder about the significance of their tasks. This question was captured in one of the most popular bits of canteen women's folklore, a poem called "IF," several versions of which circulated among canteens. The poem was a spoof, adopting Rudyard Kipling's famous paean to British military manhood to the situation of servicewomen.[48] While it seems at first to glorify women's service in homely, Kiplingesque terms, the poem can also be read as a deromanticization of women's work at the front. In contrast with male soldiers, the poem implies, the tasks and accomplishments of a canteen worker are trivial, her challenges those of a mother or housekeeper:

> If you can hold your cup, when all about you
> Are dropping theirs, and spilling tea on you; . . .
> If you can serve and not get tired of serving,
> And being asked for buns, don't deal out pies; . . .
> If you can meet each unromantic minute
> With willing labour and a smiling face,
> Yours is the Hut and everyone who's in it,
> And—which is more—you will have served your Race.

As the poem suggests, many women recognized after several months in France that what they were doing was essentially housework. Lucy Lester's catalogue of chores was typical: "We have had to make the Canteen fires, sweep, dust, sell behind the counter, cook, write letters, darn, teach French." Women were plagued by the problems inherent in housework: unskilled, repetitious, undervalued, and uninteresting, it offered no permanent or visible sign of accomplishment. Women's diaries are filled with dissatisfaction with such dull and tedious labor. Florence Turkington, a Salvation Army worker, recorded: "Each day is practically the same for me," and later the same month, "Dead day. Nothing doing."[49] More than the pressure of the hectic stretches, the tedium of the work called into question the meaning of women's service. Boredom was virtually a given in military life, and enlisted men too were frequently assigned tedious tasks. But the inescapable connection between canteen work and unpaid work in the home marked women's auxiliary service as a separate and unequal realm and undermined women's claim to equivalent service with men.

Where the fine line between patriotic service and domestic service was crossed, some auxiliary workers found their chores demeaning as well as dull. Elite, college-educated women were particularly sensitive to the lowly status of their labor. Mary Josephine Booth, a librarian from Eastern Illinois University, wrote her aunt: "The [canteen] directrice is not used to working with her equals and treats us as servants are treated." Mary Booth enjoyed setting up a small circulating library for the camp but "detested" the other canteen chores she was asked to do. "Thank fortune I don't have to wait on the officers in their mess. . . . One officer called to one girl that the fire needed coal. He probably didn't realize that the canteen workers are not servants." Margaret Hall, working in a Red Cross canteen that served both French "poilus" (enlisted men) and Americans, acknowledged that she was saved from the heaviest cleaning and cooking, probably by French hired help. Nonetheless she found the work "wearing in the end, because of the impatience with which you are viewed if you don't serve each individual the moment he appears on the scene. . . . Many of the poilus joke; some tap the counter with their cups; some call out, 'I've been here since yesterday morning'."[50] Soldiers, like children and family members at home, were importunate in their demands for women's attention and service.

Administrators for the auxiliary organizations overseas were well aware of the character of most women's canteen work. "All should understand that the primary task of women workers is . . . in the kitchen, the canteen and the cafe," wrote E. C. Carter, head of the YMCA in France, to headquarters in New York; women might find "very limited opportunities of assisting in French and other educational classes and . . . entertainments," but "ultimately the women will be in charge of the details of counter work."[51] Descriptions of this nature, it should be noted, were distinctly for internal consumption. Agency officials were concerned that auxiliary work might seem particularly demeaning to upper-class or college-educated women and that this perception might harm recruitment. "Outstanding men and women, the type most sought, were often reluctant to commit themselves without a definite knowledge of the work they were to do. . . . The dean of a women's college, for example, could not feel justified in abandoning her duties with the possibility of being set to wash dishes in a canteen." "Outstanding" men and women, the YMCA also noted in its postwar study, were difficult to manage and resisted following orders; they were "accustomed to making decisions rather than taking orders," and their refusal to "submit to rules and regulations" sometimes led to "insubordination," although their initiative, creativity, and expertise still made them invaluable.[52]

One solution to this dilemma was to create a subtle hierarchy of labor. A female Red Cross official promoted the idea that women workers "not all be of one type" and proposed a definite structure for the canteen work force. She suggested that 30 to 40 percent of women workers should have a knowledge of food preparation and that 50 percent should possess "youth and buoyancy"; these workers would compose the backbone of the canteen staff. A smaller group of women with "executive and managerial ability," approximately 10 percent, were required as canteen supervisors and administrators; such women "should be mature . . . ; should know how to organize and direct; should have initiative and good judgment and be able to create an atmosphere of happiness and good will among the workers." This commentator insisted that working women "of the school teacher variety" would not be successful in a supervisory capacity, as their career accustomed them too exclusively to "routine and red tape."[53]

The placement patterns of YMCA workers suggest that administrators followed such a model. When possible, older, educated women with organizational experience or professional backgrounds were put in supervisory positions or were shifted into special projects connected with educational, library, or religious work. Undifferentiated canteen work was reserved for younger or less accomplished women.[54] Despite the auxiliary organizations' publicity about employing America's outstanding women, working women from lower middle-class backgrounds— "women who were not afraid to work," as one YMCA recruiter put it— were regarded as crucial to overseas operations.[55] The implication was that these women would take orders more comfortably and act less independently than would women from elite or professional backgrounds.

But neither professional nor working-class women demonstrated docility. Mary Josephine Booth did not have to wait on officers' tables, presumably because of her social class and professional background; yet Booth reported that the "girls" who did do the work were "perfectly exasperated" with the assignment and with the officers' arrogant attitude. The reports of female supervisors allude to canteen workers' resistance to orders. One woman, according to her supervisor, "does not cooperate well if the task is not to her liking"; another was "not a success with fellow workers. Will not obey uniform rules. Not good under direction." Some women recognized and resented the elitism of auxiliary administrators. Mary Gertrude Ronayne, a Catholic public school teacher from New York, offered a spirited defense of her own capabilities in response to criticism by the administrators of the YMCA training program at Barnard: "I am sure my work has proven that the so-called "Faculty of

Barnard" is not competent to judge as to the efficiency of canteen workers over here." Isabel Anderson noted pervasive discontent: "many women feel they are made the drudges of the war, because they are worked hard and kept mostly at the base, and even there they are not given many administrative duties."[56]

Another feature of canteen hierarchy that caused dissatisfaction was the sexual division of labor that put male workers in managerial positions while generally confining women to housekeeping chores. The attitude of male workers was in part to blame, according to the YMCA administration: "It is clear that some of our men have the idea that the women should be assigned simply to canteen work or to the work of menials in the kitchen." Yet, until the final months of fighting the YMCA reinforced this division, distinguishing job title by gender: men were "secretaries" while women were "canteen workers."[57] In the rare instances when women were placed in executive positions, they faced considerable skepticism from male staff members. "I'm so chesty and delighted with my new promotion, can hardly bear it," wrote a woman who had been appointed head secretary of a large "Y" hut, with permission to employ an all-female staff; "It's all experimental and you can imagine how I'm plotting and planning to put it over, as we are being watched not only by Paris, but by the army here and the 'Y' men, half of the latter betting that we can't manage the problems."[58]

Even where there was technical equality between men and women, a gender division of labor and authority was maintained informally. Women auxiliary workers were expected to cook for their male coworkers as well as for soldier-customers. Male secretaries working without female colleagues managed the cooking and cleaning on their own, but when women arrived men were delighted to relinquish such responsibilities. Two female YMCA workers found a male worker's canteen in a "mess" after six weeks of solo effort, and they set to work scrubbing the place down and "setting things to right." These women took the male secretary's backhanded compliment in stride: "He told us the day before we left, that he had not believed in women canteen workers but that we had converted him. He said he never could have believed that ten days could make such a change, not only in the order and the cleanliness of the room—that was a woman's work, of course—but in the men themselves."[59]

Conflict between female canteen workers and male supervisors sometimes flared in the open. An army investigator reported a controversy between the female workers and male manager of one YMCA hut based on a chronic disagreement over activities and the use of space.[60] Gender conflict among overseas workers was sufficiently pronounced that an administrator for the YMCA Women's Division analyzed the problem in an internal memo for the "Y." In her months of canteen work, Dr. Marguerite Cockett found a philosophical and temperamental difference between male and female secretaries: the men were rigid and tried to impose their own strict standards of morality on the troops, while women had a more flexible, realistic approach that stressed the soldier's happiness rather than his morals. Cockett may unwittingly have pointed to another reason for tension: as noncombatants, male auxiliary workers were an easy target for the resentments of enlisted men, who subjected them to a stream of criticism bordering on disdain. Women workers reinforced these negative attitudes, intentionally or not.[61] Whether the source of the conflict was working conditions, values, or jealousy, the canteen reproduced the gender and class hierarchy of the businesses, offices, and schools from which most canteen workers came. For ambitious women who had come to France to find new outlets for proving their competence and value as workers, the recapitulation of male supervision and a gender division of labor was another source of disappointment.

More than any other facet of auxiliary service, the "dancing problem" dramatically highlighted the sources of women's disenchantment with overseas service and the tension between conflicting views of that service. Dancing duty for women combined two problematic aspects of auxiliary service: the domestic nature of women's work and the conflation of women's work with men's leisure. The "dancing problem" initially referred to the question of whether dances would be allowed in AEF huts and canteens. The male leadership of the YMCA overseas Executive Committee, with its evangelical Christian orientation, was resistant to this form of recreation. But military leaders and commanding officers were strongly in favor, arguing that dances were exceptionally important for military morale. Enlisted men apparently clamored for them; according to the postwar assessment of the YMCA Woman's Division, social dancing was the most popular form of entertainment among soldiers. Especially after the armistice, when concern about soldiers' morale and behavior became acute among the army general staff, the military was able to prevail on the agencies to allow their women workers to attend dances. When a company scheduled a dance, the commanding officer would send out a request for all the "canteen girls" in the region to serve as partners. With dancing duty tacked on to a full day of toil, the responsibility became burdensome, and a new "dancing problem" arose. "The other outfits are beginning to give dances and I'm in for three this week. Heaven help my feet!" said one auxiliary worker. Another remarked that "after our work at the hut was over at night we had to go to a great many dances because of the scarcity of girls—dances that were far more work than pleasure to us." Eventually the YMCA received so many complaints from women workers and other auxiliary agencies that regional directors were asked to set a limit of one dance per week.[62]

Another "dancing problem" was brewing in the AEF leave areas, which underscored the place of female auxiliary work in the structuring of sexuality by the AEF. The leave areas were casinos or hotels in some of the most beautiful resort regions of France that had been taken over by the U.S. forces and run as authorized vacation facilities for enlisted men. From the beginning, the concept of leave areas was closely connected to the military's antiprostitution and anti-venereal disease efforts. At the army-sponsored "conference on prostitution" in the summer of 1917, it was reported that General Pershing was "eager to push the scheme for an outing resort . . . as a counterattraction to Paris for soldiers on leave." At the army leave areas, unlike other auxiliary facilities, the majority of personnel were women. But the leave areas generally hired French staff to do the domestic service chores, and the entire orientation of the American women's work was to "give soldiers a good time." Reports from the YMCA catalogued the wide range of recreational activities hosted by the staff. During the day, picnics, hiking, tennis, boating, dancing, and sightseeing took place, and in the evening there were cards, games, performances, and still more dancing. "'Floating,' that is mingling with a crowd of men and being ready to listen, dance, talk or play games, was a regularly assigned duty. The mass games in the casinos, the get-acquainted children's games and the impromptu shows all required the girls' help." The high ratio of men to women meant that women's work time was regimented and tightly scheduled. "In each waltz or fox-trot, we were expected to dance with from three to seven men," one leave area worker recalled; "the girls never left the floor, even for punch, for that was brought to them where they stood." Each morning Marian Baldwin received a daily schedule filled out with her dates for the morning, afternoon, and evening. "You have no idea how strange it is to do things like these 'by order' and know that even if you don't feel like it or cordially dislike some of the men you are dated up with, you have to do it just the same and start off with a beaming smile, to laugh, talk and joke yourself and them through three or four hours on end!"[63]

These descriptions inevitably resemble those of a female worker in a brothel or commercial dance hall, and the image is ironically appropriate. The army's official leave areas were the U.S. alternative to the official and regulated brothels established by the French.[64] Leave area workers were hired "dates" intended to serve as a distraction from the prostitutes or the "loose French shop girls" whom the army feared soldiers would seek out if left to their own devices. This objectifying formulation of women's work was echoed in the attitudes of soldiers and administrators toward leave area women. The work "required versatility rather than ingenuity," according to the YMCA. The age limit for women workers was lowered to twenty-three years after the armistice expressly to provide younger women for the leave areas, and the administrators' patronizing attitude to the women was evident: "An older woman was always in charge of the groups of girls. . . . She planned their activities, arranged their hours, and solved their personal problems." According to the assessments of enlisted men, the auxiliary agencies and the AEF did succeed in creating a pleasurable atmosphere focused on the company of women. "A garden of Eden with twelve Eves and no serpent," one man described the leave area at Gervais. "The Y girls . . . will do anything to show you a good time—dance with you, take a hike, go to the movies. A man who can't have a good time with this bunch ought to go to the Old Soldiers' Home," enthused another.[65]

Women who worked in leave areas expressed stronger and more explicit dissatisfaction than any other group of workers in France. Margaret Hall, a canteen worker, described leave area women coming off duty: "Some of them are absolute wrecks. Dancing to order does not seem to agree with them. Many of them hate it there, and some who have come back say it was absolute misery. The Chalons workers who stop here on their way home begin to smile again when they land in the station." Even so accommodating a worker as Marian Baldwin felt relieved to be released from the leave area at Aix-Les-Bains. "The strain of Leave-Area work, the continual entertaining is really worse than manual labor, and I can see that we need to get off for a time." In contrast to her new placement at a canteen close to the front, which she found vital and needed, Marian Baldwin assessed the work at Aix-Les-Bains as superficial, a "gay whirl" of activity that drew on few of her resources and had no impact on the war.[66] The kind of service asked of women in the leave areas was a far cry from women's ideal of overseas service.

THE LEAVE AREA contrasted most sharply with placement at a hut or mobile canteen at the front. While the leave area or canteen was constructed as an imitation of home, a feminine sphere within the war, the front was the inverse, a realm of masculinity where war was most warlike and most removed from daily life back home. Assignment to or near the advanced section was the most coveted of auxiliary appointments, but very few female auxiliary workers served in such settings. Military officials purposely limited women's access to the front. Commanders routinely banned female civilians from the vicinity of battle. One woman assigned to the front by YMCA headquarters in Paris had her orders revoked by a major general, who warned her: "I cannot take the responsibility of allowing you to remain in the town. . . . as we are expecting a bombardment at any time, I must ask you to leave at once. I have two daughters at home just your age. I admire what you are doing but this is no place for women." The officer's statement suggests why the front was an arena of conflict between men and women. Nurses and telephone operators were quite likely to have been posted within his area of command, yet he asserted that the battle zone is "no place for women," a revealing instance of the selective erasure of working women's experience within the war effort. His statement also draws a line of connection between his own biological daughters at home and the symbolic, patriotic daughters he encountered at the front. To all these women, the realm of battle, the real masculine realm of the war, should be off limits. The argument that women did not belong near fighting was echoed by male auxiliary workers as well. The same woman who tangled with her commanding officer was also subjected to disapproval from her male coworker, a YMCA secretary: "He told us he wasn't entirely in sympathy with an army that allowed ladies to run all over the earth setting up canteens for it and that 'woman's place was in the home,' etc., and not in a gasless Ford on a dark French road in the middle of the night!"[67] Clearly, such activity on the part of women canteen workers overstepped a gender boundary to which many men clung all the more passionately the more directly it was threatened.

Yet, women auxiliary workers were determined to serve at the front, and many went to great lengths to do so, sometimes against direct military orders. Salvation Army women played an elaborate cat-and-mouse game with military officials, setting up unauthorized, makeshift canteens wherever they could. Marian Baldwin and three women companions staged a "revolt" against the ban on women: "We knew approximately where our Divisional Headquarters were situated and decided that some women ought to be there when the boys came out, orders or no orders." Invoking maternal authority, the bond of women with their "boys" (here posited as a higher authority than mere military orders), the four set off on a clandestine journey, which involved bribes and concealment, until they reached "their" division, making, in their own words, a "triumphal entry" into the area.[68]

As these conflicts make clear, men and women in the AEF had very different views of the proper place for women at war. The front was the most highly contested terrain, a realm from which men sought to exclude women and to which women fought for access. Women welfare workers could be barred because, in the end, their contribution was "auxiliary" or nonessential. Women in health care and communications created a greater strain on the careful gender divisions that were constructed around women's auxiliary service.

MOST CANTEEN WOMEN found satisfaction in their work with the soldiers, in the high-profile public role they played, and in the chance to take part in the war. Yet, women's resentment of "dancing duty" was only the most visible and vocal sign of discontent among auxiliary workers. When the initial excitement of participating in the war effort had passed, many auxiliary workers were left with a nagging sense that what they were doing was not really "useful" after all. One woman from an elite family, who had served both as a canteen worker and as a hospital letter-writer, expressed with cutting directness her own perception of the triviality of women's contribution: "Mother is right— . . . it would be nice to have some rigor in the job, but *tant pis,* there is none. . . . I have about resigned myself to being a little Sunshine."[69] The official, romanticized view of women's work was a double-edged sword; while it offered a powerful rationalization for women's service and was sometimes used by women to increase their power on the job, it also suggested that women's most valuable contribution was merely "sunshine work." The menial, unskilled nature of most canteen work and the gender hierarchy of the canteen, they believed, prevented women from demonstrating their skills and capabilities and suggested that national service for women would be little more than domestic service. Army and auxiliary agency policies that assigned women to leave areas as official dates reinforced women's sense that they were employed in war work not for what they could *do* but for what they *were.* Women auxiliary workers had come to France to shoulder a patriotic burden, to get to the center of a great national endeavor, and to expand their opportunities as workers; instead, they found themselves marginalized, consigned at the front to a domestic sphere much like the one they had escaped at home.

[4]

"The Stenographers Will Win the War": Army Office Workers and Telephone Operators

"Well, my dearest Father, this time I certainly have got one of my wishes . . . I surely am in a large institution where things go with a hum and I work with men." Elizabeth Putnam, the Radcliffe-educated daughter of a prominent Boston physician, had taken a new position as a clerical worker in the technical department of the U.S. Air Service, Paris headquarters. The job meant giving up her work with a Red Cross hospital canteen, but the employer's arguments had been persuasive to Elizabeth: the Air Service was racing to deploy airplanes, the administrative personnel was currently taxed to the limit, and an American secretary was essential. Finally, the Air Service representative suggested that Elizabeth's decision could make a small but critical difference in the outcome of the war: "He said that in his mind there was absolutely no question as to whether I ought to give up the work at the hospital or not; that where there I was helping to care for a few hundred *blessés* [wounded], here I would be helping to prevent there being thousands of *blessés*, by shortening the war." Although altruism spurred her decision, Elizabeth Putnam also made an assessment of what she stood to gain by the change. The compensations of the new job, she concluded, were "responsibility ahead and an opportunity to grow up with a thing that is growing at the rate of a mile a minute."[1]

Vital changes in technology and organization had created clerical and communications positions in the American Expeditionary Force (AEF) for women like Elizabeth Putnam. In contrast with auxiliary work, the jobs of office and telephone workers were concrete, differentiated, and skilled; no shadow of voluntarism was attached to such positions. Female office workers and telephone operators worked alongside male military personnel, in jobs that were integrated into the military structure. Experienced women workers were usually assigned by the army to high-priority military areas; women found themselves attached to offices in such critical or technologically advanced fields as communications, air service, and weapons supply. The proliferation of communications and record keeping at all levels of the American war effort led one administrator with the Young Men's Christian Association (YMCA) to remark that "she sometimes felt as though the war would be won by the stenographers."[2]

Although American women in France were doing skilled work of real value to the war effort, the War Department and the AEF command refused to grant them corresponding status or recognition. Female telephone operators and clerical workers connected with the army were placed under military discipline but were denied all military status or privileges. Military commanders, unsure of how to integrate women workers into traditionally male areas of endeavor, took a paternalistic approach, treating them as a special and protected category of personnel to be carefully monitored in their work and leisure hours. This pattern was most evident in army offices, where the new forms of work were accompanied by strict, new forms of work discipline and managerial control that fell with particular weight on women. The modern, bureaucratized military that emerged in the First World War created a place for women workers but one with little independence, responsibility, or status.

Clerks and telephone operators were determined to prove themselves in the army through hard work, skill, and individual merit. This strategy stood in marked contrast to that of female telephone operators on the home front, the most militant of wartime working women, who led a wave of crippling strikes against the Bell system in 1919. Office and telephone workers in the AEF faced many of the same problems as working women at home, but their response was notably different. They developed a work place culture that highlighted the interdependence of men's and women's work within the army bureaucracy and the significance of their own contribution to the war effort.[3] Clerks and operators in the AEF were willing to accept new work rules and military discipline as the price of equality and full recognition by the military; they grew disillusioned only when they realized that equality was not forthcoming.

IN FRANCE, MANY American participants were struck by the war's resemblance to a bustling business enterprise. A *Stars and Stripes* editorial, in a mirthful tribute to "Paperwork," noted that "up and down the length and breadth of the Army, [the typewriters] go battering their way on through service records, from-to subjects, payrolls, requisitions, transfers, court martial data, travel orders, clothing slips, passes. . . ." The U.S. war effort was in fact a big business. In France, the acquisition and distribution of people, goods, and equipment fell to the Services of Supply (SOS); at its height, the army's enormous logistical structure comprised six hundred and seventy thousand personnel. The SOS commander, Major General James Harbord, described it to his wife as "the most stupendous industrial enterprise ever undertaken by the army." The dimensions of the effort, along with the necessity for a rapid American buildup, posed an unprecedented organizational challenge for the U.S. government. Military leaders in the AEF called on the assistance of the nation's top businessmen. The managerial elite supplied officer-executives to the SOS, such as Charles G. Dawes, a prominent Chicago banker, and William W. Atterbury, vice president of the Pennsylvania Railroad, who injected modern business techniques and professional management into military administration. One of the most striking instances of business-military partnership was the involvement of the American Telephone and Telegraph Company; in virtually every aspect of telecommunications, from technical advice, research, and equipment to labor and training, the Bell System loaned its massive resources to the war effort.[4] With a new emphasis on personnel management, record keeping, efficiency, and accountability, it was indeed a new kind of war.

As war became a business, it became increasingly likely that "business women"—the growing mass of women who filed, typed, clerked, and operated telephones for America's corporate economy—would find a place in the modernized military structure.[5] Early in the war, military planners acknowledged that there might be a limited need for female typists, stenographers, and telephone operators. The official explanation for such service, the same used to justify the wartime employment of civilian women in agricultural and industrial occupations, was that the woman worker would "free up a man to fight." As one army spokesman put it, "the A.E.F. policy of employing women in offices and elsewhere" was intended to allow "every able-bodied man" to take "a man's job." A Marine Corps cartoonist offered the same argument in visual terms (see Figure 5): a woman marine stands by a desk and waves farewell to her male counterpart as he departs, gun in hand, for the front.[6]

These arguments were disingenuous. There was a significant distortion in the assumption that male and female labor were interchangeable. By 1910, the occupations of telephone operator and stenographer/typist were the fifth and seventh most feminized in the census, composed of 94 percent and 93 percent women, respectively. Women office workers and telephone operators in World War I were not substituting for men in male occupations but rather were stepping into *female* occupations now encompassed by the military. The enlistment of women in the navy predated the U.S. declaration of war; Navy Secretary Daniels based his decision to enlist women on the severe shortage of men with the typing and

5. A Marine Corps artist depicted the Navy's official explanation for female enlistment: the woman office worker would "free a man to fight." In actuality, the Navy initiated female enlistment *prior* to the war to address a shortage of skilled clerical labor. (Source: Captain Linda L. Hewitt, U.S. Marine Corps, *Women Marines in World War One* [Washington, D.C.: History and Museums Division, U.S. Marine Corps, 1974].)

stenographic skills necessary to staff the navy headquarters and regional offices. Similarly, American women operators were brought to France by the Signal Corps to replace French female civilians, not to release American enlisted men for battle.[7]

The familiar dichotomies presented by the phrase "free a man to fight"—home front vs. war front, female vs. male, auxiliary service vs. combat—obscure the essential change in war making ushered in by the First World War. Since the opening of the century, warfare has been managed by technicians, bureaucrats, and planners, and war has been conducted in the office as much as on the battlefield.[8] Workers in clerical and technical fields were thus a crucial labor force in the world's first modern war, opening the way for the military employment of women.

Yet, during World War I, policymakers were not able to come fully to terms with this change and its implications for gender relations in the military. The War Department's rejection of plans for a women's clerical corps and the AEF's ambiguous, quasi-enlistment of female telephone operators and office workers demonstrate the considerable disagreement within the military services over the proper place of women workers. Newton Baker's opposition to female enlistment was a source of frustration for military commanders at stateside facilities, who were forced to rely on women civilians to fill jobs in offices, laundries, and kitchens. The War Department's policy created an even more serious problem for army commanders in France, where no ready supply of American civilian women was available. Throughout the war, Secretary Baker and the AEF leadership engaged in a tug-of-war over women workers. Although the AEF devised an adequate solution to the problem of telephone service, AEF commanders were never satisfied with the supply of clerical workers under their orders in France.

In October 1917, General Pershing, commander in chief of the AEF, requested several units of female telephone operators for the Army Signal Corps. The AEF telephone system had been put in place quickly, but American soldiers and French civilian women had proved unable to handle the bilingual system to the satisfaction of the Signal Corps command. The chief signal officer for the AEF was bombarded with complaints about the shortage as well as the poor quality of workers. French female operators in particular were criticized by their military supervisors as "untrained and undisciplined."[9] Pershing believed that the "hello girls" of the Bell Telephone System would work with American efficiency and, if placed under military authority, could be kept on the job and disciplined by military standards. The adjutant general's office in November 1917 approved Pershing's hybrid plan to send the operators to France as civilian contract employees under special military authority. The Signal Corps policy was considered successful by the military, for it satisfied both the objections of the War Department and the skilled labor needs of the AEF; yet, it accomplished these ends at the expense of the women who served under it.

Addressing the acute shortage of skilled stenographers and typists proved more difficult. The AEF borrowed British workers of the Women's Army Auxiliary Corps and hired numerous English-speaking French and Belgian women to work in army offices. American officers and officials sometimes made individual arrangements to bring American secretaries to France, and they frequently raided the YMCA and Red Cross for office workers (as in the case of Elizabeth Putnam), convincing women that they could play a more valuable part behind a typewriter than a canteen counter. General Harbord's plan late in the war to enlist a force of five thousand American women as office workers advanced so far that news of the "WOC" (Women's Overseas Corps) reached the press, and a woman recruiter was hired in the United States. But this plan was squelched by the Secretary of War. In the end, however, General Pershing did bring several contingents of American women to France in the summer of 1918 to serve as civilian office workers with the Quartermaster Corps, Signal Corps, and Ordnance Department. In contrast with the highly publicized arrival of the "Hello Girls" six months earlier, Pershing ordered discretion and confidentiality in the enlistment of office workers, presumably to reduce tension with the War Department.[10] The majority of these women stayed on the job until the final months of the U.S. demobilization in the summer of 1919.

The status of female telephone and clerical workers in relation to the military remained a matter of controversy throughout the war and for many decades after. The military consistently maintained that the women were simply civilian employees. The women themselves, along with many officers and enlisted men, were convinced that they were members of the armed services. Telephone operators in particular regarded themselves as enlisted personnel, in part because they were required to serve in uniform and in part because, through a bureaucratic mix-up, most never received civilian contracts and were instead sworn in like soldiers. Furthermore, during their preparatory weeks in New York City, the women were put through basic military drills by the junior officers assigned to train them.[11] In attempting to clarify the status of these women, military officials made matters worse by grouping or comparing operators with army nurses, who were military personnel. In the face of this confusion, military officials were more careful in enlisting clerical workers: typists and stenographers were required to sign civilian contracts, and they were hired through the civil service. But the ambiguity of women's status was useful to the military: women, who believed they were enlisted personnel, behaved and were controlled like soldiers but received no military benefits.

Approximately five hundred American women served in this quasi-militarized capacity as telephone operators and clerical workers with the AEF.[12] This group signals an important direction of change in the military over the course of the twentieth century, the shift toward bureaucratic, noncombatant functions; the quasi-enlistment of female office and telephone workers by the AEF foreshadows the enlistment of hundreds of thousands of women in World War II, who served the Women's Army Corps and other female military corps in clerical and administrative positions.[13] Furthermore, the approach of the AEF to employing women as telephone operators and office workers exemplifies the tension between gender ideology and military necessity, a recurring theme in the experience of AEF servicewomen. In this instance, the changing labor needs of the military clashed directly with concerns and anxieties about the employment of women.

The utilization of female clerical and technical workers in the AEF highlighted the unsettling issue of the "emasculation" of warfare. Both military officials and enlisted men expressed uneasiness with the new, bureaucratic character of the military, which they contrasted with the "real blood and guts war" of the front. Noting that "the Army typewriters—male, female and inanimate—" were now omnipresent, the editors of Stars and Stripes pointed out that "a general could not send an army into action unless some other general ordered him to—usually by means of a typewriter."[14] But what kind of war was waged by bureaucrats, managers, and office workers instead of fighting men? Furthermore, the proliferation of paper, telephone calls, and telegraphs raised questions about sabotage, cohesion, and trust within the military. Not surprisingly, female office and telephone workers were at the center of the debate over these perplexing issues.

Historians have explored the impact of the machine on the traditional meanings and patterns of warfare; historian Eric Leed has asserted that World War I, with its anonymous and industrialized destruction of life, destroyed men's belief in war as a source of identity and as a test of individual will. The rise of bureaucracy disrupted the traditional connections between war, combat, and masculinity. The dilemma was especially acute for enlisted men and officers assigned as office clerks in the SOS— "knights of the crossed pen," as Stars and Stripes dubbed them—who worked alongside women in largely feminized occupations. The experience of one army field clerk illustrates the problem: judged unfit for regular service because of an eye "defect," the man was able to secure a military position based on his knowledge of stenography, yet long after he landed in France, he continued to question the legitimacy of his military service. "I have just received a letter from home saying that my mother is proudly displaying a service flag because 'yours truly' is with the A.E.F. in France. As I happen to be only a field clerk . . . I am wondering if it is right to let her display this flag. . . . I don't like to be masquerading at home as a soldier." Despite the adjutant general's ultimate ruling that the army's field clerks had equal military status with combatants, soldiers in office jobs still had to endure the ribbing and the skepticism of their peers and, worse still, their own sense of illegitimacy.[15] The debate over the status of army office workers raised some essential questions about warfare in a war in which "women's work," no matter who performed it, had come to be a crucial component of the military structure.

One strategy for resolving this conflict of expectations was to render "heroic" the work of army personnel in the SOS and other noncombatant positions. In January 1919, for example, the AEF issued "citations of heroism" to more than a dozen men of the SOS: engineers, laborers, stevedores, researchers, and others who had risked their lives under exceptional circumstances. Using terms generally reserved for combat soldiers, a *Stars and Stripes* article commended a unit of Signal Corps men for establishing phone service on an embattled hill under enemy barrage: "at the most critical point of all—in the attack on that bloody eminence which is called Hill 230—the advance was led not by tanks nor by the irresistible doughboys. Ahead of them all went the soldiers of the telephone."[16] The awkward attempt to fit office work into a familiar military mold occasionally spilled over to female workers as well. Telephone "girls" were commended for working in the advanced area, demonstrating "utter absence of nerve" under the threat of enemy air attack.[17] But on a day-to-day basis, most office personnel in the AEF, male or female, had little or no contact with danger. Judging the contribution of noncombatants by the traditional standards of combat was an unpromising solution.

The integration of female occupations into the military raised a second set of questions about the nature of modern war related to security and the control of information. The information revolution of the late nineteenth century, which allowed information to be preserved, organized, and transmitted in entirely new ways, created whole new classes of workers, many of them female, and ensured that every piece of information passed through many more hands than ever before. The question was, could women be trusted in these seemingly powerful new roles?[18] Advice literature for female secretaries and telephone and telegraph operators in this period promoted an ethos based on company loyalty and the efficient, anonymous, and detached performance of office duties.[19] But the advice pointed to an underlying anxiety: the secretary, by virtue of her access to valuable information, or simply by her key role as a middle person, has the potential to subvert the smooth functioning of business and industry. Traditional beliefs about women, gossip, and betrayal also amplified these new concerns.

As war loomed closer, questions about women and national security multiplied. The female pacifist and the woman spy were stock characters in popular culture and government propaganda of the war period. A *Ladies Home Journal* article from August 1917, for example, denounced "The Woman as War Spy: How She Carries Out the Most Despicable of All Feminine Work." Special concerns about trust and betrayal surrounded the figure of the office worker. As journalist Joseph Gollomb noted in his popular post-war study, *Spies*, "in the Great War somehow the human element in spying took on the subtlety of wireless communication, the sensitiveness of the microphone, the newness of the latest word from the science laboratories, . . . and the complexity of the age itself." Depictions of female clerical and telephone workers at the front were permeated by suspicion that their access to new technologies might pose an invisible threat to the Allied cause. In response to these concerns, military leaders implemented an extensive although crude system of security checks on AEF clerks and technical workers. It is no coincidence that U.S. military intelligence created the first internal security system for government workers during the First World War and that office workers were its primary targets.[20] As women workers set to work in AEF offices, the climate of suspicion and ambivalence surrounding their employment generated a series of efforts by the army to control their work and social lives in France. In a deeper sense, such controls pointed to more generalized fears about the growing female presence in military life.

IN APPLYING FOR a clerical position overseas, Anna Snyder captured the self-confidence and enthusiasm of the group: "I have it on good authority that our Government is seriously considering sending over a contingency of women for service at desk work. . . . *Now I want to be one of those women.* I have been in the Department now ever since last January, have learned a good deal, and like Alexander, I want 'new worlds to conquer.' . . . Incidentally, I want the experience and honor." The American women who went to France as telephone operators and clerical workers viewed themselves as a class of workers in a position to make a unique contribution to the war. A small group chosen through a highly competitive process, the clerks and telephone operators emphasized that they had answered a specific call for their services.[21] Unlike canteen workers who did undifferentiated "women's work," clerical and telephone workers brought specialized occupational skills to their positions. And the women believed that their position differed from that of canteen workers in another way as well: they perceived themselves as "militarized," or in the case of telephone workers, as full-fledged members of the army.

. Women's prewar work histories reinforced their sense of themselves as a special group. Although a few took telephone or clerical jobs for the sole purpose of enlisting, the majority had considerable experience in white-collar work. It is clear in hindsight that the 1910s were a crucial period of change in telephone and office work, as feminization and mechanization drove down the prestige and desirability of both fields. Yet, before the war both continued to be respectable work choices for white, educated, native-born women that were largely closed to black, Jewish, and immigrant women. Indeed, the fact that some college graduates still entered clerical occupations attests to their appeal. The backgrounds of AEF office and telephone workers reflected the transitional status of these occupations; as one Signal Corps woman described the first telephone contingent, "some like myself were college girls, some came from public schools, and some from private schools."[22] Yet, the commonalities within the group were far more important than the differences. Overall, clerical workers and telephone operators at the front were educated and experienced workers well prepared to take on the challenge of service for the army in France.

Despite the sometimes curious, sometimes celebratory atmosphere that greeted women clerical and telephone workers, the military was quite unsure of how to integrate women in these new work capacities. Furthermore, telephone and office work, which seemed to women like Elizabeth Putnam to hold a promise of advancement, was in fact in the process of being feminized and simultaneously de-skilled, which affected women workers at the front as well as at home. The military responded during the war to changes in the work force and the work place by imposing a myriad of controls over women workers. Women responded by devising a work place culture meant to enhance their own status, frequently by inverting or appropriating the values of military managers. This strategy, individualistic and self-confident, was in keeping with the attitudes and experiences that army clerks and telephone operators brought to their work and with their determination to pioneer an equal role for working women in the national crisis.

AMERICAN TELEPHONE OPERATORS arrived in six units between March and September 1918. Most were stationed in three large telephone centers, although during the final months of the war a few provided phone service for the advancing army close to the front. Female clerical workers followed the first telephone operators five months later; War Department opposition to the use of women secretaries delayed earliest sailing until August 1918. The majority of female clerks were stationed at SOS

Back our girls over there

Y.W.C.A.

United War Work Campaign

6. A YWCA poster of an AEF telephone operator parallels the operators' own sense of work identity: focused, skillful, and efficient, she makes a key contribution to the prosecution of the war. Created by a women's organization, this image of a woman war worker on the job was highly unusual for WWI poster art.

headquarters, while smaller groups were sent to divisional offices.[23] Most of these women were hired by the Ordnance, Quartermaster, or Signal Corps as typists and stenographers, but others served as statistical clerks, index and catalogue clerks, topographical draftswomen, and dactylographers (fingerprinting technicians). Several officers requested trained librarians to organize their filing systems. After the armistice, American clerical workers were shifted to the departments that carried the brunt of the demobilization effort.

The offices of the AEF resembled the business, government, and telephone offices at home, prompting one operator to write that "we hardly know we are at the war." Administrative organization and communications technology shaped the work experiences of female clerical and telephone employees. Telephone operators were connected, quite literally, to the machinery they operated. In the typical Signal Corps office, between five and seven operators, wearing headsets, were plugged into telephone boards lined up around the walls. The work place hierarchy was also similar to that in telephone companies at home. Operators were observed by a supervisor, who stood behind them and moved up and down the line. The chief operator sat apart, at a separate station. Because round-the-clock service was required, the women worked evening as well as day shifts; the night shift, with the lightest traffic, was covered by Signal Corps soldiers.[24]

The clerical worker's job environment was also shaped by machinery—telephone, typewriter, adding machine—but it was the human demands of supervising officers that structured her experience. A secretary's tasks were more varied and discontinuous than those of an operator. A typical work day for Elizabeth Putnam included taking dictation, typing letters and reports, filing papers, answering the telephone, and processing requisitions, all interrupted frequently by questions and requests. The distribution of tasks throughout the day was also irregular. Official army work hours for office personnel ended at 5:30, but clerical workers were frequently asked to stay late to help complete reports or take minutes for meetings. Taking shorthand notes was perhaps the most critical responsibility for female clerical workers; few enlisted men had the stenographic skill to cover meetings, where technical language was frequently used and business moved quickly.[25]

Jobs for American telephone and office workers required fluency in French as well, although later in the war knowledge of French was deemphasized in hiring, as most communication took place within the English-speaking AEF system. Clerical workers were frequently called on to serve as translators or to transcribe into English documents written in French. Not all were up to the task. The first units of bilingual telephone operators were hired specifically for their knowledge of French.

Still, the rapid French of native speakers was different from what many women had learned in the classroom or had heard growing up. All of the operators needed to learn the proper French conventions for telephone use.[26] Women operators were amused by the "doughboy French" of their male compatriots, and soldiers were astounded by the francophone abilities of some of the American women.

The bilingual component of the job had a less obvious but more significant implication for American women: it placed them in contact and competition with French women. One of the major reasons bilingual American operators were hired initially was to communicate with the French telephone system and with the portions of the American system operated by French workers. Relations between the American and French operators were far from cordial. Women in the U.S. Signal Corps complained of their difficulty in gaining the cooperation of French operators. American women attributed these problems to cultural differences, invoking the stereotype of Mediterranean languor to explain why French service was slow, erratic, or inefficient. Most asserted that "wheedling" or flattering the French workers would improve service and yield the desired results. But another operator was more insightful; she believed the behavior was intentional, an expression of resentment for their displacement by Americans: "The French girls whom we replaced had been in the office since its infancy. . . . They resented our coming, as it put them out of good jobs." In this particular office, the French women departed en masse the morning the American women arrived, leaving the newcomers to face several difficulties without assistance.[27] In fact, the French operators' resentment was justified: American women were hired to replace French women, and the alleged shortcomings of French women workers had led to the hiring of American women in the first place.

American women, French women, and American soldiers often worked side by side in large offices, creating occasions for mutual observation. Helen Scriver's opinion of French clerical workers was typical: "I have four typists but I can type more cards in a day that [sic] the four together. The French simply do not know how to concentrate." Work place competition often spilled over into social competition. At the Air Service headquarters, a popular American junior officer courted, and eventually married, a French file clerk, to the dismay of several of the American women. One wrote, with the racism typical of white Americans of the period, "Too bad. He's such a nice boy. I'd as soon marry a coon as a French person." This arrogant attitude was reflected in employment practices. French women in mixed offices were assigned to less desirable positions and given less pay than American women.[28] When the formation of the Women's Overseas Corps was announced in *Stars and Stripes*, the article speculated about whether a U.S. women's corps

7. A unit of uniformed Signal Corps operators posed before an AEF telephone office. U.S. Army Signal Corps photograph (U.S. Army Military History Institute, Carlisle Barracks, Pa.)

might lead to the massive firing of French women from AEF offices. The French women must surely have wondered themselves.

American soldiers generally greeted American women workers as a welcome distraction rather than a threat. The first female Signal Corps units arrived in a blaze of publicity. Under the headline "Hello Girls Here in Real Army Duds," *Stars and Stripes* gleefully reported:

A Melodious, Mirthful, Extravaganza . . . Produced for the First Time in France . . . Assisted by a chorus of 33—COUNT 'EM, 33—Real American Telephone girls . . . Such, in brief, might well be the handbill announcement heralding the arrival in France of the vanguard of the Hello Girls' detachment. . . . They arrived just the other day and like everything else that's new and interesting in the army—yes, they're in it, too—they were lined up before a Signal Corps camera and shot. Grouped about the base of a statue in a little Paris square, they presented a pleasing sight. (American girls always do.)[29]

Significantly, this AEF reporter insisted that the telephone workers were "in the army." Uniformed units of women who traveled together, marched in formation, and wore U.S. army insignia seemed sufficiently military to be considered "girl soldiers." Yet, the number of women was too small to raise concerns about displacement of male soldiers or to generate extensive work place conflict.[30] More extensive employment of women in clerical and technical positions might well have caused tension, as it did for nurses. Merle Egan Anderson, an operator, met some hostility when assigned to train groups of Signal Corps men "whose standard greeting was, 'If I'm going to be an operator, where are my skirts?'" Anderson recalled that "one hard-boiled sergeant . . . refused to report to a woman, until he spent a week on K.P. and decided I was the lesser of two evils."[31] The limited use of women as clerical workers and telephone operators in World War I enabled soldiers to regard them for the most part as a novelty.

The contact that most American men had with female telephone operators in France was on the other end of a telephone line; in this way, operators had an impact out of proportion to their numbers. Soldiers emphasized the positive effect the women had on their own morale; women operators eased their conversations and made them feel at home, much like canteen workers. A male journalist recorded a typical response on hearing an American woman's voice in his receiver: "It took me a full minute to recover. . . . It broke up the blues. I wanted to give three cheers for something or other." And he concluded, "I reckon the well-modulated, courteous and very American accents of a hello girl dripping in at the left ear have much the same effect on a homesick American as the soothing hand of a nurse on a sick soldier." It is interesting that this author, like many others, placed telephone work in a continuum of women's "caring" labor at the front. Women operators were praised for their tact, cheerfulness, and ability to soothe ruffled feathers; *Stars and Stripes* went so far as to assert that female telephone operators' talent for handling irascible officers was the major reason they were brought to France.[32]

But in fact, the work of telephone operators and clerical workers, in contrast with that of other women at the front, had little or nothing to do with caring for male soldiers. Secretaries and telephone operators worked with equipment to record and disseminate information. While soldiers focused on the women's effect on morale, very different assumptions and concerns about women's work underlay army policy. Accommodating civilian women within the military structure was a necessity, but commanders were determined to do so with as little change as possible by carefully controlling almost every aspect of women's service. AEF officials constructed extensive regulations and controls in three areas of women's lives: leisure time and living accommodations, loyalty clearances and security precautions, and the rate of work and work place discipline.

FOR ALL THEIR CONFLICTS with Secretary of War Baker over the employment of women workers, AEF commanders agreed that the employment of women presented special problems. As civilians, women were not technically under the army's control or responsibility in matters of housing, meals, or leisure time. Yet, military commanders were not comfortable with the idea of bringing single women to the front as workers pure and simple, and they took an active, highly paternalistic role in overseeing the women's well-being. However, it seemed inappropriate for male officers to be involved in the intimate details of women's private lives. The solution to the dilemma was found by turning to a voluntary agency, the Young Women's Christian Association (YWCA). The YWCA was in a unique position among auxiliary agencies at the front. An organization by and for women, the YWCA originally opened operations in France to provide canteens and other social services for women war workers; soon it had established a network of restrooms, clubs, and hostels for the thousands of French, British, and American women engaged in war work in munitions plants, canteens, offices, and hospitals.[33] By the time of the armistice, the YWCA had established twelve Signal Corps Houses for AEF telephone operators and had taken over responsibility for housing the AEF stenographic units as well.

The Signal Corps House served as residence, "mess hall," and recreational center and was intended to "make the life of the telephone girls . . . homelike and restful." Each house had a live-in "secretary," whose duties encompassed "general management of the billets, initiating a social program, chaperoning at social functions, . . . supervising the general physical welfare of the operating force and suggesting plans for improving matters affecting the general welfare" of the women.[34] The YWCA secretary also enforced rules of decorum established by the Y, including a policy that women always go out in groups of two or more and a requirement that women obtain an evening pass with an "hour of expiration" if they wished to be out after dark. As supervised group homes, the Signal Corps houses were modeled on the "organized boarding homes" for working women that the YWCA had established in major American cities at the turn of the century. They were also reminiscent of college dormitories or sororities.[35] Like the working women who boarded in YWCA houses in American cities, war workers in France had a mixed reaction to their accommodations. Most were impressed by the care that had been taken for their comfort. "I had visions of a dug-out and instead, a palace," one telephone operator wrote her mother; "it is much better than a telephone operator's life in the U.S." Yet, the women were aware that the YWCA houses had a moral, protective purpose as well. Another operator later described her living arrangements: "Had a French apartment house with . . . a YWCA lady in charge as a hostess and I presume chaperone."[36]

Women expressed some impatience with the regulations that hemmed in their social lives. Opera, which never ended before 11:30 P.M., was a favored pastime of American stenographers in Paris, and the system of night passes with time of return was a particular annoyance. "One rule is quite foolish, I think. They cannot associate with privates or civilians," a telephone operator noted. This regulation was conveniently adapted from the social rules for army nurses but applied in this case to civilian women. Some strong-willed telephone and clerical workers responded to such rules with open defiance. Josephine Davis, for example, dated an army enlisted man throughout the war despite the ban on fraternization. Yet, most women were themselves concerned with protecting their reputations. Equally important, the women believed that submitting to military authority was part and parcel of becoming "good soldiers." Most seemed to agree with Oleda Joure's assessment: discipline was strict, but "we accepted without question. War was serious business and not to be prolonged."[37]

In the work place, AEF officers exerted direct and substantial control over clerical and telephone workers. Coercion and suspicion were prominent elements in the security clearance system imposed on civilian workers. The security system in France was an outgrowth of anxiety over espionage and disloyalty that had been brewing in Washington, D.C., even before the declaration of war. The AEF policy took shape in the first month of overseas operation, July 1917, when G-2, the section of the AEF General Staff responsible for intelligence, instituted a requirement that the names of all civilian employees be submitted to army intelligence for investigation. The requirement, section 3 of General Order 13, evidently attracted little attention until the winter of 1918, when the U.S. army began to hire thousands of French and English civilians for work in salvage depots, construction, outdoor labor, and offices. The exponential growth in civilian employment increased the scope and inconvenience of the investigatory process according to officers in the field, who complained of the growing administrative and clerical burden.

Revised regulations, issued in February 1918, required only those with access to "confidential information," including office workers, interpreters, and stenographers, be investigated. Women were thus a prime target. The system of investigation that army intelligence ultimately devised was extensive, but crude and unwieldy. Hundreds of civilian job applicants were investigated each month, and their records preserved in a central index referred to suggestively as the "Suspect File." Army intelligence worked in close cooperation with the overseas office of the Bureau of Investigation, the forerunner of the modern FBI, scrutinizing the "national point of view," or loyalty, of the applicant, her moral conduct, and any pacifist tendencies she might have. At best, the process took more than seven weeks from start to finish. When a "problem" emerged, military intelligence delayed the case for further investigation or simply denied the applicant a clearance, causing her to lose the job. The problems were often accidental, trivial, or seemingly irrelevant. In the available files, only a tiny fraction of "suspects" were rejected, although it is perhaps possible that a separate file of rejected applicants was kept and later destroyed or lost.[38]

It is striking that the army would find it necessary and worthwhile, despite the scarcity of clerical labor, to establish an enormous, clerical-intensive program to catch what appeared to be in the end a negligible number of potential wrongdoers and spies. Once in place, however, the system had its own irrevocable momentum; in fact, the security clearance system for clerical workers was kept in place through demobilization, more than a half-year beyond the end of hostilities. Concerns with the loyalty and trustworthiness of civilian workers also extended well beyond the initial security clearance. It is difficult to determine the extent and nature of army intelligence activities, shrouded as they are in secrecy. Yet, there is evidence that telephone and clerical employees were submitted to regular surveillance in France both during and after the war. The chief intelligence officer for the S.O.S. headquarters, for example, ordered all office trash to be burned twice daily, before office staff departed for their midday meal and for home in the evening. Uniformed intelligence officers were distributed throughout the AEF and were responsible for routine security matters in the work place. Intelligence officers were authorized to work in "plainclothes" as well. The offices of auxiliary agencies were also objects of concern; one report recommended that "reliable men" inside the organizations be found "to act as informants," as the organizations were "difficult to watch" and offered a fine opportunity for "spies and grafters." The most elaborate arrangements for internal surveillance were created by the Signal Corps. Telephone operators were required to use secret code names when transmitting messages for and about the advanced section. Wiretapping, which originated in a Signal Corps program to intercept German communications, was later used to monitor U.S. employees and service personnel to ensure their compliance with security measures and to listen for signs of disloyalty. Telephone operators and office workers were a likely target for these "silent American watchers of wire talk."[39]

American women workers accepted these security measures with equanimity. Whereas military commanders fretted over the fact that civilian office workers saw and heard so much, from the perspective of women workers, access to confidential material was evidence that they were trusted, and their proper handling of such material was proof that they were trustworthy. Telephone operators and clerical workers turned their handling of sensitive, "inside" information into a source of pride. Merle Anderson, a telephone operator, reported that she and her co-workers had "advanced knowledge" of the armistice but had "carefully refrained" from discussing it with anyone. Clerical and telephone workers took pains to self-censor their letters: "Don't be afraid I will give away any State secrets, for . . . I have no desire to inform the Hun," Elizabeth Putnam wrote her family. Telephone operators felt the secrecy surrounding their work gave it an aura of romance and set it apart from the civilian work world. Grace Banker, a chief operator, recalled with both amusement and self-importance that an afternoon in the switchboard office sometimes sounded like a scene from *Alice in Wonderland,* where only the initiated can make sense of the proceedings: "Once in the mad rush of work which came before the Saint Mihiel drive I heard one of the girls say desperately, 'Can't I get Uncle?' and another, 'No, I didn't get Jam.'" [40]

Either despite or because of the stereotype of feminine garrulousness, women portrayed themselves as impeccably tight lipped. Grace Banker told a story about being "tested" on her ability to keep secrets: "One morning an officer stopped by and asked for Miss Banker. I spoke up and he introduced himself. After chatting for a few minutes he said very casually, 'By the way, when do you leave?' 'Why, I don't know,' I answered, although I had just received my sailing orders. He laughed and said, 'Well, of course, you really do. So do I. So it's quite all right to tell me. When do you sail?' 'Well,' I replied, 'if you know then there is no need for me to tell you.'" [41] The coda to Banker's story is significant. That afternoon she came across the same officer, who told her with a grin that he had been "trying her out"; the officer, she later learned, worked for army intelligence. His petty ruse, meant to entrap her, could well have justified an angry response. Yet, in recounting the story, Banker chose to stress the privilege of her access to confidential information and the opportunity it presented to prove her worth to the military.

Intelligence regulations overall had a minimal effect on the day-to-day work life of women in the AEF. Scientific management, another of the army's responses to the advent of a female labor force, had a far more powerful impact on the structure of work in AEF offices. Two issues became central in military managers' effort to assert control over office workers: the pace of work and absenteeism and tardiness. Telephone and clerical workers for the AEF generally accepted these new work rules as a wartime necessity and as proof of their skill and value to their nation's cause, just as they accepted security measures.

The AEF preoccupation with work place control was not, however, a by-product of the war; it was instead a direct outcome of prewar developments in corporate management. Changes in economic organization that gave rise to bureaucratic warfare also spawned the movement for professional management. "Taylorism," named for the most influential proponent of this reform, Frederick Winslow Taylor, was pioneered in the industrial plant, but it soon made its way to the business office. Although it was called "scientific" management, business reform was a set of attitudes rather than a strict formula; Taylorism evolved over time from its original concern with time and motion study to encompass a wide range of managerial innovations. The businessmen-officers in the AEF brought these new ideas to France as a weapon against waste and inefficiency. The Bell Telephone system was "in the very forefront" of the movement toward scientific management on the eve of World War I, which was clearly reflected in the management of the army Signal Corps.[42]

One of the central insights of scientific management was that control of time is a powerful management tool. In military offices, the contest over time management translated into a concern with the pace of women's work. Even before female employees arrived in France, AEF commanders made it clear that speed and efficiency would be expected of them. Qualifications for a clerical job with the Quartermaster Corps, for example, included the ability to take dictation "at the rate of at least one hundred words per minute" and to transcribe dictation on the typewriter "at a fair rate of speed, with neatness and accuracy."[43] The rate of work was also important in telephone service. Commanding officers of the Signal Corps struggled to accommodate a growing volume of telephone traffic in the face of an operator shortage; increasing the volume of calls handled by each operator was therefore critical. The Signal Corps, like the Bell System in the United States, used female supervisors to set and accelerate the pace of work.[44] Supervisors were responsible for "peg counts," a system by which they periodically measured and recorded the exact speed of each operator's work.[45]

The wartime career of Louise Barbour, a chief operator for the Signal Corps, exemplifies the role of female middle managers in enforcing work place control. Enlisted as an operator with the fifth female telephone unit, Barbour was promoted after the armistice to the position of district chief operator for Paris. She was responsible in this position for 66 French and American women operators distributed in five different offices. Her pocket notebook of the period was preserved and sketches the duties of

8. Telephone operators work an AEF switchboard under close observation by a female supervisor. U.S. Army Signal Corps photograph. (U.S. Army Military History Institute, Carlisle Barracks, Pa.)

her position. Barbour monitored the productivity of various telephone units by tallying the number of calls per hour handled by each operator. She was also responsible for passing on orders from above, including a prohibition against conversation during work hours. In keeping with the spirit of Taylorism, Barbour's notebook includes several references to the use of a stopwatch to measure operators' work pace. Barbour earned the approval of her commanding officers in the Signal Corps, who praised her "ability as a handler of women, as a general business woman, and telephone executive." After the war, this knack for "handling women" brought her a middle-management position at A.T.&T. headquarters in New York.[46]

Women managers and military officers were also responsible for patrolling the attendance of enlisted and civilian employees in AEF offices. Uniform hours from 8:30 to 5:30 daily, with a half-day on Sunday, were established for all SOS offices in April 1918. The practices of office workers, however, did not lend themselves to such regulation. Stints of intensive labor were frequently followed by periods when there was little to do. Evening work was common, and women employees often balanced out their schedules by arriving late when work was light or taking extended lunch hours to run errands or enjoy pleasant weather. Apparently, compliance with the official schedule was lax, for in the offices of the Signal Corps stern memos in May and October 1918 condemned infractions of these regulations. Officers in charge were informed that they would be held accountable for tardiness in their division. Office hours would be controlled by official army clocks: "For the purpose of having a standard time in the office, all clocks will be regulated with the clock in the Records Division until arrangements are completed for the installation of an electronically-controlled master clock." During demobilization, commanders intensified their campaign against tardiness. An attendance policy was established throughout the SOS, with attendance taken twice daily, in the mornings and after lunch. Similarly, after the armistice the Ordnance Department devised a system for monitoring the sick days of their American women clerks: any woman who was ill had to be examined daily by a designated medical officer, who determined whether the indisposition was "sufficiently serious to excuse the patient from duty." [47]

Despite the imposition of extensive managerial controls in the work place, telephone and clerical workers did not respond with overt protest. Acceptance of strict work discipline by AEF workers seems surprising, given the militant actions of telephone operators at home, before and during the war, over the same issues. [48] But in the AEF, managers were also commanding officers, and the risks of protest went far beyond the loss of a job. More important, perhaps, women approached their work for the army with a strong belief in individual merit, in work skill, and in their special role as female "firsts." Women appropriated or reinterpreted the ideology of military management for their own purposes, seizing on such values as speed and efficiency as a way to highlight their contribution to winning the war. This strategy was largely individualistic and had clear limitations, but it was by no means a subservient or demeaning one.

The emphasis that military managers placed on speed had a parallel in the values of clerks and telephone operators. Women prided themselves on the accuracy and efficiency of their labor. "The girls are always early at their work and their greatest pleasure in life is to give connections accurately and quickly," wrote one telephone operator. American women, according to another telephone operator, brought order and efficiency to the work in France: "Before long we had a directory made up, a more efficient arrangement of the boards had been effected, and we began to have a little system. Later on things ran smooth as clockwork." The ethos of efficiency and the ethic of hard work were also their claims to a genuine American identity, women asserted. One telephone operator described the enthusiastic attitude she shared with her coworkers as "the American woman's spirit in Uncle Sam's uniform." Speed was the special hallmark of the American telephone operator, according to officers, enlisted men, and reporters, as well as the women themselves. One operator boasted, "the American telephone girls . . . have astonished the French operators by the rapidity with which they take down a connection. Frequently, when traffic is heavy, they put up one connection with the thumb and forefinger and at the same time take down another with the little finger of the left hand, to the admiration of the French girls." Women were aware that Signal Corps commanders were exerting pressure on them to work as quickly as possible. At times, the fast pace and the volume of calls created a stressful and "hair-trigger" environment. "It was tough going," admitted one telephone operator. "[We] worked ten hours a day . . . it was a headache working in the office. It was drilled on us that every single call was so important." Yet, most women would have agreed with Louise Barbour's assessment of morale: "We were terribly busy in Sept. and Oct. and our traffic went up more than 30 percent, . . . but the girls are a picked lot and not one of us would have changed places for [the] world."[49]

In the work place culture of AEF office and telephone workers, the status and quality of their job derived in part from its position within the military hierarchy and its relationship to the vital work of important men. Like all office workers, clerical workers and telephone operators at the front compared, evaluated, and ranked their bosses and work situations. Being the secretary to a colonel was more prestigious than being the secretary to a major; being assigned to a general, even for a brief period of time, was a noteworthy development. In the working world of telephone operators, handling the calls of international leaders was part of the excitement. One operator was flabbergasted, and not a little pleased, when General Pershing called in the middle of a slow shift to ask her the time. Telephone operators who worked for the Peace Conference enjoyed handling calls from President Wilson to Clemenceau, Lloyd George, or Orlando, the Italian premier. "When Pershing can't talk to Col. House or Lloyd George unless you make the connection you naturally feel that you are helping a bit," an operator boasted to her mother, adding that such an experience was bound to make a woman feel "a real part of the army."[50]

Judging the quality of a boss involved much more than his prestige, however. Mary Lee's acerbic portraits of her various commanding officers reveal much about women's attitudes toward their work in the AEF. "The Major always drove me into a fierce rage when ever I thought about him, much less saw him, and some of those little pop-squirts . . . were so rude that it got a little on your nerves," she wrote her mother. In contrast, her favorite officer "has more to do than anyone else in Paris, I guess, but he never, never, never loses his temper. . . . Always has time to be polite to everyone, . . . and treats enlisted men and civilian employees and officers all alike as just people, all working for the same end."[51] Women workers wished to be treated with respect and shown appreciation.

For all their enthusiasm for the war effort and their willingness to put up with "necessary" military regulation, telephone operators and clerical workers were not willing to tolerate situations that they saw as compromising their dignity. Two instances of group protest by office clerks demonstrate women workers' sense of what they deserved. In the first, American stenographers working in a civilian government office demanded that they be given clean and adequate toilet facilities on the job, submitting to their commanding officer a list of their requirements, including soap, drinking water, and sufficient towels for the seventy-five women who shared the single washroom. In the second, a group of Ordnance women, departing for home in May 1919, wrote an indignant letter to their colonel to inform him that no one had arranged their passage: "After all assignments had been made to about 200 nurses and approximately 15 war brides, . . . and also several children, the 'left-over' cabins were assigned to the Ordnance Dept.," adding, "We are now aboard the steamer, and we feel it almost our duty to see that the remainder of the girls are better taken care of than we have been."[52] In both cases, the physical conditions were not the essential problem, for women workers in France frequently put up with much worse; what was crucial was their sense that they had been disregarded or slighted. This view of equality was contradictory in fascinating ways, resting on a demand for respect as well as a defense of their own respectability, a commitment to equality as well as an investment in the privileges of middle-class "ladyhood."

Above all, telephone operators and clerical workers wanted reassurance to know that their jobs were integral to the war effort. For the few telephone operators who worked near the front, constant reports of the fighting and the battle-related calls they handled were a strong affirmation of the significance of their work. Grace Banker saw a direct connection between her efforts and the success of the Allied advance: "For days I was on duty from eight in the morning until ten at night. But it seemed worth while when we gazed at the prison pen filling up with German soldiers." In offices far from the fighting, the connection between work and the war was less readily apparent. Yet, many women in these settings compared the war effort to a team or a machine, an interconnected network relying on the input of each of its component parts. Elizabeth Putnam pictured herself as part of the war machine, paraphrasing a pep talk from one of her supervisors in a letter to her family: "He feels that our great contribution to the war is airplanes, and that the quality and quantity we turn out in the next six months may determine the war, and will certainly decide whether it is to be six months longer or shorter; and that if the work failed anywhere along the line it would be the worst failure we could make; and that one place it might fail would be in the office— if they didn't have the right personnel—and that at present they lacked painfully an American secretary.[53] Putnam's construction, which stresses interdependence and the equal significance of all the parts to the whole, contrasts sharply with the hierarchical and authoritarian structure of the institution in which her work took place.

Helen Scriver, another office worker, was less confident that her work was so essential. At first her secretarial position with the American Red Cross in Paris seemed important and somewhat intimidating, much more challenging than her clerical position at the St. Paul Board of Education. But soon she had doubts, writing to her former coworkers, "I thought I would let you believe that I was holding the most responsible position in the American Red Cross when the truth of the matter is that I am still filing French cards and although it seems a little more romantic to be filing French cards than American cards still the alphabet is the same and B always comes after A whether you are in the B. of E., in the Fichier Central or in some other French Ouevre." Mary Lee also came to question the significance of her work. "I am a little low over my job just now . . . Have finally landed with the Adjutant doing the same miserable kinds of little jobs and waiting between jobs that I did [as a secretary] at the hospital."[54] The end of hostilities further eroded the romance of the work; without the grand patriotic purpose of the war to invest it with meaning, typing or connecting phone calls was simply a job.

A handful of women workers took their discontent a step further, developing a critique of military bureaucracy based on their work place observations. Mary Lee was the most articulate of these critics. The problem with bureaucracy, as Lee saw it, was that it was antihumanistic, a closed and self-perpetuating system where paperwork, policy, and hierarchy suppressed human needs. Within such a system, people quickly lost perspective and came to believe that paperwork *was* reality. Lee offers scathing portraits of officers mired in their own cynicism and boredom in her postwar, autobiographical novel, *"It's a Great War!"* In one scene, an army nurse nearly dies because a string of male officers and army field clerks insist on following the proper bureaucratic channels to secure the medication that would save her life. In another scene, on which readers and reviewers of the novel often commented, the commanding officer of Lee's hospital turns away a pair of French nuns who come to the office to make a simple request for his assistance with the help of the protagonist, Anne, as translator. Under previous French authority, the sisters recount, the hospital gave its food garbage each day to the Convent of the Holy Mother, where the sisters used it to feed their pigs; the sale of the pigs in turn fed and supported the orphaned children in their care. "The Major's eyes glazed as Anne explained this to him. Had he not just had constructed a fine incinerator behind the building? Had there not been a General Order relative to the Disposal of Garbage in Military Units? . . . 'Tell her it's all here in the orders. Tell her they say we burn it,' said the Major. . . . He waved the file of General Orders toward the doorway." Anne follows the women from the room, touching their arms and apologizing. The older woman replies: "Ah, Mademoiselle, I understand. . . . It is . . . his superiors, that oblige him to do this. They do not understand the needs of orphans." "They do not think about it," Anne said.[55]

It is significant that Lee presents military bureaucracy in gender-coded terms: the "Convent of the Holy Mother" is a counterworld to the army, an interconnected, organic, and preindustrial world of women and children. The bureaucratized military in her vision is definitively masculine. Female clerical workers have an uncomfortable position in that schema, employees of one system and members of the other. Mary Lee's was a minority voice, honed in the markedly different context of postwar America, but her writings drew on the doubts and discontents of other women workers in the offices and telephone exchanges of the AEF.

DESPITE THEIR DOUBTS, clerical workers and telephone operators had good reason to pride themselves on their work. A small, specialized force, they filled a crucial need at the front and performed admirably. Shortly after the armistice, Grace Banker, a Signal Corps operator who had served in the advanced section, reflected: "We missed the First Army with its code of loyalty and hard work. We were back in the petty squabbles of civilian life where even chief operators had 'tantrums' and where the wives of civilians attached to the Peace Conference spilled all over Paris in Army cars."[56] Like most soldiers, Banker saw her war experience as set apart from ordinary life, distinguished by a distinctive and admirable code of behavior. She expressed the differences in terms of gender, contrasting the front, defined by masculine values, with civilian life, a petty world dominated by wives and ordinary working women. In identifying herself with the masculine realm of the military, Banker laid out a vision strikingly different from Mary Lee's. Yet unlike men, who entered the military by virtue of enlistment, either voluntary or conscripted, women in Banker's situation saw their military status as something earned. As "American girl soldiers," clerical workers and telephone operators believed that their standing on the war front and their claim to citizenship derived from the loyal and efficient performance of their jobs during a national emergency.

In the post-armistice period, praise from the highest military commanders seemed to echo the women's own sense of their accomplishment and status. Major General H. L. Rogers, army chief quartermaster for the AEF, commended the telephone operators by stressing their efficiency and enthusiasm: "It has been a great pleasure to me to note the very satisfactory daily service which has been rendered by the Signal Corps telephone system since the advent of the young American women who have taken over this work. A very marked and agreeable improvement in the efficiency of the service followed their arrival; courtesy, promptness and a decidedly American intelligence in the performance of their duties have been invariable[sic] noticeable.[57] But underlying this seeming concurrence was a major difference. Commanding officers believed that businesslike service required the careful control of labor by management. The introduction of women workers, who were connected with but not *part of* the military, complicated the problem as the army viewed it, for the presence of women necessitated special forms of discipline in social life and living arrangements as well as in the work place.

Telephone operators and clerical workers generally tolerated these restraints because they regarded them as a necessary component of army life, part and parcel of the effort to win the war. It was a worthwhile sacrifice, Louise Barbour later wrote: "We women of the Signal Corps volunteered for service and most of us spent a year or more in France— a year so crowded with interest, with opportunities, and with experiences, that most of us still consider it the proudest and most important period in our lives."[58] Barbour was certainly right in one sense: Signal Corps women almost universally viewed their service as their proudest moment. But by the time she wrote these words in the 1930s, Barbour's views had diverged from most of her coworkers' in a crucial respect. These women were deeply disappointed to learn after the war that they had been civilian workers and were not entitled to military benefits. Their wartime strategy of efficient, loyal service and submission to military authority in the end yielded little in the way of public recognition or material advancement. After World War I, female veterans of the Signal Corps organized to demand the recognition from the army that they believed they had earned through their skill and labor.

[5]

"Compassionate Sympathizers and Active Combatants": Army Nurses in France

"We left Paris at noon for a destination whose name will bring a shudder to the nurses who were there in the awful days of July." Maude S. Crawford, an American nurse with Base Hospital No. 7, recollected her departure for an evacuation hospital near Chateau-Thierry during the summer of 1918. "Finally we arrived at a camp of yellow tents, pitched on a recent battle field in 'No Man's Land' near what was left of a railroad station."[1] The work was grueling and often dangerous. But Crawford was doing exactly what she had hoped to do in France. Other women workers in the war zone longed to share the experiences of army nurses, especially their access to the "no-man's-land" of the front. In this semi-fictionalized account, Anne is a civilian clerical worker and Angelina is an army nurse. "'Anne! I'm goin' to the front!' Angelina threw her arms around Anne's neck. . . . Anne ate in silence. Angelina would see the War, and she would sit here . . . Angelina would hear shells,—and she, Anne, would stay . . . typewriting in safety . . . Would nothing ever *happen* to you in this damned war?" The author, Mary Lee, envied and admired the nurses she knew and observed in France, portraying them in her fiction as independent and "soldierlike," yet caring.[2]

Nurses as well as other servicewomen shared Lee's view. Nursing brought women close to the heart of the war as servicewomen perceived it (war with a capital "W" in Lee's formulation): an opportunity at the front to share directly in the soldier's experience, risk and danger, and the potential for heroism. Military commanders considered female nurses an essential work force and recruited nurses on a mass scale. Army nurses held a military status above enlisted men and were in command of enlisted men on hospital wards. This formulation of military nursing as prestigious and important clashes with the current popular view of nursing as subservient, the quintessential and unthreatening "feminine" occupation. But to dismiss military nursing as women's "traditional" role in wartime is to collapse and ahistoricize a complex set of historical developments. In 1917, army nursing seemed to open broad avenues of advancement for women. Julia Stimson, chief nurse of a base hospital from St. Louis who surveyed the situation on the eve of her departure for France, found it "wonderful beyond belief. . . . this opportunity . . . to be in the front ranks in this most dramatic event that was ever staged, and to be in the first group of women ever called out for duty with the United States Army."[3] For women who enlisted to gain a place within the military, secure public legitimacy, and attain status on a par with men through their work, nursing came closer to fulfilling their goals than did any other form of service open to U.S. women in 1917.

As nurses experienced "real" war work, however, the reality of the war was shocking. Surrounded by the horrendous human damage of battle, nurses saw men too frightened to fight. The exhilaration of doing work more pressured, challenging, and crucial than any they had ever done before was coupled with an intense sense of futility; as nurses struggled to care for profoundly injured patients, they became frustrated at the limitations on their authority. Many nurses came to question and then to challenge military policy in regard to their own status in the army. A small minority of women became critical of the war itself.

Nursing held a special place within the spectrum of women's military service. Nurses had highly developed professional organizations and a foothold in the military through the army and navy nurse corps well before 1917, which gave nurses leadership and an infrastructure that other female war workers lacked. The trained nurses who joined the war effort had a strong sense of professional solidarity and confidence in the importance of their contribution. The status of U.S. military nurses was strikingly different from that of French nurses, for example; Catholic sisters or untrained, civilian women were volunteers in the French army's military hospital network.[4]

Still, the position of nurses in the American Expeditionary Force (AEF) was highly contested. Precisely because nursing was considered an indisputable military need, because women controlled it, and because it was thought to have the potential to disrupt gender relations in the postwar period, nursing was threatening. In Washington, D.C., where AEF medical policy was established, and in France, on the wards and in the operating rooms, nurses and nurse leaders came into conflict with men and the military establishment in more organized, concrete, and potent ways than did any other servicewomen. Unlike canteen workers, clerks, and telephone operators, army nurses turned to collective political action during the war, demanding that the state grant them the professional recognition and autonomy they believed to be their due. Yet, like other servicewomen, nurses struggled to achieve status and equality by reform from within, making their bid for recognition without challenging the framework of military authority. Ultimately, nurses were left negotiating for change with a male-dominated system that was dedicated to limiting their power.

As THE UNITED STATES entered the war in Europe, American nurses were in a strong position relative to both nurses serving other Allied forces and other American women war workers. Trained female nurses had an established place, under nurse leadership, within the armed forces, and proponents of professional nursing had access to the military through the Red Cross as well. The special position of nursing reflected both the organization of the occupation as a whole and nurses' record of military service.

The professionalization of American nursing at the turn of the century was driven by fundamental changes in American social and economic life. Urbanization, economic and political centralization, and the growth of corporate business transformed class relations and values in the last quarter of the nineteenth century, giving rise to a new middle class organized around professional identification and associations.[5] Modern medicine, which combined scientific innovations with business efficiency and rationalization, was the model of the new, middle-class professionalism.[6] From one perspective, nursing followed this model. Scientific breakthroughs—such as anesthesia and aseptic procedure, the emergence of the modern, technocratic hospital, and women's growing access to education—all opened the way for the professionalization of nursing.[7] But social scientists have questioned whether the model of professionalization can be applied to the female-dominated semiprofessions.[8] From this perspective, nurses' struggle for professional status was at best a process fraught with conflict and contradiction. Divisions of race, class, ethnicity, and education among nurses further complicated the process of professionalization, as reforms frequently advanced the interests of one subgroup of nurses at the expense of another.

At the top, however, nurses achieved an important degree of professional organization prior to World War I. A cadre of key nursing leaders, including M. Adelaide Nutting, Jane Delano, Annie Goodrich, and Lavinia Dock, were first-generation graduates of Bellevue, Johns Hopkins, and other prestigious hospital training schools. Through the American Nurses' Association (ANA) and other professional groups, they lobbied for higher educational standards and championed the use of trained or "graduate" nurses. The government acknowledged the influence of these civilian nurse leaders by appointing Nutting to represent nursing on the General Medical Board of the Council of National Defense just weeks after the U.S. entered the war.[9]

The development of military nursing not only was shaped by these professional leaders, but also followed its own course. The integration of nurses into the U.S. armed forces began with the Army Reorganization Act of 1901, which established the Army Nurse Corps (female), known as the ANC.[10] Women's groups involved in voluntary patriotic service, especially the Daughters of the American Revolution and the American Red Cross, had lobbied for the bill. More important, however, was the impressive record of the twelve hundred female "contract" nurses employed by the army during the Spanish American War, who battled typhus and the other tropical diseases that were ravaging U.S. troops in Cuba and in training camps. This successful use of female nurses with the armed services, including an overseas expeditionary force, was a powerful counterweight to arguments that women were not fit for military service. The plan for a permanent military nursing service was designed by Dr. Anita Newcomb McGee, a prominent Washington-area physician with elite political and social connections who had organized the contract nursing program. The legislation mandated that the superintendent of the ANC be a graduate nurse, ensuring that leadership would come from the professional hierarchy, and established the ANC Reserve, a register of nurses eligible for military service. The ANC was located in the office of the Surgeon General, which facilitated nurse leaders' relationships with army physicians and War Department personnel.

Jane Delano, who served as superintendent of the ANC from 1909 to 1912, cemented the links between the military and the civilian nursing hierarchy. During these years, Delano also directed the newly organized Red Cross Nursing Service and the ANA, the leading professional organization for nurses. Under her administration, the registration list of the Red Cross Nursing Service became the official ANC Reserve.[11] The close relationship between civilian and military nursing was an agreeable symbiosis for both sides. The Red Cross gained legitimacy and a semiofficial governmental status, while the ANC gained access to skilled womanpower and the experienced professional leaders of the civilian nursing organizations.

When war mobilization began, the ANC and the Red Cross Nursing Service were ready. In the eighteen months of the war, the ANC and ANC Reserve increased from a force of less than four hundred to more than twenty-one thousand, with more than ten thousand nurses in the AEF and the rest in stateside military camps and hospitals, an impressive performance by all accounts.[12] Nonetheless, the military medical establishment in 1917 was divided over the proper position of nurses in the mili-

9. Jane A. Delano (1862–1919) was responsible for linking the realms of professional and military nursing and for establishing the American Red Cross Nursing Service as the nation's official reserve corps for nurses. Daughter of a Union soldier killed in the Civil War, Delano served as superintendent of the Army Nurse Corps from 1909 to 1912, a position she resigned to devote herself full-time to the work of the American Red Cross. During the war she ably coordinated the nation's military and civilian nursing needs, in the United States and overseas, as director of the American Red Cross Department of Nursing. Delano died in Savenay, France, in 1919 while undertaking an inspection tour of Red Cross work. (Source: National American Red Cross, *History of American Red Cross Nursing* [New York: Macmillan Co., 1922].)

tary, and during the course of the war there was considerable conflict and negotiation over their status, rights, and responsibilities. One striking example of this ambivalent attitude was the army's refusal to equip or uniform its own nurses. The army required the Red Cross to provide these necessities, in much the same way that it had traditionally utilized voluntary women's organizations in wartime. The Red Cross was compelled to provide each nurse with a package of equipment, including a hat, an outdoor uniform, a coat, a cape, gloves, shirtwaists, woolen underwear, pajamas, a sleeping bag, a blanket roll, a raincoat, three pairs of shoes, and one pair of rubber boots, no small task for a nongovermental organization.[13] A Treasury Department ruling in October 1918 similarly treated nurses as a category apart: army nurses, unlike male military personnel, would not be paid when held as prisoners of war. This decision provoked a furor among nurse leaders and was later overturned. Nurses were also excluded from retirement benefits, although they were entitled to some army privileges.[14]

The military's ambivalence about the integration of women was most apparent in its response to two major issues of nursing policy: military rank for nurses, and the engagement of nurses' aids, as they were called at the time. These issues provoked a level of controversy in the United States that no other women's war work inspired. The medical military establishment was adamantly opposed to granting rank to women. Unlike the yeoman(f)s of the navy, who were enlisted personnel, army nurses were officers, but officers without rank. This designation raised an obvious question: Who is required to take orders from an officer without rank? Military nurses initially worked without any clarification of their authority or status. In response to a wave of complaints early in the war from nurses in stateside hospitals and camps, who claimed that enlisted men assigned as ward attendants and orderlies would not follow their orders, the War Department issued Regulation 1421 ½ on July 6, 1917. The regulation read: "As regards medical and sanitary matters and work in connection with the sick, members of the Army Nurse Corps and the Army Nurse Corps Reserve are to be regarded as having authority in matters pertaining to their professional duties (the care of sick and wounded) in and about military hospitals next after the medical officers of the Army." But the parenthetical phrase, nurse leaders pointed out, could be interpreted to mean that the professional duties of a nurse pertained solely to the person of the patient and did not encompass such sanitary conditions as heat, light, ventilation, cleanliness, and supplies, over which the nursing profession had claimed authority. Matters of sanitation were precisely the domain in which nurses and orderlies most often interacted. From the nurses' perspective, this ambiguity could not be tolerated. When the War Department finally issued amendments to

10. Army Nurse Corps nurses sterilize hospital laundry in an AEF hospital facility. U.S. Army Signal Corps photograph (U.S. Army Military History Institute, Carlisle Barracks, Pa.)

Regulation 1421 ½, nursing leaders found them inadequate, and if anything, more confusing.[15]

Leaders in civilian and military nursing, armed with complaints from the field, lobbied for legislation granting nurses relative military rank, the plan used by the Canadian and Australian armies.[16] Prominent suffragists and female reformers supported their campaign. Harriet Stanton Blatch, a suffragist strongly identified with the cause of wage-earning women, organized the New York Committee to Secure Rank for Nurses.[17] On April 16, 1918, the House Committee on Military Affairs held a hearing on the proposed legislation, organized by attorney Helen Hoy Greeley. Professional and lay leaders, including Jane Delano; Harriet Stanton Blatch; Julia Lathrop; Dora Thompson, superintendent of the ANC; and Lenah S. Higbee, superintendent of the Navy Nurse Corps, argued that giving nurses officer rank would increase the efficiency and quality of medical care. Several middle-ranking members of the Army Medical Corps and Reserve also defended the proposed legislation. But the only opinion that mattered to the Congressmen was that of the War Department. Four days after the women's testimony, Surgeon General William Gorgas voiced his opposition to rank for nurses. Gorgas and his supporters on the Medical Board of the Council of National Defense did not see the "necessity or the advisability" of creating "30,000" female second lieutenants "with the stroke of a pen" and insisted that nurses' current status was entirely sufficient to enable them to perform their duties. The proposal was set aside for the duration of the war, until a coalition of nurses and suffragists revived the campaign in 1919.[18]

As this controversy shows, military policymakers regarded equality of rank for women as unworthy of serious consideration. Their response to the proposed use of nurses' aids was more complex. Plans to use minimally trained aids to assist trained nurses at army hospitals dated from before the war and were modeled on the British Voluntary Aid Detachment (VAD) system. In the spring of 1918, as concern about the nursing supply mounted, a Red Cross plan to mobilize aids gained increasing attention. Although the debate over this plan is usually portrayed as a struggle between the professionalizers and their opponents, it was, rather, a conflict between two different professionalizing strategies within the occupation.[19] Nursing leaders who were aligned with the military, including Dora Thompson, Jane Delano, and many of the chief nurses in France, supported the nurses' aid plan as a necessary compromise. These women were committed to the "advancement" of nursing through the education and registration of nurses, but they believed that superior performance and full cooperation with the armed services was the surest path toward professional recognition. Their strategy was to control the enlistment and training of aids through the Red Cross. Chief nurses had selected nurse's aid units (which were never mobilized) as part of their base hospital preparations before the war, and they expressed confidence that such women could be used successfully. Furthermore, the contact of AEF chief nurses in France with British VADs had convinced them that college-educated aids would pose no threat to hospital-trained nurses after the war.

Civilian nurse leaders, on the other hand, were staunchly opposed to the use of paraprofessionals, convinced that any dilution of standards would jeopardize the professional status they had fought so hard to attain. Their alternative plan, devised by Annie Goodrich, professor of nursing at Columbia Teachers College, and promoted by Adelaide Nutting, who was serving on the Medical Board of the Council of National Defense, called for increased recruitment of private-duty nurses, full utilization of nursing school enrollments, the employment of student nurses in military hospitals, and the creation of an Army School of Nursing with branches at several major military bases.

This plan received substantial support from the military medical establishment and its civilian advisory boards. Many medical leaders supported the professionalizing agenda of the civilian nurse hierarchy, seeing it as part of a larger program to enhance the quality and prestige of medical care. Army medicine had been modernized during the progressive era: military medical experts had established optimal nurse-patient ratios; had put into place a network of base hospitals; and had been dispatched to Europe to investigate and assess the Allied treatment of mental health, venereal disease, rehabilitation, and other wartime medical concerns. In joining the war in Europe, medical practitioners wanted American medicine to outperform all others, including the Germans, leaders in the field; yet, recently the military medical establishment had been stung by accusations of incompetence from Congress and the public, who were shocked by epidemic illnesses at stateside military facilities.[20] The General Medical Board of the Council of National Defense and the surgeon general and his staff were willing to cooperate with the professional nursing organizations; the ANA in particular was considered vital to mobilizing quickly the enormous number of nurses needed by the military.

In the end, this concern with recruitment was the dominant factor in the military's response to the employment of nurses' aids. The military was willing to respect the wishes of the professional nursing hierarchy only as long as it was convinced that professional nursing could meet its quotas. Whether there was a "nursing shortage" in civilian or military health care during the war has remained a matter of controversy.[21] It is clear that nursing shortages in the AEF were never due to a shortage of nurse enlistment but rather resulted from transportation and organizational problems beyond the control of the nursing services. The War Department's refusal, until the postwar influenza epidemic, to enlist any of the trained and eager African-American nurses suggests that "shortage" was a flexible notion.[22] Still, military medical leaders remained anxious about the nursing supply, and in the spring of 1918 more of them came to endorse the plan to mobilize aids. Ultimately, the civilian plan, using recruitment and student enrollment in lieu of aids, did prevail, although only through the intervention of Secretary of War Newton Baker. Once again, male leaders demonstrated their ambivalence about the integration of nurses into the military; willing to work with professional nursing when their goals coincided, they were equally willing to use nonnurses in army nursing jobs if the military considered the supply of trained labor insufficient.

Perhaps the most intriguing aspect of the controversy over nurses' aids is the enmity against nursing and nurses that it brought to the surface. The most vocal advocates of nurses' aids, and the most virulent opponents of organized professional nursing, were neither military leaders nor nurse leaders in the Red Cross or the ANC but rather civilian doctors, hospital administrators and trustees, patients, and members of the public. On the surface their concerns related to the protection of servicemen, but self-interest lurked just beneath the surface of the debate. Military recruitment ate into the civilian nurse surplus and slowly drove upward the low wages of private-duty nurses. Doctors found it more expensive to obtain help for their middle-class and working-class patients and directed their anger and frustration against the nursing profession. Some doctors, patients, and community leaders advocated the use of trained aids to "protect" the civilian supply; some hospitals anticipated this plan by initiating their own "shortened courses" and training programs for workers they variously called hospital attendants, aids, and nurses.[23]

These discussions also provided an opportunity for the airing of deeper and more long-standing resentments. Hospital administrators, community doctors, and editorialists attacked the very idea of professional nursing, criticizing scientific training for women as "brainstuffing" and claiming that it unsuited women for the practical work of nursing. Doctors, according to a *New York Times* editorial of April 5, 1918, "have found their work hindered, not helped, by nurses whose education along medical lines had been carried too far." Now such arguments had the added weight of patriotic concern. More sophisticated critics also expressed seething anger at the professional nursing organizations, calling them obstructive, bureaucratic, repressive, and wrapped in red tape, terms that in wartime were a shade away from an accusation of disloyalty. With each victory for organized nursing, opponents lashed out at the "power" of nurses. The approval of the Army School of Nursing and the dismissal of the plan to employ aids prompted a sputtering letter to the Secretary of War from Dr. S. S. Goldwater, director of Mount Sinai Hospital in New York and a member of the General Medical Board of the Council of National Defense: "The fact of the matter is . . . that Miss Goodrich, Miss Nutting, and their nurse associates, who by their zeal, perseverance, determination, one-idea'd intensity (and mild hysterics) appear to dominate the nursing program of the Army, seem to be blind to the hazards of the game."[24]

This sense that nursing was powerful, and therefore dangerous and in need of containment, was also expressed in more covert ways during the war. The multilayered response to nurses reveals the complexity of popular consciousness and the multiple meanings expressed through popular culture. In wartime media, nurses were sometimes lauded for their courage, patriotism, and loyalty, an image that held great significance for nurses themselves. More often the figure of the nurse was sentimentalized, drawing on the traditional iconography of nurse as mother, virgin, or saint.[25] At the same time, nurses were simply less visible in the culture than their numbers would warrant, far less visible than canteen or auxiliary workers. The canteen worker, or "Y girl," was the predominant model of military womanhood during the Great War, while the nurse seldom appeared in magazine articles or photo spreads.[26]

Nurses were, however, the primary subject of gossip about women with the AEF. Rumors about American nurses in France, which were striking for their violence and veiled sexuality, swept the United States soon after the first nurses departed for overseas service in the fall of 1917 and peaked in the early spring of 1918.[27] The rumors had two components, or came in two forms. On the one hand, they described atrocities committed by German soldiers against American nurses, usually mutilations of the hands, but sometimes of the feet, eyes, or tongues. In a typically gruesome story, which was brought to the attention of the American Red Cross in Washington, D.C., a woman from New Albany, Indiana, claimed to have seen two Red Cross nurses on a train "lying on cots with their eyes gouged out and their tongues split from the tip back to the root." On the other hand, the rumors involved the sexual immorality of nurses and alleged that pregnancy and venereal disease were rampant among American nurses in France. A typical tale might be that five hundred nurses were sailing home "to become mothers" or, more colorfully, that an entire wing of the Sloan Maternity Hospital in New York was dedicated to expecting army nurses. Beliefs about the sexual promiscuity of working women underlay these stories, but the war emergency prompted their uncontrolled growth.[28]

In some instances the themes of vulnerability and promiscuity were combined: one gentleman heard ("fifth-hand," from a man whose closest neighbor's father was the neighbor of the family of one of the unfortunate women!) that five Red Cross nurses were all pregnant and had had their hands cut off by the enemy after being "common property for German soldiers." But usually the themes were separate, for they tapped into different veins of anxiety. In the first, the nurse is delicate and helpless, like the "frail American nurse" of one newspaper account who was deceived by one of her patients, a "great bully" of a German officer: after praising and thanking her for her ministrations, he took both of her hands in his and crushed them, breaking "all of the bones, ligaments and tendons. He then said to her that . . . she would never be able to nurse another American. . . . He escaped and the doctors later found the little American nurse in a faint on the floor. She is helpless and will be for the rest of her life."[29] The underlying message in this story is clear: a dangerous war zone was no place for this or any woman; a woman who ventured to support herself "with her own hands" would soon be returned to helpless dependency.

The theme of sexual impropriety was more complex because it was unclear whether the nurse was a victim, a villain, or both. As it was put by Mrs. Frank E. Jennings, a local member of the Council of National Defense in Florida involved in recruitment, "I have encountered frequently . . . a story that nurses are specially subjected to temptations of sex—and that young girls who have been reared in a sheltered way by prudent mothers are placed in training schools with girls of doubtful character—and are liable to moral disintegration. . . ." The implication is that war is the wrong place for respectable women because corruption or sexual danger awaits her, just the opposite of the message given out in recruitment campaigns. Questions of male sexuality and responsibility were usually sidestepped in these stories, and American soldiers were never implicated; in one particularly resilient tale, the guilty perpetrators were identified as French doctors who "victimized" a boatload of Canadian nurses, an interesting instance of cultural distancing. But most rumors insinuated that women were to blame, that nurses became loose, dangerous, and uncontrollable once their "moral and physical resistance" had been weakened in the war zone. In some versions, the nurse's evil is actively malignant rather than latent, as in a rumor about an American nurse who poisoned her soldier-patients or the nurses who "gave" venereal disease to American boys.[30]

Red Cross officials condemned the rumors, accepting the War Department's assertion that they were German propaganda spread by spies to hamper nurse recruitment, but no evidence supports this assertion. Recent work on cultural and psychological attitudes toward nurses suggests that the rumor campaign was based on an underlying fear of nurses' power, of what Barbara Melosh has termed the "sexual inversion" of nursing. Female nurses confront male patients in a state of childlike or feminine helplessness and dependency; the nurse handles male bodies, violating social taboos and taking the part of sexual aggressor or castrating mother.[31] In this sense, the rumors reflected a belief that female sexuality was a threat to men at war and that the "power" of nurses called for a counter-response, for some form of containment or retaliation.[32] In other words, the rumors were a covert way to project the same resistance to professional military nursing that was expressed more concretely in the denial of military rank and benefits for nurses and in the promotion of the employment of aids. American society was caught uncomfortably between its dependence on this group of skilled women workers and its unwillingness to cede them the civic equality to which their new position entitled them.

NURSES IN THE AEF formed a unique community, strengthened from within by a professional ethos based on their training and work experience and a belief that they, almost alone among women, were participating in the "real war" alongside men. Army Nurse Corps and Reserve nurses were by definition nurses trained at large hospitals, many of which were affiliated with universities and medical schools. The practice of keeping nurses from the same parent institution together underscored the training-school tie and boosted the esprit of each nursing unit. A nurse with Base Hospital No. 50, for example, called her unit "a very friendly bunch" who were "dedicated to doing a good job of taking care of our patients in the best possible way." All were volunteers from the University of Washington, and most "had known one another previously."[33] Nurses in the AEF identified with their profession as well as with their institutions; for example, nurses made reference in their letters home to medical lectures they had attended and to articles they had read in the *American Journal of Nursing*. Although some women were taken directly from nurse training, especially during the final months of the war, more often army nurses had had significant work experience, some in supervisory positions; some in such specialties as anesthesia, orthopedics, and mental health; and some in public health nursing.

Nurses, like clerical and telephone workers, had a sense that they possessed a special set of skills and competencies. Yet, in contrast to clerks and operators in the AEF, nurses enjoyed expanded autonomy and increased authority, although this development was vigorously contested by men. Nurses also believed that their skills were essential to winning the war and that it was their duty to offer their services to the country, which distinguished them from canteen workers. The woman who volunteered for auxiliary service knew that she was as likely to be turned down as accepted, given the great number of volunteers, and all who made it overseas acknowledged their good fortune. Trained nurses, on the other hand, were well aware of the nursing shortage. Newspaper headlines and nursing publications insisted month after month that military or community service was a nurse's wartime duty, and nurses took up the refrain. "Won't you think it over and see if, conscientiously, you can refuse to bear your part of the burden for your country's sake, your profession's and your own?" one army nurse asked her colleagues in an open letter to the *American Journal of Nursing*. It is not surprising that so many nurses gave as their reason for enlistment their belief that "their country needed them." As Mildred Brown put it, "I was a graduate nurse R.N. and thought I could help the cause. . . . A good trained nurse was a valuable asset to any organization who need that kind of service."[34] Army nursing seemed to embody the soldier-citizen role that servicewomen sought.

This set of attitudes about work and work identity was the underpinning of nurses' work culture in the AEF.[35] Nursing culture both defined work relationships in military hospitals and served as the filter through which nurses made meaning of their experiences. At the same time, nurses' experience of the war—their social relations in the hospital, their daily working conditions, and their exposure to combat—also altered their views and attitudes. In military hospitals, nurses both conflicted and cooperated with enlisted men, doctors, and military officers in ways that had lasting consequences. In combat situations they responded with courage and often with horror to the consequences of the warfare they helped to wage.

NURSES LIVED AND WORKED alongside enlisted men and officers of the army medical corps. Several of the large hospital centers were located in former resort areas, where hotels made awkward hospital wards but comfortable living quarters. Many of these formerly elegant facilities were in tattered condition. At the other end of the spectrum were temporary barracks and facilities: at best, sturdy but plain; at worst, muddy, makeshift, leaky, cold, and vermin infested. Mobile hospitals were composed of tents and looked like the circus, many nurses noted with good humor; the tents were also frequently sunk in deep mud. One nurse pointed out the irony in the fact that many army nurses had formerly worked in public health: "Hadn't we fought flies in the alleys of our cities, begged window screens, netting for covering the babies? . . . but here we were in an army proud of its sanitary record, and the flies eating the food out of our hands, dropping into our coffee." [36]

Nurses were organized into base hospitals, the standard unit of medical care in the AEF. Each had roughly forty officers, one hundred nurses, and two hundred enlisted men. [37] Every base hospital was organized around a standard, hierarchical pattern of gender and occupation. At the top was the hospital's commanding officer, who generally held the rank of colonel or lieutenant colonel and was responsible for all hospital functions: personnel, physical plant, supplies, and medical care. The medical services were headed by chiefs of surgery and medicine, who usually held the rank of major; they directed a staff of male physicians, all of whom were officers in the Army Medical Corps. (Female physicians, although they agitated for admission, were barred from service with the Army. [38]) The nursing service was headed by the chief nurse, an administrator whose responsibilities included paying, housing, and assigning nurses; taking reports; monitoring overall nursing care, reporting to her superiors; and implementing orders from above. The chief nurse assigned day and night supervisors for the operating rooms and wards. Beneath the nursing staff were the two hundred "corpsmen," enlisted men in the Army Sanitary (Hospital) Corps, the largest labor force in the hospital. Although they usually worked as orderlies on the hospital wards, corpsmen could also be detailed to work on the numerous hospital facilities or in the kitchen, laundry, and offices. At the very bottom of the hierarchy was a group of approximately fifty domestic service workers—French women, girls, and sometimes disabled or elderly men—who were

11. Nurses on duty in the AEF, in work uniforms, paused for a picture, January 1919. U.S. Army Signal Corps photograph (U.S. Army Military History Institute, Carlisle Barracks, Pa.)

hired from the surrounding villages to cook, clean, and wash linen. In areas where such assistance was in short supply, corpsmen could be assigned to these tasks.[39]

On a daily basis, nurses worked most intimately with the corpsmen assigned to duty as orderlies. Of all hospital relationships, this was the most complex, for while the intensity of the bad times or the long dull hours of night duty could build an easy comradeship between these men and women, relations between them were also rife with conflict and competition. At best, such relationships were characterized by mutual respect and the teasing informality of mixed-gender work places. In the original base hospital units, the enlisted men were volunteers drawn from the same communities as the doctors and nurses, and the two groups had a similar mix of class and ethnic backgrounds. Nurses and orderlies exchanged army nicknames and involved one another in elaborate inside jokes. A limited amount of social interaction between nurses and orderlies received official approval, such as the amateur theatricals they staged in certain hospital centers. The sources attest to other social activities, such as playing and listening to popular music and going on "joy rides," which were strictly against the rules. In fact, the ingenious methods they devised for getting around army regulations was one of the strongest ties that bound nurses and enlisted men together.[40]

Such easy camaraderie concealed an underlying problem: nurses technically held authority over enlisted men and noncommissioned officers when the men were assigned to orderly duty on the wards. As officers, nurses were in command of orderlies' labor, a highly anomalous situation. Nowhere on the war front were traditional gender work relations more severely strained or challenged, and nowhere was male resistance more explicit. The "orderly problem" was nursing shorthand for the range of conflicts surrounding nurses' authority over male workers. "The military does not define distinctly enough the authority of the nurses over these men but we must have it if we are to be responsible for the care of the sick and wounded," Carrie Hall wrote to her family. In nurses' arguments on behalf of rank, the insubordination of orderlies toward nurse supervisors and ward nurses was the major complaint. According to one ANA leader, "we get letters all the time from women overseas telling of the petty annoyances and the friction and the generally disturbed morale that result because the authority of the nurses to give orders to men of the enlisted personnel is not plain and is not made plain."[41]

Nurses were forced to compete with noncommissioned officers, called "ward sergeants," for the labor of enlisted men. One nurse, for example, watched her orderly leave the floor half washed when the sergeant ordered him to wash windows, a task far less crucial to medical hygiene. "In the hospital where I was stationed, the head nurse of our operating room had to go to the officer in charge before the men . . . would do any work whatsoever or even report for duty.. . . They absolutely refused to take orders from the nurse," one woman noted; "I discussed the corpsmen problem with nurses from three other units and found conditions much the same." "Whenever I took an orderly to task for his neglect," a nurse testified, "he either did not answer me and put on his hat and went out to the top sergeant and asked to be taken off my ward because he could not work with me, or he was most insolent and impertinent."[42]

Numerous AEF nurses reported that orderlies' work was sloppy or incompetent. An overworked nurse was frustrated when an orderly refused her order to bathe several new patients, claiming that he did not know how. Certainly, many such incidents came from a genuine lack of knowledge. Yet nurses suspected at times that orderlies feigned ignorance: "If he personally liked the nurse, he might get along, but if he preferred to drive an ambulance or do something else, he would simply make himself so useless that he would eventually be changed to the service he preferred." Some tales were perhaps apocryphal, such as the story of the orderly who doubled a patient's pulse rate when recording it in the chart because "it seemed to me too darned fishy that he should have 36 when the rest of them guys had 65 or 70." But the fact that such stories had entered into folklore in France was itself significant. Perhaps most telling, nurses and chief nurses found good, capable, or hardworking orderlies worthy of special remark. "There is a remarkable spirit of . . . glad service everywhere. . . . It does one's heart good to see the way men who are Ph.D.'s can do regular orderly work," Julia Stimson wrote in a letter, although she acknowledged that her group also had its share of "grumblers."[43]

Enlisted men themselves noted the tension between nurses and orderlies, although they failed to explore its sources. With some sympathy a corpsman penned, "If Sherman thought war was H__,/ When the South he marched across,/ He should have been an Army nurse,/ With orderlies to boss." Another enlisted man was less charitable: getting along with the nurses was "the only disagreeable part of this ward orderly job." According to corpsmen's writing, the most important quality in a nurse was a pleasing personality, a "cheerful disposition," and a "sunny smile." A number of nurses were praised for their constant readiness to supply a tired orderly with hot coffee, toast, and other "eats." The most popular nurses were those who preferred enlisted men to officers and "treat[ed] the men as equals." The profile of the "good nurse" was very similar to that of the good canteen worker, yet canteen workers were employed explicitly to be pleasing to the men whereas nurses were not. Conversely, orderlies criticized nurses for being haughty, arrogant, standoffish, argumentative, or strong willed. Enlisted men did express admiration for women who were hardworking and dedicated to the patients, yet being overly professional or a stickler for rules was considered a fault in a nurse. These preferences reflect the anti-elitism of soldiers, but they also suggest that enlisted men felt threatened by nurses who were authoritative or commanding—who, in other words, attempted to carry out their role as officers.[44]

From the perspective of corpsmen, the structure of work on the wards was threatening. Orderlies had little or no training in patient care, and they were being managed by women with superior knowledge and skills. Enlisted men found the military authority of nurses ambiguous, which it certainly was. Lacking rank and insignia in a system almost wholly reliant on such markers of power, nurses were entirely dependent on cumbersome War Department Regulation 1421 ½ to back up their orders. Some noted sardonically that the "½" in the title was peculiarly appropriate for a regulation that never really clarified their authority. When the officer status of nurses was acknowledged by enlisted men it was usually treated derisively, as in a Stars and Stripes cartoon (Figure 12). Two ambiguities about nurses' status in particular fostered confusion: did an unranked nurse fit into the military chain of command above or below a

12. "Never flirt with your superior officer," warned popular doughboy cartoonist Private Abian "Wally" Wallgren (1893–1948) in *Stars and Stripes* 1 (April 19, 1918): 11. His depiction of the nurse as an emasculating authority figure is part of a long tradition in popular culture. The cartoon captures enlisted men's negative view of nurses' claim to rank.

noncommissioned officer of the Sanitary Corps? Technically speaking, nurses outranked "noncoms" because nurses held the "theoretical rank" of lieutenant, a commissioned office. Yet typically, a sergeant or corporal "regard[ed] himself as outranking the nurse because . . . in his opinion she is only a private." And did the jurisdiction of the nurse include the sanitary conditions of the ward, including its cleanliness and temperature, or was her jurisdiction confined to the person of the patient? In disciplinary hearings, nurses pointed out, enlisted men cited such ambiguities as a defense for insubordination.[45]

Men's resentment of taking orders from women was undoubtedly exacerbated by the menial character of their work. Enlisted men performed the back-breaking, endless "grunt work" of the hospital. Peeling potatoes in a hospital kitchen, scrubbing down the floors of an operating room, and preparing bodies of the dead were hardly the glamorous stuff of male war heroism. One medical orderly summarized corpsmen's insecurity about their role: "The fact is that we were a little on the defensive. In the peace-time army the Medical Corps is looked upon with considerable condescension, not to say contempt, by the combatant troops."[46] Most of the tasks performed by orderlies were closely associated with women's work back home, the domestic service that working-class women performed in their own homes and that immigrant women, black women, and black men performed for wages in middle-class households. Enlisted men may well have felt that their work was feminized and degraded, exacerbating the undercurrent of hostility between nurses and orderlies at the front.

Nurses clashed with their superiors as well as their subordinates. "We hear much said about the necessity for rank for nurses on account of the enlisted men," remarked one chief nurse. "My experience is that we need . . . [it] much more on account of the officers. . . . the officers were at a complete loss as to how nurses should be treated." Medical officers could be close colleagues; nurses and doctors, particularly those on surgical teams, often forged close relationships in the excruciating conditions of a major drive. In their postwar evaluations, medical directors and officers sometimes praised the heroism, loyalty, skill, and self-sacrifice of their nursing colleagues. In general, however, American doctors and nurses in France were divided by the same gulf of class, gender, and authority that divided them in their prewar working lives. "The medical men are just as temperamental and exacting here as at home," Carrie Hall wrote a friend. Nurses at times displayed a sort of inverse snobbery toward doctors. Ethel Pierce, an army nurse posted at Rouen, France, pictured herself as a front-line fighter against disease and disparaged the physicians, who "wouldn't dirty their delicate hands" to help with dressings.[47]

In reports and investigations, nurses complained of the "discourtesy" of officers, both medical and military. Lack of concern for their living conditions and inappropriate orders and requests were chief annoyances. One head nurse noted with resentment that an officer told her to "look after" his luggage while he went up to his room. Furthermore, nurses found that officers trivialized or ignored their requests and complaints. One nurse who reported a problem with an orderly to her commanding officer received an unsatisfactory response; in her assessment, the officer, "as a military man concerned chiefly with men's matters," was "unaware of the significance of the difficulty complained of." Nurses' concerns were "quite likely to be overlooked or put aside as unimportant," she concluded.[48] Perhaps for lack of alternative recourse, one army nurse penciled and posted a bitingly humorous catalogue of fifteen indignities that nurses faced at the hands of officers, asserting equality for women in the work place as well as claiming certain courtesies traditionally paid to ladies. Under the heading "Etiquette for officers as a nurse sees it (with humble apologies to the very few to whom this does not apply)" she wrote:

Never offer a graduate nurse a chair. They enjoy standing.
When addressing a nurse put your feet on the desk, lean back and be comfortable.
When an operation is to be performed never notify the operating room. Ought to be ready.
Never do dressings in the morning. The nurses enjoy doing them in the afternoon.
When addressing the nurse in charge of ward, never call her name, just yell "Nurse" and see what happens.
Never ask the nurse about her patients. She might be able to give you some information.
If you see any candy on the desk help yourself but don't ever bring any.
Whenever possible cigarette ashes and butts are to be scattered around; it almost makes us feel at home.
When all is said and done, bid the nurse "good night" and smile, even if it hurts at first.[49]

Discourtesy at times shaded into more troubling behavior. Glimpses of sexual harassment appear in nurses' stories. Shirley Millard, an American nurse's aid in a French military hospital, described this incident with a surgeon whom she barely knew:

He stared at me in an odd sort of way and would not let me pass. Then he took the tray from my hands, set it on the window ledge and without further ado, grabbed me in his arms and kissed me vigorously. I struggled free with some difficulty, and he gravely handed me the tray again and began walking along beside me as if nothing had happened. . . . I tried to hurry away from him but he deliberately kept step with me and although he looked exactly as if we were discussing medical matters, he was calling me all sorts of French pet names and asking me when I would go to Paris with him.

"Nearly all of us had some similar adventure to report," Millard concluded, although she deemed the behavior a "natural" male response to the pressure of wartime. Ethel Pierce, who was also propositioned by an officer ("come to Paris with me" was apparently the standard line), had a more straightforward explanation for this activity: "his pecker was bothering him, cozy old devil!"[50] In a work place setting, such behavior is an assertion of power and an expression of hostility; recent studies of women in nontraditional fields, including the army and navy, suggest that harassment is especially common or virulent when men feel a need to "defend their territory" against the encroachment of women.[51]

The chief nurse who maintained that male officers were at a complete loss about how to treat nurses was at least partially correct. In civilian life doctors had interacted with nurses in carefully differentiated roles, as student nurses in the hospital or as private-duty nurses taking doctors' orders. Conditions at the front were profoundly different from the calm, order, and regimentation that were the ideal of the most prestigious, modern hospitals. By necessity, nurses were given tremendous autonomy in their work, a situation that they welcomed and built on. Physicians and nurses were both placed under military authority and labeled officers. Nurses seemed to embrace this position, taking up military slang and jargon and adopting such army nicknames as "Conkie," "Al," "Hawks," "Jeff," or "Pete," unisex or masculinized versions of their own given or family names. Some AEF nurses bobbed their hair, which their male colleagues found unsettling. These new behaviors disrupted expectations about proper genteel, womanly behavior that had been the promise of nurse training programs, if not always the result. The nurses at one base hospital gleefully flouted gender proscriptions: baseball games between nurses and doctors were a favored pastime; in the evenings, the chief nurse noted, the nurses were sewing uniforms for their male opponents, replete with girlish but bulky skirts! The doctors' reaction to this mischief was not recorded, yet the joke may well have touched on some underlying tensions.[52]

Male officers' response to this blurring of gender roles was not the sort of resistance put up by enlisted men, but rather the imposition of tighter control. Commanding officers were in a position to assert their authority by regulating nurses' social behavior in ways that both paralleled and diverged from the controls placed on other women workers with the AEF.

Regulations concerning the hours, places, and forms of recreation, restriction of callers, and daily dormitory inspections were typical. The "Rules for Nurses" issued by one camp commander give an indication of how petty and oppressive such regulations could be:

> Outside the hospital there must be no social relation between the Nurses and Officers or Enlisted Men of the Camp, even casual conversation must be avoided. . . . Visiting in the Hospital when off duty, or in wards other than those which you are assigned to duty, is strictly prohibited. . . . Doors to Nurses' Quarters must be kept closed at all times. . . . The presence of patients in the building where the Nurses are quartered imposes the necessity of reducing noise as far as possible. Especially when passing through the corridors, loud talking, singing and laughing is to be avoided . . .[53]

Of course, the arbitrary imposition of power is intrinsic to military organizations and institutions. But nurses were well aware of the sexual double standard in base hospital discipline, which restricted their social freedom much more than it did that of enlisted men, not to mention the male officers who were theoretically their counterparts. The politics of dancing are illustrative. The universal ban on "fraternization" with enlisted men gave rise to a "dancing problem" for nurses that was the inverse of the problem for canteen workers: for nurses, social dancing with American soldiers was a tabooed recreation rather than an official assignment. At the same time, officers on most bases expected nurses to attend their own parties, which included dining and dancing.[54] The inconsistency and variation in social rules for nurses underscored the fact that this regulation arose from anxiety and mistrust, not from military necessity.

Nurses were already accustomed to strict regulation of their work and private lives; the "Rules for Nurses" resemble the rules imposed on student nurses in hospital training programs.[55] But this was precisely the problem: army nurses were experienced and mature working women, and many had previously been head nurses and superintendents. Most found the reversion to student nurse discipline infantilizing and unnecessary. "Treated too much like kindergarten children," one nurse declared curtly. Julia Stimson demonstrated far greater insight into nursing culture when she opted for a supervisory style stressing trust and self-discipline.[56] Nurses in fact seem to have been an exceedingly well-behaved group; there were few official complaints about their behavior and very few incidents of serious punishment. Nurses, who saw themselves as capable of self-control, found it demeaning when their superiors issued rules that were arbitrary, petty, or severe in tone.

But they soon discovered that in the military there is little recourse for such grievances. Nurses, like enlisted men, could bend or break minor rules. They could also request transfers out of particularly repressive hospitals, but transfers required the approval of the base commander and were difficult to obtain. Most often ward nurses turned to the nurse supervisor or chief nurse to intervene on their behalf, and chief nurses frequently attempted to advocate for their staff. Florence Blanchfield was so distressed by the unreasonable strictness of the commanding officer at her hospital that she joined the nurses in requesting a transfer. But ultimately, chief nurses found that they had little recourse themselves. "I feel much like the fly that has accepted the spider's invitation. . . . We are . . . hemmed in with so much military routine and regulation, all of it necessary, no doubt, that there seems no avenue of escape," Carrie Hall wrote in June 1917. By fall her battles with the military hierarchy had strained her patience further: "Just at present I am saying, 'D___ the army.'"[57]

Army nurses expected to be treated with fairness and respect in the work place by both superiors and subordinates. Embedded in these expectations was an understanding that women's work for the army earned them certain rights and recognition. Some nurses translated this understanding into a specific demand for formal equality within the military in the form of full military rank. Submitted as testimony during the House Hearings, for example, was a letter from one nurse to representatives of the ANA: "I hope you are working diligently to give us rank; you know the veterinarians have it, and while I do not begrudge the animals anything, I would like to see nurses work recognized. It has never been by the United States Government. . . . The nurses almost to a woman are women of whom the United States Government may well be proud. Interested and capable, they are as much entitled to this acknowledgment as any officer I have ever seen."[58] Most nurses argued for army rank and benefits for nurses on altruistic grounds. Yet, in their commitment to autonomy and economic independence for women, to work place rights, and to gaining access to opportunities from which women had been excluded, nurses shared many of the views of the wage-earning and professional women who became active in the 1910s in the movement for women's rights. It is significant in this context that army nurses aligned themselves with Harriet Stanton Blatch in their fight for rank; Blatch was one of the feminist leaders responsible for moving feminism in a new direction, emphasizing women's paid work as the basis of social rights and equality.[59] After the war, this conception of rights became increasingly prominent in the way nurses and other servicewomen evaluated their wartime experience and took up their own cause in the political realm.

Whereas the tensions in nursing back home revolved around class and professionalism as well as gender, in the military hospitals of France gender conflict was a far more prominent feature of daily life. Nursing culture in the AEF, which emphasized professional pride and a sense of equality, set up confrontations with enlisted men and officers. In light of the role nurses took on and the work they did, it is not surprising that they aroused such hostility, for the medical care system in France and the men who worked within it were dependent on nurses' labor in new ways. The position of nurses in the hierarchy temporarily altered social relations between men and women at the front. The daily activities of hospital nursing also changed the women and their understanding of their work role.

FOR WOMEN AS WELL as men, the "real war" was the experience of combat, what orderlies sometimes referred to as the "mud-and-blood" work. Although American nurses serving overseas were seldom wounded by enemy fire, the majority worked and lived under conditions that some historians regard as "combat situations."[60] Nurses were frequently exposed to strafing, bombing, and submarine attacks—or the threat of such attacks—as hospitals, transport ships, casualty clearing stations, and base camps came under fire. Most nursing memoirs report air raids, bombing, and overhead strafing in the vicinity of the hospital.[61] Several dramatic incidents occurred in the very early stages of American involvement and were widely reported. One nurse had her eye blown out when the tent in which she was sleeping was bombed. Base Hospital No. 5, the first U.S. unit to reach France, was bombed during its fifth month of service, in September 1917; several men were killed and a nurse was wounded while on duty. Under the headline "Woman Nurse Courageous," a Chicago newspaper reported: "Although the exploding bombs created horror in the hospital there was not the smallest sign of panic. . . . The American nurse, although struck in the face by a fragment of steel from the bomb, refused to be relieved and worked on." Such incidents fed the public perception that nursing involved risk and danger and helped establish the notion that the pinnacle of female war heroism was attending faithfully to hospital duties while under fire. By the end of the war, nurses had embraced this expectation. "I am glad to say there was not one coward among our nurses," wrote Sigrid Jorgensen, describing how nurses carried stretchers and tended patients during a bombing episode during the last months of the war. Julia Stimson praised the nurses of ARC Hospital 107 for their comportment during a raid: "All the nurses behaved like bricks, as did the Aids. No greater courage or devotion could possibly be expected."[62]

Accidents and disease, although less glamorized, posed far greater dangers to nurses, as they did to all members of the AEF.[63] Hospital workers were routinely exposed to contagious diseases such as meningitis, measles, typhus, scarlet fever, dysentery, and the Spanish influenza.

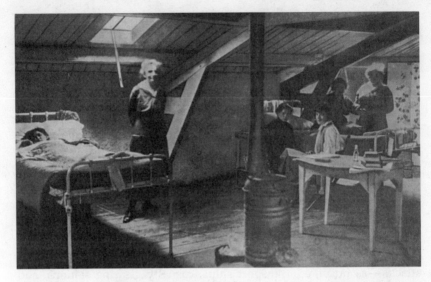

13. Sick nurses are cared for by their colleagues on a special ward. The Sick Nurses' Quarters, US Navy Hospital No. 1, Brest, France. Nurses in the AEF were exposed to high levels of disease. (Source: National American Red Cross, *History of American Red Cross Nursing* [New York: Macmillan Co., 1922].)

Base hospital centers set up special infirmaries for their nurses, and two convalescent hospitals for servicewomen were established by the American Red Cross in France. The army did not publish figures on the number of nurse days lost to sickness, but it was the exceptional nurse who escaped illness in the course of overseas duty. Julia Stimson was careful to point out that nurses were sick no more often than were their male counterparts in the military. Although the flu pandemic did not reach the same catastrophic proportions in the AEF as it did in the United States, it was a significant health crisis among nurses and hospital staff by October 1918. One army nurse veteran recalled that forty corpsmen and twenty nurses in her unit had pneumonia or influenza at the height of the epidemic, and two nurses and two corpsmen died.[64]

A total of 296 women died in war service or as a result of injuries sustained during war service, more than one-third of them overseas. This number was minuscule compared with the death and injury rate for men in the AEF. Yet, the impact of nurses' deaths was out of proportion to their numbers. As Julia Stimson explained, "there were few units which did not lose one or more nurses by death," and the deaths were all the more devastating since many of the women had trained together at the same sponsoring institution and been friends for years. For one base hospital, which buried twelve nurses in a single month, the point that nursing could be mortally dangerous was brought home with painful clarity.[65]

Nurses were acutely aware of the potential risks they faced, and the sense that their work involved danger was an important aspect of nursing culture in the AEF. "We were often in great danger, but very few, if any, had any thought of fear for herself," declared Alice Kelley, an ANC nurse on temporary assignment with a shock team near Verdun. At some hospitals it was a practice among nurses going on special duty at the front to make out informal "wills," bequeathing their equipment, chocolate supplies, and photographs to their coworkers. Routine military practices such as lifeboat drills and gas attack training also heightened nurses' perception of danger. Carolyn Clarke, one of the small number of nurses' aids who served with the AEF, was given her gas mask at Red Cross headquarters along with the warning that she had been assigned to "a position of extreme danger." Later, a Red Cross official took Clarke and two other women aside and asked them how their parents would feel if they were killed; the answer from all three was that "they wouldn't mind at all," for their parents were certainly prepared for the possibility that their daughters might die in the war.[66]

This response might seem startling, but it is characteristic of the way in which AEF nurses spoke and wrote about going to the front. One nurse aptly summarized the ubiquitous enthusiasm of her peers: "We always looked forward to the day when we might be chosen to go to the front, and you can picture our joy when the word came for us to get ready." The most powerful evidence about nurses' attitudes toward danger comes from their overwhelming response to service at the casualty clearing stations. Universally regarded as the most dangerous situation for nurses, the casualty clearing stations were the furthest forward position to which nurses were assigned. Julia Stimson found these the most coveted nursing positions of all and estimated that there were always ten times more volunteers than there were places.[67] Nurses clearly wished to be judged by male standards of courage, risk taking, and heroism. Nurses shared telephone operators' and canteen workers' fascination with the battlefront, but their routine access to the front and the danger in which they were placed indicate that their response was more than fantasy or bravado.

Yet, war only rarely requires heroism in the face of death, and much more often demands physical endurance in carrying out dull, routine tasks. When asked whether she had experienced combat, one AEF nurse veteran answered tentatively yes, if one could count the nursing of wounded men.[68] The majority of AEF nurses came face to face with the "real war" not under the extraordinary circumstances of direct combat but in the daily care of patients. Nurses performed a highly skilled job under circumstances entirely unique to war, and in the course of their duties they were immersed in the immediate consequences of battle.

Wartime nursing differed from both other women's work at the front and civilian nursing. The daily work experience of nurses was shaped primarily by the chronic shortage of Allied nursing personnel, the system by which men were routed from the front to the hospital, and the technology and character of injury in World War I. First and foremost, the work experience of AEF nurses was tied to the forms of destruction used in the war. Rifles, machine guns, and various types of explosives were responsible for most wounds in the fighting in France. Shrapnel, the exploding fragments of metal shell casings, was especially dangerous, as it traveled at low velocity and cut ragged wounds deep in the flesh, carrying bits of clothing, dirt, metal, and bone into the wound. Nurses' roles included work in the operating room, administering anesthetics and participating in operations; in triage, sorting the patients and preparing them for surgery or transfer; and on the wards, providing aftercare.

Care of wounds and amputations was critical because infection was rampant. The infamous mud of the trenches was heavily fertilized with animal and human feces; bacteria in the dirt, including the dreaded "gas bacillus," lodged in wounds and rapidly spread infection. One of the primary responsibilities of an army nurse was tending to surgical dressings. Once a wound was "debrided," that is, when all foreign bodies and damaged or infected tissue had been cut away, it was covered with bandages and left open. The wounds then were washed or "irrigated" regularly with an antiseptic and redressed until all infection was eradicated. One corpsman found this nursing task the hardest of all, for the nurses were in "constant contact with dreadful agony, which expressed itself in irrepressible moans and shrieks."[69]

The use of poison gases was a novel challenge for medical personnel. Two classes of chemical weapons were used extensively on both sides. Lung irritants such as chlorine, phosgene, and chlorpicrin caused vomiting, suffocation, or asphyxiation and could be fatal. Vesicants or blistering agents—the infamous mustard gas of the trenches—burned or blistered all parts of the body, especially moist tissues such as the eyes, nose, and throat. Painful burns and temporary blindness were the common result, although in high concentrations mustard gas too could be lethal. Nurses contended not only with coughing and choking and with burns that were highly prone to infection, but also with the emotional distress of victims of these strange and damaging new technologies.

Fighting in France had other psychic costs for soldiers, and nurses were called on to respond to the psychological needs of soldier-patients. Male hysteria or "shell shock" was a notable feature of disability in

World War I; its etiology, significance, and treatment were matters of controversy among contemporary medical practitioners.[70] Soldiers emerged from the fighting with strange and troubling symptoms: hysterical blindness, deafness, and mutism; paraplegia, hemiplegia, and gait disorders; and stammering, shaking, and trembling. Most nurses found the helplessness of "the shell shocks" painful and "pitiful." "These shell-shock cases are always falling out of bed," was a common observation. "The other night the explosion of shells could be distinctly heard, and almost all [the men] . . . shook as though they were having convulsions all night." Ironically, despite nurses' sympathy for these patients, the goal of specialized psychiatric nursing in military hospitals was to return the men to the trenches as swiftly as possible following a "therapeutic" period of rest and recreation.[71]

The intensity of military nursing was exacerbated by oversized patient loads of desperately ill men, far greater than was customary in any civilian hospital. Nursing shortages in France were chronic and, during the final drive of the war, severe. In the summer of 1917, the Surgeon General estimated that 22,430 nurses would be required for an army of a million men; yet, for an expeditionary force of two million, the number of nurses never exceeded ten thousand. At the time of the armistice, the Army Medical Department estimated that the nursing service in France was short of six thousand women. For AEF nurses, this translated into patient loads that were sometimes thirty, fifty, or more, and occasionally in the hundreds.[72] The greatest portion of American nurses arrived at the very height of fighting, in the final summer and fall of the war, when nursing services were most heavily taxed.

Nursing shortages did not mean that all medical staff worked under regular, constant pressure; in actuality, periods of intensive, at times overwhelming, work were interspersed with periods of inactivity, at times even to the point of boredom. The characteristic ebb and flow of nursing at the front depended on the system through which wounded men were routed from the battlefield through successive tiers of medical care and treatment. An injured soldier received first aid on the field and was then carried by stretcher to an ambulance and transported several miles back to the casualty clearing station, the first of the facilities staffed with nurses. At every step along the way, nurses, corpsmen, and doctors sorted the men by the seriousness of their injury and the immediacy of the care they required, the goal being to transfer patients as quickly as possible away from the front and open up beds and resources for the next round of wounded men. Patients could be treated at the casualty clearing station for shock or given critical surgery, but most had their wounds dressed and were prepared for transport. Large convoys of patients were sent to the evacuation hospital for surgery or treatment. After three weeks, or sometimes much less, patients were sent on to base hospitals, convalescent camps, convalescent hospitals, or specialized facilities for fracture, rehabilitation, or neuropsychiatric care further behind the front.

The nursing shortage, the nature of injury in trench warfare, and the practice of clearing large convoys of wounded men all at once created what nurses, doctors, and enlisted men called "the rush," the period of intense labor, often lasting forty-eight hours or more, in which one hospital received and treated hundreds of patients. The arrival of each convoy strained the resources of the entire hospital to the limit. Yet for nurses it took on special significance. The rush was nurses' equivalent of "going over the top," an initiation rite in which the nurse's will and strength were tested. In American nurses' memoirs from World War I through Vietnam, the rush symbolizes the horror of war and, in compressed form, stands for the entire experience of war nursing.[73] In some cases it also held the seeds of disillusionment, when the nurse came face to face with the consequences of war and began to question the part she played.

The hospital rush was the nurses' direct link to the front. Temporally it immediately followed a major battle and slowed as the drive slowed, giving nurses the sense that they were but a "few hours behind the actual events." Nurses identified their hospital work with particular battles. Maude Crawford, for example, wrote: "Chateau Thierry is a name that the American boys will never forget, and a name that will bring a shudder to the nurses who were there in the awful days of July." Nurses experienced the battle through their patients: "We who cared for the boys lived through each battle as it was retold for us, either by a patient right from the scene or by one under ether, whose descriptions were often more vivid." But the rush as nurses perceived it was itself a kind of battle, in which they became fighters against time and death. "We were no longer compassionate sympathizers but active combatants," Shirley Millard wrote. "This time it was different. . . . This time . . . the shells exploded in our very hearts. . . . " Chief nurses remarked on the overwhelming volume of patients handled during a rush. "It is only numbers that would give you any idea at all of what we have been doing," Julia Stimson wrote her family. "No one over here thinks in any numbers less than 50 or 100." Bodies stacked or strewn on every surface transformed the hospital into a shadow of the battlefield. One nurse's aid eloquently described the sensation of working amid the sights, sounds, and smells of men in agony: "Hundreds upon hundreds of wounded poured in like a rushing torrent. No matter what we did, how hard we worked, it did not seem to be fast enough or hard enough. More came. It took me several days to steel my emotions against the stabbing cries of pain. The crowded, twisted bodies, the screams and groans, made one think of the old engravings in Dante's *Inferno*."[74]

For nurses, the rush was a "baptism by fire," as Stimson put it. One nurse acknowledged that she "went all to pieces" on her first night when left to care for ninety men, many of them "in the most awful condition," but she soon learned to maintain her composure. Stimson noted her particular concern about a group of replacement nurses, "young, inexperienced little things," fresh from their training at a small Kentucky hospital, who were plunged into the midst of a large drive on their first day of duty. The new nurses survived admirably the "unbelievable hell" of their first shift, Stimson found, and she hoped that they would soon be seasoned like her other nurses. Long after they had adjusted to the shock, nurses expressed extreme ambivalence about working through a rush. On one hand, they found the work deeply fulfilling. Many would have agreed with the young Kentucky nurses, who stated that this experience was exactly "what they had come for." The value and urgency of nurses' work in a desperately overcrowded hospital was beyond question. Women were driven to work twenty hours or more without a break because they knew how mortal even a few hours could be as infection advanced or bleeding continued. "If we went off duty, it only meant that much longer for them [the patients] to wait," commented Sigrid Jorgensen. Jorgensen recalled her arrival at a mobile hospital, which had received a thousand wounded patients in twenty-four hours: "About a dozen tired but cheerful nurses greeted us and told us they were glad we arrived as there was more work than they could possibly describe. . . . Help was needed and needed quickly."[75]

At the height of a rush, nurses worked with virtually no oversight and were free, if not compelled, to make decisions independently. Informal "promotions" were not uncommon, as in the case of a nurse's aid who found herself in charge of a tent of 105 gas and shell-shock cases and an isolation ward next door; she handled these patients on her own, consulting with a nurse or doctor only when she "occasionally" needed advice. Nurses were much more than an extra pair of hands. The absence of an experienced surgical nurse or a nurse-anesthetist would paralyze a surgical team, and nurses on shock teams were involved in life-and-death procedures. Maude Crawford portrayed them as "too busy to do more than give [the patient] a smile or an encouraging pat as they pass by," in other words, as too busy for the traditional, maternalistic work of comforting the ill.[76] Nurses embraced this autonomy, understandably proud of their contribution.

Although the rush intensified AEF nurses' belief in the centrality of their work to the war effort, it also brought into sharp focus the horrific consequences of war. Nurses' pride in their work was mingled with sorrow, regret, horror, and, at times, disillusionment. One AEF nurse veteran found these feelings inexpressible: "It would be very hard to portray the real horror of the trench warfare. [I] still get a lump in my throat when I think of their suffering."[77] Other nurses summoned up words and memories that bore eloquent witness to the dark side of their experience.[78] For Ethel Pierce seventy years later, the memory is unwrapping a bandage to reveal a wound writhing with maggots. Indeed, for many women the disruption or distortion of the war is emblematized by a moment of seeing or doing the obscenely unimaginable. Grotesque images appear in nurses' accounts: watching a man's lungs pumping through an open chest wound, grasping a man's severed hand or severed foot, holding a soldier's eye in her cupped palm.[79] Such violations of the body represent in nurses' accounts a vision of life gone haywire, of the world mutilated through war.[80] In contrast with the apocryphal tales of sadistic Germans mutilating their enemies, these impersonal mutilations were all too real.

The rush left nurses with an unsettling paradox: the responsibility and autonomy of the situation gave nurses a feeling of professional empowerment, yet the number and difficulty of the cases gave them a lurking sense of powerlessness and futility. In civilian life, nurses had worked with dangerously ill cases, and most had previously lost patients. But the numbers of seriously ill men, the kinds of injuries they suffered, the youth of the patients, and the constant presence of death set this experience apart. In many cases the nurse could do nothing but watch a patient die. Ethel Pierce recalled treating a British soldier, whom she believed to be fourteen years old, who was shot in the stomach. "'Sister, I can't keep it down . . . it won't stay down.' I said, 'I know you can't son. Just try, try taking a little sip. . . . Of course he was dying, and what could you do? It was awful. . . .'" Nothing could be done for patients with profound burns. "One of my most stolid nurses came to me . . . and said, 'I just don't know how I am going to stand it'," Julia Stimson wrote; "that day we had so many sick men to look after . . . and several nurses got hysterical and I felt things were just too much. Any one would have thought so if they had seen our poor gassed men who are so terribly burnt." Often nurses could not even do the work of comforting or easing death, finding that their touch brought agony and suffering rather than comfort: "Their garments are caked with mud from head to foot, so that to get the things off without causing excruciating pain is almost impossible. 'Leave me alone, will you!' they scream wildly and resist my ministrations."[81]

Some nurses wondered why they healed men simply to send them to the front again. "It chokes me every time I see the men march away . . . thinking . . . [that] many of these would be coming back, as those mangled things were in the ambulances," Julia Stimson wrote. Carrie Hall remarked: "You see I am where I am seeing something of the *business* of war. There is no glamour whatsoever about it. The men who go to the front for the first time go with cheering and vim. Those who go back for the second and third time go in silence and go because they are sent."[82] Nurses were also troubled by the impersonality of death. Ethel Pierce went to see the burial of her 14-year-old patient and determined she would go to no others: thirty-six men were buried at once in a long trench and, she observed, the body bags did not correspond with the crosses on the embankment. The most critical nurses came to see the war as a machine, endlessly chewing men up and spitting them out, a calculated technological process rather than a natural one.

Nurses and orderlies on the wards were the most emotionally vulnerable, since they interacted with patients as individuals, listened to their stories and hallucinations, and came to know them as people immersed in family relationships. Nurses learned to distance themselves from patients, using toughness, briskness, humor, or cheerfulness as a protection against despair. Yet, caring invariably involves a certain kind of identification, and the impulse to empathize broke down this protective distance again and again. Nurses' stories often tell of a particular patient who broke through the facade by virtue of something that set him apart: a special sweetness or innocence, unusual stoicism, contact with his family, or simply the extremity of his injury. "There are two cases I shall always remember particularly," wrote Alice Kelley, a surgical nurse with an evacuation hospital. The first man had wounds in the left leg and arm, and had lost his left eye, his right leg, and right arm. The second patient, "a lad of twenty-one," had a leg so badly infected it was necessary to amputate near the hip. Touched by this patient's tenacity, Kelley wrote to his parents when he died.[83] Ethel Pierce only wrote to one patient's mother, and promised herself she would never do it again.

Feeling compassion for patients as individuals could have another unsettling effect on nurses. Of all the women in the AEF, they had the most intimate contact with the "enemy"; it was not uncommon for a nurse to be assigned to a ward of German prisoners. For some women, this experience called into question the very concept of "enemy." Shirley Millard struck up a friendship with a German soldier, a 16-year-old "youngster" who had happy memories of visiting his uncle in Milwaukee. "His right leg was gone above the knee, and his right arm was so shattered he would never use it again. His eyes were large and gentle. . . . He looked gray and undernourished, and often told me, very confidentially, that he hated the war." As a general rule, nurses regarded German officers as arrogant and overly demanding, but German privates usually evoked a kinder response.[84] In some hospitals, it was the practice to use German convalescents as ward orderlies. Ethel Pierce, who was stationed in Rouen, France, recalled that one of the German "boys" was so gentle and tender with the American patients that he was the only person who could make one particularly difficult patient comfortable. Such attitudes are not surprising, for nurses came into contact with German soldiers as frightened, sick boys, who were often a decade or more their juniors. Yet, recognizing the personhood of the enemy had the potential to undermine one of the basic underpinnings of war.

The experience of nursing posed a challenge to underlying concepts of war in another way: nurses experienced the war not as a political conflict with a clean and definite ending but rather as a multifaceted human event with consequences stretching well beyond the cessation of fighting.[85] For nurses, this raggedy quality of the war was quite concrete: sickness and death did not cease at 11:00 A.M. on November 11, 1918. Military hospitals stayed busy in the following months, in large part because the flu epidemic in the AEF peaked just as the war was ending. But even the morning of the armistice there was fierce fighting, an irony of World War I immortalized by Remarque in *All Quiet on the Western Front*, so that many hospitals were in the midst of a new rush even as bells pealed to celebrate the end of the war. Some nurses reacted bitterly to the news. Shirley Millard remarked: "There is no armistice for Charley or for any of the others in that ward. One of the boys began to sob. I went and talked soothingly to him, but what could I say, knowing he would die before night?" Ethel Pierce recalled, "It was awful to think of the Armistice being signed—I was in a hut . . . and they had the flu, and the flu was awful." "I am glad it is over but my heart is heavy as lead," Shirley Millard wrote in her diary.[86]

THE "RUSH" EPITOMIZED nursing on the war front. Intense excitement, autonomy, control, and the conviction that their special skills were indispensable reverberated in the experiences of army nurses. Backed by a sense of professional identity and a strong female leadership, nurses believed they were in a unique position to claim a place for women in the war. Yet at all levels they encountered severe and frustrating limits on their authority. Working in a rush highlighted the importance of their contribution, but it highlighted as well the ineffectuality of their efforts. The journey to the heart of the war raised troubling questions for nurses about the dimensions of the destruction, the futility of their work, and the nature of the war itself.

[6]

Serving Uncle Sam: The Meaning of Women's Wartime Service

On September 30, 1918, President Wilson urged the Senate to support the woman suffrage amendment to the Constitution. Wilson was a latecomer to the cause of votes for women; less than a year earlier, in the wake of the New York State suffrage victory, he had reaffirmed his commitment to the principle of states' rights in matters of voting qualifications. Now he declared the immediate enfranchisement of women "vitally essential to the successful prosecution of the great war of humanity in which we are engaged." Women have been the "partners" of men in this war, he asserted. "Shall we admit them only to a partnership of sacrifice and suffering and toil and not to a partnership of privilege and of right?" Justice demanded enfranchisement, as did the international reputation of the United States as the guarantor of democracy. "Democracy means that women shall play their part in affairs alongside men and upon an equal footing with them." Wilson's speech linked women's citizenship with women's war service in ways that had been unimaginable even nine months earlier. In January 1918, when the House had passed the suffrage amendment, debate had revolved around abstract questions of democratic rights and state sovereignty. Then came the horrific last summer of the war, when the U.S. army turned the tide in Europe toward an Allied victory. Thousands of American men died in those campaigns, and thousands of American women streamed to France to back their efforts. Now Wilson placed women serving with the American Expeditionary Force (AEF) at the center of his argument, reminding his listeners that "the tasks of the women lie at the very heart of the war." His references to women workers in the war zone were unmistakable: "This war could not have been fought . . . if it had not been for the services of the women . . . rendered in every sphere,—not merely in the fields of effort in which we have been accustomed to see them work but wherever men have worked and upon the very skirts and edges of the battle itself."

Wilson's language militarized women's service, adding rhetorical strength to his argument. Women's war work had involved "service and sacrifice of every kind"; women were not "slackers." Now Congress had a debt to pay to women, and Wilson urged the senators to "show our women that you trust them as much as you in fact and of necessity depend upon them."[1]

Many factors contributed to the passage of the nineteenth amendment, most importantly the broad-based suffrage movement itself. Yet, as Wilson's speech makes clear, the war had dramatically altered the terms of the debate by the autumn of 1918. A year earlier, Alice Paul and other members of the Congressional Union had been jailed and denounced as disloyal for stating the same arguments that the president now offered to the Senate. Wilson's speech is notable for its clear linkage of women's equality claims with their service for the AEF, promoting the citizenship claims of all women on the basis of their partnership with men in the prosecution of the war. He emphasized the dependency of the state on women's labor in the war zone, the "heart of the war." For a brief, significant moment, the historical strands of women's suffrage and women's war mobilization were woven together in a dramatic and public way. Wilson's speech also reveals prevalent attitudes toward women's service at the close of the Great War. During the final months of the war and over the years that followed, male and female military officials, veterans, and civilians reflected on the meaning and implications of women's military service. Although women's mobilization had been greeted initially by uncomfortable silence or antagonism, by the end of the war servicewomen seemed to have won wide respect from officers, soldiers, and the public, even the president. One journalist called servicewomen "America's true war heroines"; another dubbed them "Uncle Sam's nieces." In big cities and small towns, women returning from Europe were welcomed home with accolades and celebration. One nurse recalled being taken from the dock in New York City and "whisked up Fifth Avenue through the big white Victory Arch."[2] The passage of the woman suffrage amendment seemed a sign of the nation's gratitude for women's patriotic service.

But would the wartime expansion of women's work have lasting consequences, redefining women's public and civic opportunities? Emily Newell Blair was skeptical. During her two years on the staff of the Woman's Committee of the Council of National Defense, she had listened to inflated rhetoric about women's role in the war effort. "When speeches were made to mothers of boys, woman was the strongest power of the world, the noblest jewel in America's diadem; when food was wanted, she was the foundationstone on which our whole economic structure is built; when labor was needed, she was the great reserve of the industrial world; when pain and anguish wrung the brow or threatened to, she was a ministering angel," Blair wrote in her postwar report. "But when she asked for a definite status in the scheme of things, when she asked for the privilege of deciding how she should serve her country and what her contribution to victory should be, her status varied according to the group of men to whom she applied. . . ."[3] Blair captured an unsettling underlying truth. As the war came to an end, organized servicewomen began to ask for the benefits to which they felt entitled and to seek expanded opportunities for public service. Official responses, as Blair suggests, were "nebulous," shifting, and ultimately evasive. Women's contributions to the war effort had been defined as an extension of their femininity, and working women's struggle to redefine their own role did not succeed in moving beyond the wartime work place. The suffrage amendment was the first and nearly the last public acknowledgment that military service had transformed women's relationship to the state. Women's place in the civilian labor force was not transformed by their wartime employment in the male-dominated military, and their labor itself was not seen as an attribute of citizenship; rather, women's wartime work was subsumed by their gender.

Drawing on official postwar reports, media and propaganda materials, published memoirs and private journals, this chapter examines competing formulations of women's service at the close of the war in three major constituencies: the military and government leaders of the war effort, civilian organizations that recruited and supervised women workers for the AEF, and servicewomen themselves. These groups invested women's wartime labor with different meanings and used it to support their own goals. While organized women veterans looked for an expanded definition of their role and a recognition of the equality that they had earned through wartime service, government, military, and civic leaders worked to limit and contain the consequences of women's military service. By the mid-1920s, they had succeeded in erasing the more radical, egalitarian implications of women's work with the AEF. The meaning and memory of women's service was fixed in the postwar period in a conservative patriotic frame, which emphasized themes of voluntarism and subservience. In this reactionary political climate, women veterans narrowed their own concerns, struggling to shore up the gains they had already achieved rather than to enlarge women's opportunities; former servicewomen increasingly focused on the contested issues of benefits and official military status. Women veterans advanced as individuals, but war service failed to enhance their group status as citizens.

FROM THE TOP echelons of the army downward, the official, public assessment was that the employment of American women in the war zone had been a notable success. As General John J. Pershing wrote in his 1919 report to the secretary of war, "the various societies, especially their women, including those of the theatrical profession and our army nurses, played a most important part in brightening the lives of our troops and in giving aid and comfort to our sick and wounded." Pershing's compliment was part of a wave of appreciation for women workers that crested at the close of the war. Pershing's remarks are also revealing, for they typify the strategy of domesticating women's service with the AEF. This discursive strategy posited a continuum of women's care work, in which all roles played by women—nursing, transport, telephone operation, canteen work, marine and naval yeoman service—were translated into a version of domestic caring labor. Pershing did not distinguish among various female occupations or between civilian and military personnel, distinctions that servicewomen regarded as crucial; all belonged to a single group, marked and defined by their femininity. In this approach, the war front is made continuous with the home front, and women's service with the AEF is reconfigured as an extension of their natural role within the family. This concept was laid out with special clarity by Major General Helmick in a speech to female auxiliary workers gathered at Brest, France, during demobilization: "It makes no difference what you are, whether a nurse in the hospital or a Y worker creating the home atmosphere at the front . . . everywhere there is the same beautiful spirit and the same wonderful influence that has its effect on our soldiery."[4]

While Pershing and other top officials praised women in public for their feminine, nurturant qualities and their positive impact on morale, internal military reports also judged women on the basis of "merit." Using "overall efficiency" or "specific job qualifications" to measure women's accomplishments established an objective, gender-neutral set of criteria. By these criteria, too, military officials deemed women's work "decidedly a success." Women telephone operators, for instance, had shown that "they were more skillful in the manipulation of a board than are the men," and their arrival had brought a "great improvement" in the "smooth and efficient functioning" of communication, according to the chief Signal Corps officer for the AEF. Surgeon General Merritte Ireland commended the "splendid" work of military nurses at the conclusion of the war: "The service of the nurses have [sic] been efficient in the highest degree and their work both in this country and abroad has been very highly recommended." The quality of women's work equaled and often exceeded that of men doing comparable tasks, according to military observers. As an AEF intelligence report on auxiliary agencies concluded, "the women as a rule were more aggressive and hard working than the men, they were more cheerful and optimistic, and did not become so irritable under strain as did the men."[5] In short, women workers were credited for their hard work, skill, and positive attitude.

What accounts for military officials' almost uniform praise for women workers? The majority of AEF officers were genuinely impressed by the work of their female subordinates. Military commanders also may have stressed the valuable contribution of women at least in part because they felt compelled to justify a controversial new policy, which many Americans (including the secretary of war) had difficulty accepting. Commanders in the AEF had deemed women's labor a necessary and effective solution to their manpower problems, a practical approach as well as a fair and enlightened one. But women's "success" in the war was also problematic, for it could imply an acknowledgment of women's equality with men. This problem is apparent in Major General Helmick's speech to women war workers. "You women . . . have made a new place for yourselves in war . . . and I venture to say that never again will the American man go to war without demanding that the American woman come with him," he began boldly. Helmick compared servicewomen with servicemen in ways that highlighted equality and sameness. "The American soldier knows that the American woman is not afraid; she is just as anxious to get to the war and into the field as he. She has shown that shot and shell do not keep her from performing the duties she came here to perform; they have been gassed and wounded and yet they have performed their duty." Helmick's rhetoric has far-reaching implications: women were not cowards; they did not crack; they endangered their lives for the cause; their zeal never flagged; in short, they took war like a man. Significantly, Helmick went on to connect women's war service with political equality. "You are going back home very soon . . . to greatly changed conditions," Helmick noted, referring to women's role in the triumph of prohibition and the growing momentum behind the federal suffrage amendment. "You are going to be shoulder to shoulder with men in the future. Upon your shoulders is going to rest the responsibility of the success or failure of the future of our great country."

Despite his image of women as equal partners with men in national affairs, Helmick was not a feminist. For commentators such as Helmick and Theodore Roosevelt, the fine wartime performance of women workers posed a problem of logic and policy. For both men, the solution was a second-class citizenship in which women, with their "beautiful spirits" and "wonderful influence," would serve as helpmates to the primary citizens, the red-blooded American men who emerged from the war as new model citizens.[6] Helmick's rhetorical solution to the dilemma of women's success became the dominant strategy of policymakers, a strategy of "gender containment," to adopt Elaine Tyler May's term.[7] Its pur-

pose was to limit the possibilities of change while allowing and even ap-
plauding certain narrower advancements. Containment was a compromise position that accepted a place for women in the war but relegated
them to a secondary and separate status. Through policy as well as propaganda, the state expended considerable effort to control the subversive
potential of women's overseas service. The urgency of this task was enhanced by women's own demands for change, most notably the nurses'
movement for rank and women's mobilization for peace and suffrage.
The strategy of containment and the policies it generated can be seen
clearly in two major arenas of struggle for servicemen and servicewomen
during the war: work and sexuality. The army's resolution to these wartime dilemmas had important implications for the postwar task of making meaning out of women's war service.

Ambivalence about women at war is evident in the army's handling
of servicewomen's sexuality, a theme developed in earlier chapters. The
deeply held belief that American women could help keep the AEF
"clean" and sober had been an early justification for women's military
service. For Pershing the fight against venereal disease necessitated the
employment of women in many capacities. The "pretty," "younger girls"
urged on auxiliary agencies by AEF headquarters were intended to
temper the "white-hot intensity" of the natural "male appetites," which
were assumed to increase in combat situations. Leave areas and canteens, army dances featuring American women as dance partners, the
"Substitute Homes" program, and the Young Men's Christian Association's (YMCA's) entertainment division all used women to address the
sexual and emotional needs of U.S. soldiers. While commanders believed
that a measured dose of female sexuality could be beneficial to army
morale, they also feared that rumors of sexual permissiveness in the AEF
might erode trust and morale back home. Managers of the war effort
worked hard to present the army as a safe and paternalistic institution, a
task made urgent by the controversial selective service system. Secretary
of War Baker promised to provide American "boys" with "an invisible
armor" of morality, an "attitude of mind" that could never be penetrated
by "anything unwholesome."[8] This guarantee of sexual protection for
America's fighting men was an important underpinning of public support for the military and for women's warfront service.

At the same time, concerns predictably arose about the sexual protection of women in the war zone. The mother who insisted her daughter
wear glasses to conceal her attractiveness while on duty in France was
not alone; public and parental anxiety about the purity of American
"girls," alone in a sea of homesick and unattached American men, ran
just below the surface throughout the war. Elizabeth Marbury, a prominent wartime lecturer for the Knights of Columbus, expressed these con-

cerns in a widely publicized speech: "I think anybody who has any control over a young woman is doing very wrong to let her go to France and entertain soldiers, dance with them and so on. . . . Hundreds of them went to get new sensations but in my opinion it is most unsafe."[9] The lurid rumor campaign against nurses was both symptom and cause of this anxiety. The stories of rape, brutality, promiscuity, and pregnancy that swept the United States in the spring of 1918 exacerbated fears about the danger of military service for women and heightened doubts about the appropriateness of sending women into a war zone. Misogynist rumor campaigns occurred during World War II as well, directing smears of promiscuity and lesbianism toward the Women's Army Corps; the similarities between the two campaigns suggest that the rumors sprang as much from ongoing fears of gender transformation as from the specific circumstances of the two wars.[10]

Ironically, the army's own handling of sexual issues may have contributed to this negative attitude toward women workers at the front. Themes of sexual danger and female betrayal thread the discourse of World War I. Many scholars have suggested that the view of woman as whore, seducer, and betrayer of men has deep historical and ideological roots in western traditions of warfare. Klaus Theweleit places male fear and hatred of female sexuality at the very center of militarist violence.[11] Anxieties about female sexuality were also expressed in the propaganda and folklore of all combatant nations during the Great War. Prophylaxis campaign posters presented women as conduits of debilitating sexual disease; female spy stories emphasized the mortal threat that female temptresses posed to their own countrymen. *Stars and Stripes* printed doughboy humor about allegedly unfaithful wives and sweethearts back home. Military intelligence repeatedly warned doughboys not only about the danger of sexual relations with prostitutes but even against casual conversation with women.[12]

Overall, the AEF's formulation of female sexuality was paradoxical. When meticulously managed, female sexuality could be a valuable tool of the war effort; but uncontrolled female sexuality was a threat to the Allied war effort and the effectiveness of the armed forces. These mixed messages placed AEF women on a moral tightrope. While there was no tolerance for female sexual autonomy, women were counted on to be pleasing and desirable to soldiers. The solution to this dilemma was sexual containment, a carefully controlled boy(ish)-girl(ish) eroticism in which flirtation was acceptable but more direct forms of contact were forbidden: look but don't touch. Comparing the World War II army pinup with her counterpart in World War I, one is struck by the AEF's cult of cuteness, the clean-scrubbed, kid-sister image that figured so prominently in military lore. The quintessential image of female sexu-

14. Salvation Army "doughnut girls." This hometown girl with a "helmet halo" was the best-known and most popular image of women war front workers during World War I. U.S. Army Signal Corps photograph. (U.S. Army Military History Institute, Carlisle Barracks, Pa.)

ality in World War I was no doubt the Salvation Army "doughnut girl." Images of the doughnut girl were consumed at the front through song, story, and, most powerfully, photograph. Army photographers' depictions were widely distributed both in France and at home (Figure 14). In this iconic image, the doughnut girl is shown with rolling pin or apron, marking her connection to home and the domestic sphere; her helmet "halo" is at once integral to the image and charmingly incongruous. Her job is to *be* there for her male admirers, plucky and optimistic but also vulnerable to the dangers of the war zone. Salvation Army materials describe her purity in semireligious terms, an image that was often echoed in the writings of enlisted men: "there is something about her delicate features and slender grace that makes one think of a young saint." The doughnut girl's virginal "sisterliness" contributed to her inaccessibility and kept her off limits to the doughboys. "No wonder these lassies were as safe over there ten miles from any other woman . . . , alone among 10,000 soldiers, as if they had been in their own homes."[13]

Here once again is the "essentialist" war myth, based in notions of inherent gender difference. The doughboy was fighting to protect the American woman, symbolized at the front by the doughnut girl. When his job is done, he can go home and marry a girl just like her. At war, he is dedicated to protecting her purity, not just from the brutal Hun, but from the baser instincts of himself and his compatriots in arms. Ultimately, the girlish purity of the Salvation Army lassie, successfully preserved even in the war zone, is a promise that women's sexuality can be repressed and placed at the service of men, even in the unconstrained and uncontrollable environment of war.

Elements of ambivalence were also apparent in the treatment of women's work for the AEF, as earlier chapters showed. If women were praised for their competence and American know-how in official military evaluations, they were often ridiculed for these very qualities in more informal AEF sources. Women were criticized for being small-minded rule followers who reveled in bureaucracy, even as they were praised for following orders. Women were applauded for their efficiency but ridiculed if they took themselves or their work too seriously. Nurses who insisted on the authority of their position were the butt of enlisted men's jokes; in cartoons and stories they were portrayed as "battle-axes," desexualized and emasculating.

Doughboy humor was frequently used to cut women down to size, to undermine their authority, as in the Wallgren cartoon for *Stars and Stripes* shown in Figure 15. Enlisted men were threatened by female authority and grumbled about "taking orders from skirts." One poem printed in *Stars and Stripes* used the theme of unskirting to express anxieties about wartime labor and the disruption of the gender status quo. Called up for overseas service, the man hastens home from training camp to say farewell to his family. There he finds his child, alone and unfed, and his wife out on the street, engaged in military drill.

> That voice, with love once soft and low,
> Was shouting "Right by section HO!" . . .
> The swish of dainty skirts was now
> No more; instead were—khaki trou!

This soldier's poem, titled "I Loved an Amazon," draws out a dire string of consequences from a woman trying to wear the military "pants" in the family, from the preemption of male authority to the disruption of the American home and the desexing of the American man.[14] Ambition and authority were regarded as inappropriate traits for women workers; they threatened to disrupt proper gender relations and destroy army morale.

SK IN HOSP (IN LINE OF BEAUTY)

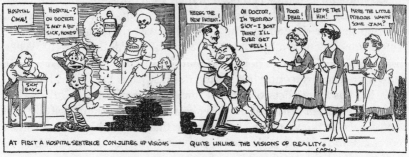

15. Cartoonist "Wally" Wallgren shows a soldier's fantasy about AEF nurses: not equal partners in the war, they are instead doting mothers or sexy playmates in this *Stars and Stripes* cartoon. *Stars and Stripes* 1 (April 19, 1918): 11.

At the same time, women workers' "feminine" qualities were emphasized and presented as a liability at the front. Overly personal and excessively emotional, women might form or maintain bonds that would prevent them from carrying out their duty to the impersonal cause, the abstract nation. As Jean Bethke Elshtain has shown, Western notions of the essentially private nature of woman have led thinkers since Machiavelli to regard women as untrustworthy players on the public stage of war.[15] During the First World War, the "brother-sister" rule imposed by the AEF, a ban on accepting female relatives of AEF soldiers for overseas service, was meant to staunch the disruptive flow of feminine emotionalism across the Atlantic. Anxieties about woman's nature were also expressed in military intelligence practices. The danger of women's employment at the front could be minimized if women's "talk" could be carefully controlled through the many security measures and mechanisms created by G-2 and directed toward women workers.

The pattern of containment is evident in regard to women's labor in the armed services: women were welcomed to the war zone as workers in female occupations so long as they carried out the orders of male superiors, uncomplainingly and efficiently, without pushing for advancement. The strategy of the war's managers was to accept limited change, but *only* in a separate and subordinate female service sector. Although yielding some ground to women, this strategy was most certainly a way to protect male privilege of other sorts. It is worthwhile to recall the areas where working women pushed for entry during World War I and were rebuffed: female physicians were not commissioned in the army medical corps, female war correspondents were not granted credentials, and military nurses were not given rank. Allowing women entry to those opportunities would have placed them in direct competition with men for authority, prestige, and expertise, and so these areas remained sacrosanct. What the army yielded to women is what we have come to describe as the pink-collar sector: a feminized, subservient, and carefully delimited domain of work in both the civilian and military economies. From the dominant perspective, it is a second-rate contribution and as such is defined as unthreatening and controllable.

This set of attitudes about gender, work, and authority within the military has continued from World War I forward. Margarethe Cammermeyer, a decorated Vietnam veteran who achieved the rank of colonel in the Army Nurse Corps, recalls from her early military career that army nurses, even with full rank, were regarded as subservient and therefore acceptable by their male colleagues: "the real source of my protection in the male military world was that, performing in a supposedly subservient capacity—as a nurse—I was not perceived as a threat to any man's position." Cammermeyer was dishonorably discharged in 1992 when she chose to reveal her lesbianism; only when she confronted the army with the specter of female authority, self-assertion, and sexual independence was she judged to be unacceptable. Cammermeyer takes this to be the meaning of her experience: "As I and other women step out of 'inferior' roles and compete with men, we become more frequent targets of male hostility and subtle abuse."[16]

But the very notion of a subordinate, pink-collar sector is a historical construction. Nursing and clerical work are not inherently inferior occupations. On the contrary, the case of World War I suggests just the opposite, that the status of female service work was in a state of flux during this formative era. Wartime policymakers and enlisted men alike were aware of and anxious about the power inherent in many aspects of women's work at the front. Caring for men who are weakened, helpless, and dependent; handling important and sensitive military information; asserting professional independence and authority—themes of female empowerment run through perceptions of women's work in World War I. They suggest that such potentialities were still present in female service occupations, at least at that historical moment. The hostility directed toward nurses and clerical workers and the trivialization of their work can be seen as attempts to cut women down to size, to establish and codify their inferiority. The containment of women's work roles during World War I was one stage in the process by which the female service sector was constructed as a subordinate sphere of female employment, a significant legacy of the war.

THE VOLUNTARY AGENCIES were a second major site for the evaluation and interpretation of women's service during and after the war. Because of women's contested status within the armed services, auxiliary organizations such as the YMCA and the American Red Cross worked closely with AEF women, recruiting, training, supervising, and, in the case of canteen workers, employing them. Like military leaders, the leaders of the auxiliary organizations publicly had nothing but high praise for the women who served under their auspices. But, the voluntary agencies also looked at women's wartime service through the prism of organizational self-interest, and the divergent interests of the organizations gave rise to divergent perspectives. The contrast between the YMCA and the American Red Cross Nursing Service is most striking. Auxiliary agencies such as the YMCA had been forced into a far greater reliance on female workers and administrators during the war than they had intended. To the male leaders of these organizations, women's wartime advances in the Y were certainly not meant to presage permanent change. The commitment of YMCA leaders to reasserting the status quo after the war meant undercutting or dismissing women. The Red Cross Nursing Service, which was led by women, took a different approach. Its leaders shared the goals of the American Red Cross, to see the organization maintain its position as the government's officially recognized guardian of public health. But as leaders of a professional and service organization of women workers, they also represented the occupational and political aspirations of nurses. The goal of the Nursing Service at the close of the war was to commemorate and extend the wartime contributions of nurses.

The American Red Cross Nursing Service, under the direction of Clara D. Noyes, issued its own official summary of women's war record in 1922. This lengthy, meticulous history related the story of wartime nursing as a remarkable tale of female achievement. Women are not handmaids in this account; on the contrary, they are the central actors, and this history of the war is told in large part through the voices, words, letters, and reports of nurses themselves. The authors of the Red Cross history challenged head-on the popular view of the nurse as the "angel of the battlefields," "set high above the ugliness and stench of combat, unperturbed, serene, and holy by reason of [her] beauty of person and character, a shining ideal toward which the dying soldier turned his glazing eye." Nursing leaders were dissatisfied with this passive icon and were determined to replace her with an alternative figure, fully as heroic but far more practical and corporeal.

Instead of the flowing white veil and the immaculate uniform of popular fancy and postered fame, the Red Cross nurse wore the utilitarian cap of the graduate nurse and the practical gray uniform of the field; some times she was muffled up in a slicker, with storm boots on her feet. . . . Instead of a seraphic-faced girl, she was far more frequently a woman of mature years. . . . Highly-trained instrument in the care of the sick that she herself was, she could manifest no reactions . . . of her own emotions. Though her throat might ache with sympathy, her mind must be alert, her eyes must be clear, her hands steady for the performance of her manifold duties.[17]

Red Cross authors described nurses as dispassionate professionals with specialized, scientific knowledge. "Training" and expertise, rather than the supposedly inherent feminine qualities of sympathy and caring, were central to nursing leaders. Nurses were still engaged in a struggle for professional status in the medical community and larger society, and the clinical and professional success of U.S. army nurses in World War I was crucial evidence for the champions of nurse training. "Scientific" facts and figures, nurse leaders believed, could demonstrate the value of the graduate nurse best of all, and their history is crowded with data: five of every six men who were sent to U.S. military hospitals were returned to active duty; nineteen of every thousand men of the AEF died of disease, as opposed to twenty-six of every thousand during the Spanish-American War.[18] These statistics seldom meet current standards of evidence. But, in the rhetorical battle over the professional reputation of nursing that took place during the 1920s, Red Cross leaders used the war record of American nurses as ammunition.

The contest over representations of women at the front was dramatized in a conflict between the Red Cross Nursing Service and the War Department over a poster depicting the military nurse (Figure 16). The Red Cross poster was never used during the war, but was reprinted in its official history. Like the facts and figures compiled in the text, this image of the nurse underscores the efficacy of her work and the power of her knowledge. The American Red Cross poster differs sharply from the widely distributed "mater dolorosa" poster of the British Red Cross, one of the Great War's most famous images. Captioned "The Greatest Mother in the World," the British poster is modeled on a pieta scene, with a stylized virgin-mother-nurse in habitlike uniform, seated and frozen with grief, her eyes turned heavenward, cradling a small stretcher in her lap.[19] The American poster, in contrast, portrays the nurse as a physically active figure, heroically fending off the shadow of death with one arm as she supports her patient, a severely wounded soldier, with the other. This poster was planned and commissioned by the nurse leaders of the American Red Cross Nursing Service, who had hoped to use it during their recruitment campaign. But it was "withheld from distribution" by request of the War Department, ostensibly because the image of the helpless doughboy on the verge of death would be harmful to morale on the home front. This powerful depiction of the military nurse also clashed

16. A poster planned and commissioned by the American Red Cross Nursing Service presents the nurse as a lifelike and actively heroic figure, laboring to save a severely wounded soldier. The poster was withheld from distribution at the request of the War Department. (Source: National American Red Cross, *History of American Red Cross Nursing* [New York: Macmillan Co., 1922].)

with officially sanctioned representations of women war workers, which emphasized their dependent status and secondary role.

Red Cross nursing leaders, while acceding to the War Department's wishes on this matter, cherished their autonomy and exercised it frequently during the war. Jane Delano, who died during the winter of 1919 while on an inspection tour of U.S. military hospitals in France, had a bold vision of what the insider-outsider status of the Red Cross could accomplish for the public health and for nurses. Delano had resigned as superintendent of the Army Nurse Corps in 1912 to dedicate herself to the Red Cross. Under her direction, civilian nursing charted an independent path during the war. In Europe, despite the absorption of nursing resources by the war effort, the organization sponsored extensive projects in maternal and child health and developed nurse training courses and programs. Delano was not afraid to criticize the War Department, even in the conformist atmosphere of wartime Washington; she did so in the controversy over nurses as prisoners of war and when supporting relative rank for army nurses.

The course that Delano set to advance nurses' status is illustrated during the immediate postwar period by the second major attempt to secure full military rank for nurses. The committee formed by Harriot Stanton Blatch during the war was revived and reconfigured in 1919 as the National Committee to Secure Rank for Nurses. Clara D. Noyes of the American Nurses' Association and the American Red Cross was vice chair, although, tellingly, the male leadership of the American Red Cross's executive committee turned down Noyes's request that the American Red Cross endorse the measure. Leaders of the renewed campaign, including many nurse-veterans, were determined to gain actual rank this time around, convinced that the scheme for relative rank, which they had earlier supported, was an undesirable compromise. During the summer of 1919, bills in support of relative but not full rank were introduced into both the House and the Senate. It soon became clear that only relative rank had any chance of success, in large part because Secretary of War Baker and Surgeon General of the Army Ireland both continued to oppose even this concession to women. In the end, the relative rank proposal was passed.[20] Red Cross leaders were ambivalent about the result. They were especially distressed that even this half-measure was opposed by the new superintendent of the Army Nurse Corps, Julia Stimson, a distinguished AEF nurse and former Red Cross administrator. Stimson was likely conforming to the wishes of her superior, the surgeon general; her lack of independence and her inability to act on behalf of working women underscores the strength of Delano's insider-outsider approach. Delano, like other Red Cross women, was an open advocate for professional women. To these nursing leaders, the war had been an important opportunity, and the meaning of women's military service was clear: nurses' performance at the front had demonstrated working women's competence and their readiness to handle increased public authority and responsibility in the future.

The leadership of the male-dominated auxiliary agencies had a more conflictual relationship with women workers. The official assessments of women's service by the directors of the auxiliary organizations, like the public pronouncements of military officials, were effusively positive. They echoed the praise of Raymond Fosdick, chair of the Commission on Training Camp Activities, that "the work of the women was even more essential and even more important than the work of the men." The special value of women workers was their femininity, their moral and domesticating influence.

But, in fact, auxiliary organizations promoted and expanded women's work for rather different reasons. Over the course of the war and demobilization, auxiliary leaders became aware that women workers were, quite literally, their greatest asset. Women were an unexpected success not only with the troops in France but also with the American public, which kept pouring funds into the coffers of the organizations through patriotic aid drives. At the outset, the agencies had intended to rely on male secretaries to staff their programs for morale building and moral uplift at the front. But male workers proved to be an unanticipated public relations disaster. Male workers for the YMCA and other groups were subject to a storm of accusations as the war proceeded, charged with embezzlement, sexual indiscretion, drunkenness, and favoritism toward officers. Doughboys viewed the men with suspicion, as shirkers, cowards, and moral hypocrites who tried to force religion down their throats while avoiding real service. The criticisms implied that "normal," patriotic American men should fight and kill, not opt for safe, "womanly" work caring for other men. In this case, as in many others, rigid gender roles shaped the wartime expectations placed on both men and women. Virtually all of the charges against male auxiliary workers proved to be false. But what mattered, right or wrong, was what soldiers thought. And although American servicemen responded to male welfare workers with an alarming level of suspicion and hostility, they adored women doing comparable work. "The work of the women seems to have been universally popular," concluded a G-2 investigator in the spring of 1919, "and many officers and men during this investigation have expressed themselves as believing that a larger portion of the Y.M.C.A. work would have been better managed had it been controlled by women." When the work of female auxiliary workers was criticized in the press as immoral and frivolous, AEF newspaper editors were flooded with letters from servicemen defending the women.

Because of the popularity of female auxiliary workers and the seeming failure of men, the organizations' male leaders were forced to accede to the plans of female administrators and turn increasingly to women workers. Auxiliary organizations relied ever more heavily on women as the war progressed. By the time the Jewish Welfare Board organized its overseas services in 1919, the formula for successful canteen work was well established. Bibles alone would never win the support of the "Jewish boys" in the AEF, field representatives wrote back to New York; they would need cookies, coffee, chocolate, and smokes "in liberal quantities" if they wished to compete with the Christian organizations, and they would need Jewish women to distribute them. "I hope by the time this letter reaches you, you will have sent us here a number of first-class women," enjoined the Jewish Welfare Board director for the AEF, "as I find that from many points of view women are far more desirable as welfare workers than men."[21]

The central role that women played in army welfare work created a dilemma at the close of the war. Women had proven themselves to be highly capable under the most trying circumstances, and women workers had reason to believe that their success in wartime France would translate into a strengthened position in these organizations back home. In the YMCA, the issue came to the surface at war's end in a lengthy memo from the women's bureau. Women workers sought to claim a role in the largest and most influential of the auxiliary organizations. Titled "A Home Room in the 'Y': Comments on the Value of Women's Work as a Permanent Factor in the Y.M.C.A.," the memo drew on the experience of women's work in the AEF to make a comprehensive case for employing women as YMCA secretaries. The authors proposed that "there be added to the staff of any Association one uniformed woman secretary (or possibly two), women with unusual qualifications . . . specifically trained for this difficult and important work." The authors hastened to reassure Y officials that the proposal would in no way alter the basic mission of the organization or its fundamental policy of strict gender segregation. "It does not imply that the Association should work *for* women. It does not imply structural changes in the organization of the Association. It does not imply that women should go on boards of directors. It does not imply that an Association shall introduce *groups of volunteer women workers* into the lobby or other parts of the building." But the authors did add that gender integration at the staff level "probably ought" to lead to some cooperative work with the Young Women's Christian Association in "offering young men and women in the cities a moral life." As moderate and diplomatic as the proposal was, it was clearly out of step with the thinking of the YMCA Executive Board in the 1920s. The women's position paper was apparently received with profound silence, and the women's bureau was closed down completely in the late fall of 1919. It was not until the mid-1930s that the organization granted women professional status as YMCA secretaries, and the question of finding a place for women and girls in the YMCA received no serious airing until the 1940s.[22]

The pervasive wartime representation of auxiliary workers as substitute mothers or sweethearts, which was a powerful rationalization for women's war work, yielded in the postwar period to a vision that was far more limiting for women. In a speech given in 1919, Fosdick looked ahead to the postwar gender system and offered women some advice: "Those young men over there . . . have been fighting for you, they have been dying for you, and it is to you, the Helens of America, that those young fellows are coming back home when the war is done and you have it in your power through your magic touch to make and shape the manpower of America for a generation to come."[23] Fosdick's speech invoked the most deep-rooted traditions of women's role in war: having launched the war with her beautiful frailty and need for protection, having caused this worldwide disaster, the American woman must now bind the warrior's wounds, a process that had emotional, physical, and perhaps sexual dimensions. His speech also alludes to a reproductive task; out of this reunion of men and women will come babies, a new generation to serve in future wars. Fosdick's words represent a deeply conservative vision of postwar relations between the sexes, a profound reaction against the changes in women's roles that occurred during the war.

WOMEN'S OWN STORIES of war intersect in complicated ways with these official formulations, demonstrating the dynamic relationship between public culture and individual consciousness. The major sources documenting the meanings women made of military service are personal narratives, memoirs, and reminiscences, some created during or just after the war and others written or told years later. Their narratives suggest that servicewomen were highly selective consumers of the dominant wartime culture. Almost universally, servicewomen belittled the assertion that women's true and highest wartime calling was to "keep the home fires burning." "My mother . . . told me soothingly that . . . I could do plenty at home, knitting and selling Liberty Bonds," Shirley Millard recalled; but, she declared, "this was not enough for me. My imagination had caught fire. . . . I wanted to go overseas!" Although parents and others tried to persuade them otherwise, women who had joined the AEF viewed service at home as "safety and tedium and a passive helping to 'win the war.'"[24]

The domesticated vision of women's role at the front did not appeal to
servicewomen either. They evinced little interest in being the obedient,
self-sacrificing daughters of an avuncular national state, the "Uncle Sam's
nieces" or girls-next-door that were relentlessly paraded in the wartime
media. It is striking how infrequently women made use of the official
image of the AEF woman as an icon of the American home and family.
Even when women's narratives appear to embrace the domestic vision of
women's overseas service, they do so with profound ambivalence. One
narrative, *A Red Triangle Girl in France,* illustrates the resistant quality of
many women's stories. This canteen memoir in the form of letters is on
one level a "family" story. The book is prefaced by the woman's father;
the anonymous author literally has no identity other than girl or daughter, for the father has "concealed . . . very carefully her . . . name." Her
story is artless and "wholly unconscious," he explains, composed of letters "dashed off rapidly . . . to members of our family circle." The military
is also depicted as a "family," and the soldiers are portrayed as affection-
ate older brothers, teasing and doting by turns. The author's presence
serves as a catalyst for strengthening real home ties, as in this conversation with a soldier: "He said that when he came here he hadn't written
home for nine years, but he had been looking and looking at me and at
last had written home. The very day before he had received a beautiful
answer from his sister, enclosing a photograph of herself (a very sweet
looking girl)." Here the author has worked her womanly magic, not by
anything she has said or done, but simply by being looked on, becoming
the object of the male gaze. The anonymous woman writer of *A Red Triangle Girl in France* seems to have acquiesced to the dominant wartime
construction of women's role, which Jane Marcus calls the patriarchal-
militarist "plot" about war. Yet, the text itself gives cause to doubt this os-
tensible meaning: *A Red Triangle Girl in France* is a narrative at war with
itself. To begin with, the patriarchal preemption of this young woman's
story is undercut by the actual conditions of her overseas enlistment: the
letters reveal that she joined the YMCA over the direct objections of her
parents, an act of independence they deemed inappropriate and dangerous. Furthermore, although the author states that her letters home were
written to console and reassure her family, they do anything but that. Her
accounts of her own daring and dizzy exploits cannot have been much
comfort to a father who feared that overseas service would expose his
daughter to moral corruption, danger, and a lower class of people.[25] Rife
with defiance, her letters belie the stance of daughterly obedience and patriotic self-abnegation that the book presents on its surface.

Many women's narratives show signs of internal resistance to dominant versions of womanhood in wartime, and these tensions or contra-
dictions are the key to their interpretation. On the surface, women's for-

mulations of their own wartime service pay honor to the forms and conventions of patriotism. My country needed me; I was ready to sacrifice myself to the cause—across social class, level of education, and occupation, women expressed fervent loyalty to their nation at war. Even long after, women veterans remembered with great immediacy the patriotic pride which imbued their service. Responding to a veterans questionnaire at age 94, Mildred B. Byers declared, "I am proud I was chosen to serve in the war of 1918—I consider it the most important years of my life," adding in her strong but shaky hand, "May Old Glory wave as long as I live—I love her." [26]

This patriotic rhetoric has led some scholars to view women's wartime service as an extension of their traditional feminine role as supporters of men. Other scholars have argued that the patriotism expressed by women represents their integration into a system of militant nationalism, a process of militarization inherently at odds with their struggle for emancipation.[27] But other messages are equally evident in women's stories of war: the search for self-definition, the longing for change and opportunity, and the desire to participate directly in the defining event of their generation. If women saw their work as patriotic service, they also viewed their service to the wartime state as a step toward liberation.

A survey of servicewomen's narratives reveals numerous themes and gestures of liberation, if not as foreground then as fault line or subtext: release from the social constraints and restrictions of middle-class womanhood, freedom from family control, and opportunity to pursue male-defined options for identity, prestige, and success. The most immediate and obvious opportunity presented by the war was the chance to engage in work that had formerly been considered male. Many women noted with pride that they had successfully carried out such tasks as carpentry, driving, and auto repair. "I've been hammering and sawing until my lily-white hands are rough as a man's," marveled one YMCA worker. In the "topsy-turvy" world created by the Great War, women were "doing things" they had "never done before." The suffrage press highlighted this development, but suffragists were not alone in their attention to such gender-role disruptions. Servicewomen of all backgrounds remarked with satisfaction and solidarity that women workers performed these new tasks well when given a chance; coming themselves from highly feminized occupations, they took special note in their diaries and letters of the many French and English women employed as train porters, tram drivers, and streetcleaners. This commentary on work and gender is one clue to servicewomen's view of female equality and competence in the work place.

Like the anonymous "Red Triangle" girl, many servicewomen attached a special prestige to activities within the male sphere associated with speed, strength, and power. This sentiment could crop up in unexpected places: a Salvation Army worker relished the target shooting lessons she took from two enlisted men, describing in her diary the pleasure she took in her Colt 45 revolver. Driving, fixing, and riding in automobiles was a preoccupation of women at the front. As at home, access to a motor car meant independence and mobility; but at war, it also meant access to dangerous, masculine work.[28] Servicewomen shared the wartime fascination with airplanes and aviation as well, and when they could, they flew.

For the vast majority of servicewomen, the most palpable and immediate gesture of liberation was donning a military uniform. The restrictive fashion conventions that were still firmly in place before the Great War were not only clearly unsuitable for the war zone but also symbolized the restrictive home life of middle-class womanhood. Putting on dark wool uniforms and heavy boots marked a woman's shift from civilian to military status. Servicewomen perceived this change of costume as both a practical and a highly symbolic act. Reflecting on her stint in France, one canteen worker noted in her journal: "For eighteen months I haven't worn white gloves, or silk stockings, or a veil, no, nor even powdered my nose," adding with conscious irony, "the worst of it is, these things don't seem to matter any more." Like army slang, which women adopted with enthusiasm, the AEF uniform was a sign that women now belonged to the world of the military. Even in later years, many veterans cherished those uniforms, and dressing in them was a ritual of servicewomen's reunions, provoking nostalgia as well as humor.

Clothing styles were controversial matters at the front. For some women, dressing in uniform was glamorously "mannish," an exciting and adventurous experiment with a new identity (much like the hair-bobbing craze which ran through the community of women war workers in France). Soldiers worried about an army where the "women wore the pants," and the rivalry between men and women was often expressed through games of skirting and unskirting: baseball-playing nurses sewed skirts for their physician-opponents to wear, for example, and enlisted men stole Katharine Prest's clothing and dressed up in drag to mock her. Surprisingly, AEF women appear never to have raised the possibility of actually wearing pants, a sensible innovation for the freezing cold and muddy conditions at the front. Coveralls and pants were widely adopted by women at home who were employed in traditionally male occupations, such as railroad workers and the Women's Land Army. Women in the AEF may have looked down on wearing pants because their social class aspirations and concern with respectability led them to prefer a costume associated with business or professional status to the pants worn by industrial and agricultural workers. In contrast with pants, the uniform was a sign of importance and official status. Wearing the uniform of their country gave women a feeling of being serious, authoritative, and professional, of having a real job to do in the war, as Elizabeth Black put it.[29]

In a similar way, embracing violence could have been another strategy of release from gender norms for servicewomen. Violence was the central fact of "real war," and it is a common, powerful, and troubling theme in women's war stories. Abstract expressions of belligerence, for example, are fairly common in women's narratives. An auxiliary worker wrote with vehemence: "I hate to think of anyone being pro-German. If I were a man and fifteen years younger I would volunteer for the Front. I feel that I would LIKE to kill a Prussian."[30] Significantly, in making this unladylike statement, the writer chose to call attention to her womanhood. Expressing hatred of the enemy was a violation of a deeply held gender taboo, embracing what was perhaps the most masculine aspect of the war. Some women may have experienced belligerence as daring or liberatory in much the way that a shooting lesson was: a release from gender expectations that was bound to shock others. Likewise, servicewomen's fascination with the fighting front is one of the most striking and universal themes in women's war narratives. Women from all occupations craved the opportunity to work in close proximity to battle and envied those who had the opportunity to do so. Women's narratives privileged the front as the realm of authentic—that is, male—war experience, suggesting that the real war was about violence and killing, and that for women to take part in the real war it is necessary for them to experience this violence as directly as possible.

An account of a trip to the front by the "singing sweetheart of the AEF" exemplifies these attitudes in a staged and purposefully theatrical form. Elsie Janis, a celebrated vaudeville performer, was invited by a general to visit troops at the front and "take part" in battle. Her account can be read as a burlesque or masquerade in its formal sense: a strategy involving emulation of the other, an inversion of roles that reverses expected norms and relationships. Her description of the event, a gruesome burlesque of women in battle, is worth quoting at length:

> At nine this morning we went with General A. up to the woods right back of the lines where the big guns nestle in sweet seclusion. We got out of the motor . . . and got onto the cutest little narrow-gauge railroad, on a little car that usually carries shells. . . . We passed many big guns, all camouflaged by natural trees, and finally arrived at a battery of one hundred and fifty-fives. The General gave the word and the show commenced. Boom! went one on our left some distance away. Boom! on the right. . . .

"Now, Miss Janis, kill a few Huns," said the General.

I took the little piece of cord . . . , and thrilling as I have never thrilled before, I stood at attention and waited for my orders. "Battery ready! Fire," said the General, and I *pulled.* I was so excited I forgot to jump. "Always the same!" came the command, and I pulled again. I would be there still pulling only for the fact that the observation posts reported that there was nothing left of the position we had been shelling. . . . They told me I was the only woman who had fired regular hundred and fifty-five power hate into Germany.[31]

Janis's experience at the front—part AEF publicity stunt, part seduction scene—was of course artificial. But it expressed a fascination with masculine power and violence that typified the attitudes of many women.

Janis's story was typical in another sense as well: like all women, she was only a visitor to the violence of war. In a world of killing and combat, women were necessarily outsiders, and when traveling to the terrain of no man's land, definitively a "no woman's land," they did so as tourists. Themes of voyeuristic interest in violence appear in women's stories of war. Touring the trenches after the war and picking up gruesome battle-front souvenirs, women's narratives suggest, was a relatively common practice among servicewomen. On her first trip to Verdun, France, a canteen worker recounted matter-of-factly, "there were still good pickings for the souvenir-hunter by the way; shell-cases, helmets, gas-masks lying along the roadside." Margaret Hall claimed to have met both nurses and canteen workers who were collecting body parts, a phenomenon she found both degrading and intriguing. "Two women of the canteen are taking home skulls as 'souvenirs,' and some of the nurses pull belts and boots off the dead Germans. Sometimes the feet come off in the boots, but that seems to be no objection!"[32] The perversity of these actions is disturbing, although recent scholarship on the history of U.S. warfare suggests that male soldiers also engaged in acts of voyeuristic mutilation.[33]

More women openly claimed to desire access to the front as an opportunity, not to kill, but to die for the nation's cause. Isabel Anderson, a wealthy volunteer canteen administrator, observed that women "want a chance to work at the front, where they can be of the most service, not coddled in comparative safety at the bases. After all," Anderson asked rhetorically, "hasn't a woman just as much right to die for her country as a man?"[34] Some women may have regarded the "right to die for her country" as an attribute of full citizenship. Yet, the two hundred deaths of AEF women resulted not from direct combat but from a horrifying change in the nature of war; in modern warfare, the death toll among noncombatants has regularly rivaled or outstripped that of regular soldiers. Contemporaries were unable to recognize that World War I marked the beginning of a transformation that uncoupled death from masculinity and militarization. Not only were more noncombatant positions being created within the armed services for men and women, but unbelievable numbers of civilians—women, children, and old people alike—would soon be killed in the massive bloodletting of the twentieth century. With this hindsight, Anderson's comment about women's "right to die" for the nation surely resounds with a bitter irony.

Women's war narratives also contain evidence that some women abhorred the violence of the war. In 1916, U.S. nurse Ellen LaMotte published an account of her work in a French military hospital, *The Backwash of War,* which is an outspoken deconstruction of the wartime cult of heroism. But open expression of such attitudes during the war was clearly exceptional, a fact underscored by the suppression of LaMotte's book after the United States entered the war in 1918.[35] Still, antiwar memoirs and novels of U.S. servicewomen, most written by elite and educated women, were published in the more receptive 1930s. Glimmerings of antiwar sentiment can be found even in the wartime writings of rank-and-file servicewomen, including nurses, Salvation Army workers, and Young Women's Christian Association workers. Women's questioning of war frequently began with a simple act of identification with its victims. Army nurses could identify with their patients, soldiers from both sides. Auxiliary workers more often identified with other women. The French women hired to cook and clean in the canteens alongside American women were a source of heartrending information on the devastating consequences of war for civilians. So too were the American parents who passed through canteens and rest rooms in France in search of their sons, only to find their sons' graves. "The last few months have brought dozens of wives and mothers and sisters," reported Harriet Dunn, a YWCA worker who headed the American Women's Club in Paris. One story told by Dunn was a counterpoint to the propaganda about "Mother" so vigorously promoted by the army and auxiliary agencies. "She had come from a little town in Pittsburgh, . . . determined to find the grave of her son. He was her only child and had run away when only fifteen, was wounded in the Argonne and died in the American Hospital at Neuilly. We found that this little woman could neither read nor write . . . and that for two long years she had been making quilts to earn enough money to pay her way over to France." Dunn's portrait is sentimentalized, but hers is not the abstract American mother in service to the state; rather, she is a real and vulnerable woman who must personally suffer the consequences of state policy.[36] In these instances, servicewomen identified with civilian women rather than with soldiers, recognizing violence itself as the real enemy.

These dissenters were minority voices. The sources from the Great War contain no evidence to suggest that as a group, women were more pacifistic or more conciliatory toward the enemy than were men.[37] Most women responded to the war's violence as male soldiers did, regarding it as a condition that lent life-and-death intensity to their experience but without closely scrutinizing the violence itself. When they were forced to confront violence directly, they responded as men did: sometimes with fascination and desire, sometimes with revulsion and horror, and sometimes with a blend of these emotions.

Ultimately, what gave meaning to war experience for the greatest number of women was an ideal of patriotic service that embodied both their desire to give to others and their drive toward emancipation. One canteen worker summed up this notion of service concisely during her week of YMCA training at Barnard College:

> We make no claim to courage
> But we claim the right to work.
> Give us service!
> We'll promise not to shirk.[38]

Women workers did not aspire to become soldiers, but they did assert a right to serve their country. The meaning of the word "service" for women war workers is worth close examination. In its nineteenth-century incarnation, "going out to service" meant doing domestic work, household drudgery marked as degraded by the race, sex, and class of those who performed it. "Service" for women who enlisted in 1917 retained its association with domestic service, which was still the single largest category of paid employment for women; it was also associated with the services that women provided to their families in the domestic sphere. But the scope of women's service had gradually expanded from the household to the community; the notion of service to others as the distinctive mission of middle-class women had been widely accepted since the late nineteenth century. Now, the Selective Service Act of 1917 cemented a new association, that of national military service, a masculine and militarized role accompanied by a range of public privileges. Women too embraced the term service to describe their contribution to the war effort. By the end of the war, AEF women had taken a new name for themselves, *servicewomen*. They codified its meaning in 1921 through a new organization, the Women's Overseas Service League (WOSL), the first veterans' organization of women.

The concept of service also had a personal and private dimension. Women's narratives suggest that, at the start of the Great War, many felt that typical women's lives were trivial or lacked meaning; "a few months ago I was comfortably enjoying the . . . futile pleasures of what I considered life," wrote one. Like this war volunteer, they hoped that military service would provide them with a sense of purpose. The word that appears repeatedly in this context is "usefulness," as in a revealing passage from the letter of Mary Josephine Booth, a YMCA auxiliary worker, to her aunt: "I know that you are glad to have me of use in this greatest of all times—you have no one else to fight for you and I must do this work for both of us—you know how my mother used to pray that I might be a useful woman and I feel that I should not be giving my greatest usefulness in any other place than here. . . . If I were married and had children I might feel differently but I am the last of the race of grandma and I want to do all possible to help save the world for freedom."[39] Booth recast the nation's war aims in female terms: she would fight for freedom as part of a legacy of useful, dedicated service passed from mother to daughter.

Booth's language and the Barnard anthem make another important point about women's concept of service: AEF women believed that the medium through which they would fulfill their service to country was work. Here they were setting themselves apart from the homemakers who knitted socks or conserved flour for the war effort; that was service too, perhaps, but of a private or domestic sort. In contrast, the working women who volunteered for overseas service considered their work to be both an important source of identity and a form of engagement in a social contract, a vital connection to the public and national realm. Many contemporary trends fed into and shaped servicewomen's views of work. Female progressive reformers had opened opportunities for women in social service, while the female professions of nursing and social work had legitimated women's expertise in public health and welfare. The "New Woman," with her expanded opportunities for mobility, self-definition, autonomy, and even adventure, was especially attractive to servicewomen, not in her leisured, college-girl incarnation but in the form of the independent career or "business" woman. Feminism appealed to servicewomen to the extent that it championed the cause of wage-earning women and spoke to their desire for equality and independence. Building on these traditions, women who enlisted in the AEF viewed work as central to their wartime service.

Military service was the ultimate form of national labor. It was also an opportunity to participate in the most masculine and privileged of public arenas. Journalist Margaret Deland observed that women workers enlisted for service in France out of a "desire to stand up beside the boys and say, 'Here! Look at me! I'm just as good a soldier in my way as you are in yours!'" Some women, according to Deland, linked this demand for public recognition with the acquisition of equal political rights. "When the war is over, . . . the men will be ashamed not to give us the ballot!" one auxiliary worker declared.[40] Deland's observation was prescient. In the postwar period, service women would struggle to gain recognition for their war service and to establish their wartime labor as an entrée to equal citizenship.

SERVICEWOMEN RETURNED HOME in 1919 to the vote and its promise of a wider role for women in the civic and public life of their nation. "Uncle Sam's nieces" were for the moment celebrated as a new model of citizenship for American women. But the flush of victory soon faded. Women whose sense of themselves had been profoundly transformed by their overseas service encountered a society that not only failed to comprehend their experience but also seemed bent on restoring the prewar status quo. "It seemed so lovely to be on this side of the Atlantic again that I reveled in all I saw," wrote Ona Rounds, a demobilized YMCA worker, of her days in New York City. Yet, she felt "strangely aloof" from "the people on the streets [who] looked so calm," and she "feared sometimes they would be conscious I was staring at them." Rounds found herself gravitating toward others just back from France. "There were many returned soldiers everywhere, and without knowing it we would hasten toward each other and compare notes on New York this time instead of France. It all seemed strange, and we wondered if we would ever fit into the scheme of civilian life. . . . Our uniforms made it easy to talk and to consider our problems together." Women and men alike felt some anxiety about readjustment to civilian life. But for women, as for African-American soldiers returning from France, getting out of uniform meant a more dramatic change than it did for white male veterans.[41] Women returned from military service with an altered sense of self and an uneasy feeling about how their new identities would fit conventional expectations of feminine behavior. This dynamic affected the relationship between men and women veterans. The parting words of Rounds's male soldier friends—"Get some real clothes and send us a picture. We want to see you just as a woman"—suggest that for many in the United States, the return to normalcy would be a return to prewar gender relations, based on white male dominance.[42]

Gender containment shaped the process of reconstituting postwar gender relations. To the extent that servicewomen aspired to establish their wartime labor as a basis for social and political advancement, they were disappointed. Yet, as *individuals,* most women veterans were strikingly successful in postwar America, finding personal mobility and wide opportunity in their postwar careers. Women's work at the front had no measurable impact on the larger contours of the civilian labor market for women or on the structures of women's work in the postwar period. The transformation of the U.S. economy during the 1920s, although problematic for many working people, generally benefited the women who returned from the war.[43] Expansion of the service and financial sectors, growth in state and local government, and the continuing rigidification of gender segregation in hospitals, offices, and schools ensured that servicewomen would find a place in the labor force. While the feminized occupations to which war workers primarily belonged began to decline in pay, status, and working conditions during the 1920s, the female service sector contained its own internal hierarchy, and many women veterans found a niche as managers of other women, constituting an elite within the female occupations. Most had already been self-supporting before the war; after the war, they constructed careers that brought them independence, security, and a measure of status.

Mobility was not universal. Poor health and disability accompanied some women home from France, and other veterans faced unemployment and poverty later in the decade. A 24-year-old nurse from McKeesport, Pennsylvania, for example, was discharged on medical grounds in April 1919 and sent back to the United States; although she soon found employment as a school nurse in her hometown, her medical condition, presumably tuberculosis, continued to limit her capacity for work in the succeeding years.[44] During the decade following the war, WOSL units identified and aided 1,456 women who were "rather seriously incapacitated" by physical or mental illness.[45] Female veterans, like their male counterparts, suffered primarily from tuberculosis and mental illness, according to figures released by the Veterans' Bureau in 1924.[46] By the 1930s, poverty consequent to unemployment, underemployment, and widowhood was the primary concern. The Veterans' Bureau recorded a 31 percent increase in admissions of female patients in the wake of the stock market crash. Neither patriotic service nor impressive white-collar credentials were a buffer against hard times, as a 1933 advertisement poignantly attested: "Overseas Girl—A.R.C. interested in securing management or assistant management of shop, store or department. . . . Has had 5 years of business management, 3 years of Department Store Personnel Work."[47]

Although military service brought poor health and indigence to a few, for most it led to modest but real gains in social and economic status, sometimes through marriage but just as often through singlehood and employment. Exservicewomen used their wartime experience and contacts, their training, and their access to public and corporate employers to establish themselves in the labor force. The experience of former army nurses exemplifies this process. Nurses faced significant obstacles in the postwar period. Nursing school enrollment had burgeoned during the war years. After the war, a drop in the demand for private-duty nursing, coupled with the oversupply of trained nurses, led to unemployment and underemployment; what had been a chronic problem during the 1920s became a severe crisis during the 1930s. Nonetheless, former army nurses seem to have had little difficulty securing employment on their return from France. Their success was caused in large part by the distinctive pattern of their employment: while the majority of trained nurses in the 1920s, 57 to 70 percent, continued to work in private duty, nurse veterans seemed by and large to find employment in hospitals. They anticipated by a decade the revolution in nursing that would take place during the 1930s, when private duty would virtually disappear and hospital nursing would become the norm.[48] Former army nurses were poised to take advantage of the rapid expansion of the hospital industry during the 1920s, particularly in military and veterans' hospitals. The number of hospital beds increased by 56 percent over the course of the decade to a capacity of nearly one million. The Veterans' Bureau was created in 1921 to establish and administer a network of hospitals and other services for the veterans of the Great War. By the end of the decade, the Veterans' Bureau operated forty-seven hospitals, most of them newly constructed, with a combined capacity of 22,732 beds. The Bureau was staffed in 1925 by a work force of more than twenty-seven thousand, and more than twelve thousand were women.[49]

Nurse veterans were especially likely to find positions in government hospitals. Clara Bowhuis, for example, wrote to Congresswoman Edith Nourse Rogers during a controversy over benefits for nurse veterans: "On February 21, 1945, I will have personally completed 24 years of service with this Government in the care of veterans of all Wars suffering from nervous and mental disorders. I graduated in 1917 and in 1918 entered the United States Army Nurse Corps and served one year overseas in France." She went to work for the veterans' hospital system around 1921, and was made chief nurse of the hospital in Lyons, New Jersey, in 1929. As early as 1925, the Veterans' Bureau had a stated policy of extending preference in hiring to exservice personnel. The inclinations and values of army nurses also contributed to their concentration in military hospitals. Nurse veterans were accustomed to working in a military milieu and to caring for soldiers. The variety of patients in the hospital, the pace of work, and the contact with other medical personnel came much closer to approximating war front nursing than did private duty. As one nurse veteran who returned to private duty declared, "how one misses the comradeship of life over there."[50]

Nurse veterans also gravitated toward public health nursing, another growing field during the 1920s.[51] Exservicewomen found employment in municipal, industrial, and employee health; rural nursing; and maternal and child care. Public health was an obvious choice for nurses returning from the front. Of all fields of nursing practice, it offered the greatest degree of autonomy and freedom. Former army nurses, who had relied on their own judgment in life-and-death situations, relished the opportunity to take charge and to work in a setting of obvious need. Many regarded public health as an opportunity for adventure, emphasizing the "pioneering" aspects of the work, whether it be nursing in an urban tenement or on an Indian reservation in the far West. Former army nurses also placed special emphasis on the "public" aspect of public health. Birda Hunt claimed that war service changed her career goals and her sense of social responsibility; she returned from France with "a larger scope of what nursing meant and what could be done," so she joined the Public Health Nursing Association in Indiana and worked in rural communities. Others were on call for nursing during floods, epidemics, or other domestic emergencies, such as the devastating floods of 1937.[52] For these women, war service was not an isolated incident but rather generated a whole new relationship to the civic realm, which entailed both obligations and privileges.

Telephone operators also found their wartime work experience well suited to the postwar economy. The telephone industry was a major area of economic growth between the war and the depression; Bell System employment nearly doubled from 1917 to 1929, and the field became more technologically and administratively complex.[53] Ordinary operating jobs with the phone company were readily available to women on their return from France. Signal Corps veteran Kathleen Hyatt McKee declared with confidence that she "could have become a telephone operator in civilian life," but she enrolled in business college instead. Although the industry offered an abundance of jobs, security, and benefits, routinization and managerial control of telephone work continued to increase in the postwar period, and the status of the operator's job declined correspondingly. But the emergence of a female managerial stratum in the telephone industry translated into high-status, middle-class careers for other exservicewomen. Some managerial jobs required the same supervisory functions that Signal Corps women had performed creditably in France; new fields such as personnel, training, engineering, publicity, and finance were also opened to women. The Bell corporation began to publicize its "opportunities for women" during the 1920s and 1930s. Signal Corps veterans, virtually all of them single, were relatively successful in gaining entrance to these middle-management positions.[54]

For women veterans from the auxiliary and clerical services, information on postwar employment is much less systematic; still, some patterns do emerge. Most continued to work in the female-dominated, pink-collar or semiprofessional occupations that had characterized the group on enlistment.[55] They did not always do so by choice, however. Mary Lee applied after the war for a position as a news reporter on a Boston daily paper but was told definitively by the editor that he would never consider a woman for such a position. Many women veterans found work in the growing public sector or expanding service industries. A report on the Portland unit of the WOSL illustrates these patterns: one AEF clerical worker had become a clerk in city hall, a Red Cross auxiliary worker had become a clerk in the county office, and a Signal Corps worker was employed as a telephone operator. Only one veteran in the group had departed from the norm of feminized employment by becoming a dentist.[56]

Exservicewomen may well have been locked into a small number of female white-collar occupations. Still, the most energetic and motivated women often managed to find an outlet for their ambitions in clerical-managerial fields. In the booming consumer economy of the 1920s, many veterans went into business for themselves, entering such fields as real estate and retail sales. Women ingeniously exploited their overseas experience for financial gain. Lingerie, frocks, and hose with a decidedly French flavor were the specialty of the Flaurance shop operated by a member of the Chicago unit of the WOSL. The mystique of European travel, like that of French fashion, was a marketable commodity, and a number of exservicewomen offered their services as tour guides to the cultural monuments of France, England, and Italy. *Carry On*, the WOSL magazine, reported: "Miss Stella Saxton, who served for some years in the American Red Cross, . . . is conducting interesting trips through Italy. Miss Saxton . . . has never returned home since 1918." Travel agencies and vacation resorts, taverns, and tea rooms, even a dude ranch run by exservicewomen, were described in *Carry On*. The wide-open opportunity for those with business savvy and a sense of adventure was highlighted by the story of Celeste and Olive Rauch, "city-bred girls" from St. Louis and Red Cross canteen workers overseas, who developed Pima Estates, a ranch resort in Arizona. The author of the article in profiling their adventures, herself an exservicewoman, praised them in military metaphor. "I cannot begin to tell you . . . of the battles they have fought and mostly won—of the seemingly insurmountable obstacles that have loomed before them, only to see them rally to the fore with the old war cry 'Carry On.'"[57] Although this language was a journalistic device, it also pointed to something deeper. The ambition and independence that had pushed certain women into military service found an outlet after the war in entrepreneurship, a realm where individualism, independence, and ambition were requisite, if not inevitably rewarded.

FOR MANY WOMEN, individual success and economic mobility were a satisfactory payoff for their work in the AEF—or, perhaps, veterans recognized that these were all that they could attain. Other servicewomen continued to demand a fuller measure of recognition for the service they had rendered their country during World War I, but their collective efforts to secure full integration into the military and civilian auxiliary agencies bore frustratingly few results. Organized groups of working women continued their campaigns for increased political power and expanded economic opportunities during the immediate postwar years. Helen Hoy Greeley, the suffragist attorney who had lobbied for military rank for nurses during the war, made the most expansive demands on the state. In a series of addresses given to the National League of Nursing Education in June 1919, Greeley called on women veterans to seize the hard-earned benefits of national service and build momentum for long-term change. In the next and future wars, women must be "equal participants with adequate channels for the expression of our intelligence and our professional training," Greeley insisted. "We want to be servants in the very largest sense, but we do not want to come in as clerks, messengers, errand girls, and domestics," she said, expressing the new notion of women's national service as distinct from traditional female service work. Greeley's words also reveal the social class aspirations embedded in this formulation; women expected their new role to offer social and economic mobility as well as enhanced prestige. Greeley's critique of women's position in the recent war focused on their lack of authority, from the hospital work place to the War Department. As a champion of working women within the mainstream women's movement, Greeley was sensitive to the devaluation of women's work and the subjugation of women workers. In the military, women faced structural barriers to their advancement, and their labor was taken for granted. Greeley exhorted her audience: "We must see to it that in the future there shall be women sitting in the seats of the mighty who will understand women's problems, even in the midst of war." Greeley called for the creation of female executive positions—a woman in the United States War College, a woman on the Army General Staff, and a woman as third or fourth assistant secretary of war—to oversee and advocate for army women, although in doing so she failed to consider how beholden these advisors and advocates would be to the men who put them in power.[58]

Greeley and other feminists hoped to take advantage of public gratitude to veterans by strengthening the role of women in the military. They were soon disappointed. During the 1920s, military and civilian leaders pursued a quiet policy of gender retrenchment. The Army Reorganization Act of 1920 granted only relative rank to the members of the Army Nurse Corps. Although this achievement was symbolically important, its limitations were apparent. The system established a hierarchy among nurses and gave women formal authority over other women, but it did not grant women formal authority over men. When the War Department turned its attention to women's concerns during the 1920s, it concentrated almost exclusively on creating a positive image of the army in the minds of female voters, partly in response to the reemergence of feminist pacifism in the wake of the war. The secretary of war appointed Anita Phipps director of women's relations for the army general staff and charged her with presenting the army to women as "a progressive, socially minded human institution" rather than a "ruthless military machine." War Department officials intended to appeal to women as patriotic housewives, not as potential armed services personnel. Phipps, however, prepared a comprehensive proposal for a Women's Army Corps, which projected a war emergency need for one hundred seventy thousand women workers in a subsequent war. Phipps's plan was formally rejected by the general staff in August 1926, and her position was eliminated soon after.[59]

The most significant setback for women in the military occurred in 1925, when the navy closed its doors to women, this time on a de jure basis. The Naval Reserve Act of 1925 eliminated Josephus Daniels's famous loophole, by limiting naval enlistment to "male citizens of the United States" instead of "all [capable] people." The highly capable women who had served the Navy during WWI testified to the Senate Naval Affairs Committee that the new wording denigrated their contribution in the Great War and excluded worthy women from service. No navy officials supported their position at the hearing. The bill passed and the navy reverted to an all-male institution—a situation that caused considerable difficulty in 1941 when the navy once again required a massive infusion of women's labor.[60]

Women were excluded even from the most traditional arena of women's involvement in military matters, the protection of soldiers' morals and morale. During the twenty months of war, historian Nancy Bristow has shown, male and female progressive reformers had gained unprecedented influence on army policy through the Commission on Training Camp Activities. After demobilization, responsibility for recreation and hygiene work was absorbed directly and permanently into the structure of the armed services, undermining the role of reformers. Female reformers and welfare workers were more decisively and completely disempowered than were their male counterparts. In 1923, the War Department held a conference "to consider plans for a more intensive general program of moral training for soldiers, to develop community contacts, and to recommend those policies and activities which will strengthen the religious program for Regular Army posts and stations and safeguard young men who enter the various training camps." Women had developed a fine reputation for administering and staffing such programs during World War I. But women were quite literally given no seat at the table; no women were among the ninety-four invited guests, who included representatives of all the major auxiliary organizations as well as religious groups. Not only had real women disappeared from army welfare programs, but their symbolic counterparts were strikingly absent from military rhetoric. In World War I discourse, the army would protect the soldier's morals by preserving home values and domestic influences; in postwar rhetoric, the soldier would be removed from his home setting and improved by the army so that he could return to and uplift his community.[61] This reformulation obviated the necessity and the justification for employing women in welfare work. The militarization of moral uplift and morale building marked the demise not only of progressive influence but also of significant female involvement in this aspect of military life.

Faced with eroding support, women veterans organized to institutionalize the memory of their military service and defend their status. The WOSL, the most significant organization of women veterans, engaged in this effort. Members believed that their war service, like that of men, should be recognized and rewarded. Throughout the 1920s, the WOSL focused on obtaining veterans' benefits for women. Like the movement for rank for army nurses, the issue of benefits arose out of women's experience of the war as work and involved issues of workers' rights. But the struggle over veterans' benefits was more than a matter of money; it was also a struggle over definitions of citizenship and the impact of wartime service on women's postwar civic status.

The organization's first goal was securing admission for women to U.S. veterans' hospitals and homes. In September 1923, after lobbying the Veteran's Bureau and securing the intervention of Secretary of War Weeks, the WOSL scored a "real victory": for the first time, facilities were set aside for women at two government institutions, the Danville Soldiers' Home and the Northwest Branch Milwaukee Veterans' Hospital.[62] The opening of veterans' hospitals and soldiers' homes to enlisted women was accomplished in increments, culminating in full access during the 1930s. But army welfare workers, telephone operators, and clerical workers, who had served in World War I as civilians, were not eligible for any of these benefits. Accordingly, WOSL leaders presented two bills to Congress providing hospitalization and benefits for women who had been employed by the army overseas. The WOSL's political strategy was formulated by Lena Hitchcock, an occupational therapist who had worked for the Army Medical Corps during the war and after the war was assigned to Walter Reed Hospital in Washington, D.C., and Faustine Dennis, a Vassar graduate who worked for the Library of Congress. Hitchcock served as national president of the WOSL from 1927 to 1929, and Dennis served as legislative chairman from 1929 through 1933

and as national president from 1933 to 1935.[63] Under their leadership, the
WOSL's legislation was circulated annually until it was withdrawn by the
WOSL as an act of patriotic cooperation with President Roosevelt's emer-
gency economic plan in the early New Deal.

The WOSL held a vision of equal rights for military women,[64] but the
organization never articulated or identified with a broader feminist
agenda. The fourth annual convention of 1924, for example, adopted a
resolution calling for 100 percent voter registration and participation and
exhorting exservicewomen to study the Constitution, a decidedly vague
and insubstantial position. Articles on women and politics began to appear in *Carry On*, the official publication of the WOSL, during the 1920s.
"Are we good citizens?" asked Faustine Dennis; "we cannot criticize an
action of Congress if we played golf on election day instead of voting. . . .
Let us all stand united for good government. . . . Let us in our thinking
be statesmen."[65] Although the WOSL championed the entry of women
into public life, its leaders avoided taking any stand on a wider women's
agenda for social change, such as that put forth by the Women's Joint
Congressional Committee. Neither did they take a stand on the Equal
Rights Amendment. The WOSL resembled the postsuffrage women's organizations described by historian Nancy Cott as "associational," special
interest groups based not on an encompassing vision of womanhood
but rather on diverse and specialized needs and identifications among
groups of women.[66] Like these groups, the WOSL functioned in part
through exclusion. Women in the WOSL, for example, set themselves
apart from women who had served stateside during the war, including
enlisted women from the navy and marines. During the early 1930s, they
distanced themselves from the impoverished male veterans who were
agitating for an acceleration of their service bonus. The political identity
of AEF servicewomen was a middle-class one, and they felt no kinship
with the down-and-outers of the bonus army, even though they had
similar goals.[67]

The WOSL employed an increasingly narrow, militarized version of
citizenship, termed "martial citizenship" by one historian. This definition, which makes political rights contingent on military service, has his-
torically excluded the vast majority of women from many benefits of the
welfare state set aside for male citizen-soldiers and veterans.[68] Yet, by
the late 1920s, WOSL leaders had embraced this formulation, arguing for
servicewomen's benefits not on the grounds of social responsibility or
compassion but solely on the basis of the civic rights that women had
earned through military service. The citizenship argument was summarized by WOSL president Mildred Taubles in a nationally broadcast
radio address in October 1930: "How many of my listeners know that

22,000 American women served their country overseas in the last war? How many of you know that only 49 percent of that number are the Army and Navy Nurses, who have the benefit of Government Hospitalization? . . . All these women did something for the comfort of the men of our country who were in the war. And all these women braved the dangers of the submarine and the air raid and stood the same chance of disease—yet have no hospitalization privilege." She went on to ask: "Do you feel that a woman who served gallantly and who gave of her strength when she was needed should go to charity for help if she is friendless and without funds? Our League does not. We have pledged ourselves to bend every effort to get a bill through Congress which will give Government Hospitalization to every woman who served overseas in the war, just as is given to our Army and Navy Nurses."[69] Taubles's speech adopts a highly masculine vision of citizenship. Gallantry, risking death, sharing men's risks—these are the acts, she asserts, that give women a claim on the public. Like other groups in the emergent postwar political system, the WOSL engaged in interest group politics of a markedly narrow and restricted sort.

Women veterans of the Signal Corps, a small group with a strong sense of cohesion, were the most vocal and organized group seeking recognition during the 1930s and beyond. One Signal Corps veteran, Helen Carey, laid out their sense of entitlement in a letter to her former AEF supervisor, Louise Barbour, who was by then a middle-level Bell Telephone company manager. Having gotten together with a group of "Signal Corps girls," Carey explained: "for some time we talked over 'Why we weren't recognized by the Army'. . . . You know we are considered 'Civilian Employees.' No Bonus! no recognition! Why? We all think that our services should be recorded just as well as women in Navy and Marine (they didn't get across [to France]). . . . We are not interested in Bonus or Insurance but we would like an 'Army Discharge.' I think we are entitled to it. I decided before we were old and bent we better get going."[70] Forty years and three major U.S. wars passed before these Signal Corps women achieved their goal. In 1979, Congress and the Department of Defense granted official army status to AEF telephone operators. Several dozen women veterans of the Signal Corps, all in their eighties or nineties, were honorably discharged from the U.S. Army. Television cameras recorded the "hello girls'" departure from the army as photographers had celebrated their entrance in 1918. Rank-and-file servicewomen had worked persistently to gain what they viewed as a significant symbolic advancement for women's rights.[71] These women, who had ties to the suffrage era, found strong support among second-wave feminists; the National Organization for Women, in keeping with its equal rights feminism, championed their cause and worked with the WOSL. Defense officials had additional motivations for belatedly conceding their military status; at a time when the armed services were struggling more fully to integrate women, the positive publicity surrounding World War I telephone operators was a small public relations boost.

Former servicewomen of the AEF made another public appearance in 1979, this time in symbolic form, during the hearings on women in the military conducted by the House Committee on Armed Services. One witness who addressed the committee was Major General Jeanne M. Holm of the U.S. Air Force (retired), former director of the air force secretary's personnel council. General Holm invoked the legacy of women's service with the AEF in her brief remarks recounting the story of General Pershing's reliance on women workers and reviewed the history of women's service to and within the military from 1917 forward. According to General Holm, "history has shown that whether we have a draft or an all-volunteer force, women are essential to national defense, a resource we cannot afford to waste." Holm insisted to the committee that the issue was not one of gender equality but simply of the best and most rational approach to national defense.[72] But the issue of women in the military continues to be deeply connected to larger social questions about gender; its meaning is as highly contested now as in 1919.

World War I was a defining moment in the evolution of the U.S. gender system. The war heightened and thus made visible the underlaying contradiction between prevailing definitions of womanhood on the one hand and women's increasing participation in the waged labor force on the other. Domestic definitions of women's roles could be stretched to encompass some aspects of women's work for auxiliary agencies, in hospitals, and as assistants in army offices, but they could not contain women's own sense of themselves as essential, expert, and authoritative participants in the war effort. Women's labor and skills were more integral to both the civilian and military economies than armed service and government planners could admit, and the exigencies of wartime allowed women workers more autonomy than most enjoyed on the home front. Furthermore, the fact that women worked for the wartime state lent political significance to their labor. Women's new sense of entitlement to citizenship was based on their full participation in the work of the nation. This emergent definition of citizenship, which had been articulated by a radical minority within the prewar suffrage movement, became dominant after the war, as working women joined middle-class feminists in the suffrage victory. For the rest of the twentieth century, women would work out the implications of basing their full membership in the nation state on their activity in the labor force. Ironically, the armed forces may be the last domain in which women achieve equality, although women's military service during the First World War signaled the beginning of this movement.

Service at the front in World War I wrought no dramatic transformation in women's social position in the United States. Yet, the war connected the women who served directly to the nation state, and it gave them a sense of entitlement shared by few of their counterparts on the home front. Women enlisted out of a deep sense of patriotic duty and out of a desire for personal advancement, equality, and respect. The medium of their contribution was work, and it was in the work place and in matters of workers' rights that women asserted their claim to equality. In exchange for their contribution to the war effort, AEF servicewomen demanded equal access to opportunities and responsibilities previously reserved for men. They also lobbied for equality of benefits with the male veterans of World War I, a political program that had both practical and symbolic meanings. Servicewomen's goal of equality, however, was not to be earned through the strategies they employed. Women's conception of their own service clashed with the needs and expectations of the government and the army during World War I. In the context of wartime mobilization, the state regarded women first and foremost as workers, but as workers of a separate and unequal class. The state was ready to use women's labor in the war but not to grant them equality as the ultimate reward for their service. Women in the AEF were pushing for an expanded definition of their role and a chance to participate in the public realm as equal citizens. The meaning of war experience for them was a liberatory one; it represented an opportunity for patriotic service, public respect, and personal mobility. But the state was determined to establish and maintain a separate sphere for women at the front, to contain and limit changes in gender relations set in motion by the army's decision to employ women workers. Here, then, is the central tension of servicewomen's experience during World War I: women's patriotic duty, a duty the wartime state asked them to accept unquestioningly, was defined as upholding a conservative vision of womanhood embedded in the privatized sphere of home and family. But other trends and cross-currents at the time, which had led to new patterns of employment and self-support, also underlay women's military service. Women were motivated to enlist because they felt confined by that same domestic vision. Their search for new models of female competence, professionalism, and public engagement led them to define a new role for themselves, as *servicewomen*, working for the national state at war.

Notes

Introduction

1. "Stars and Stripes of Boston Unit," *Boston Transcript*, 7 May 1917, 2; "Harvard's Sons in Khaki Parade in Boston," *Sunday Herald*, 6 May 1917; "Bishop Blesses Harvard Base Hospital Flag: Impressive Ceremony Brings Women to Tears," *Boston Herald*, 7 May 1917; "Hospital Unit Goes to Church," *The Boston Post*, 7 May 1917; "Moving Religious Service for the Base Hospital Going to War Zone," *Boston Daily Globe* (extra), 7 May 1917.

2. The unit at departure numbered 244: 25 officers (mostly physicians), 153 enlisted men, 1 chaplain, and 68 women. Women formed more than one-quarter of the unit; however, some enlisted men were away for training, so women composed an even larger proportion of those present at the dedication service.

3. Women's labor has been used by the military in every war in U.S. history, but until World War I their employment was either very limited or the conditions under which they worked were informal, unorganized, or voluntary. See Nina Bennett Smith, "The Women Who Went to War" (Ph.D. diss., Northwestern University, 1981); Mary Denis Maher, *To Bind Up the Wounds: Catholic Sister Nurses in the U.S. Civil War* (Westport, Conn.: Greenwood Press, 1989); Agatha Young, *The Women and the Crisis: Women of the North in the Civil War* (New York: McDowell, Obolensky, 1959); Portia Kernodle, *The Red Cross Nurse in Action, 1882–1948* (New York: Harper Brothers, 1949).

4. There are no definitive figures for the number of women who served with the AEF. In part, this problem reflects questions of definition, for the military status of women was hotly contested by the military hierarchy and servicewomen during the war. Because my primary interest is the relationship between women workers and the state, in daily life at the front as well as in policy, I have adopted a functional definition of women's service with the AEF, including all women who served under the authority of the U.S. Army, in uniform or with AEF insignia, and performed work directly for the American military effort; it does not include the thousands of additional U.S. women who worked for welfare and relief organiza-

tions. My estimate of sixteen thousand five hundred is composed of ten thousand members of the Army Nurse Corps, five hundred clerks and telephone operators, and six thousand auxiliary or welfare workers. This estimate is considerably lower than the figure of twenty-five thousand used by Dorothy Schneider and Carl J. Schneider in *Into the Breach: American Women Overseas in World War I* (New York: Viking Press, 1991), p. 1, and Appendix A, pp. 287–89, which includes American women who worked with the French and British armies and with other civilian relief agencies.

5. Anonymous, *Red Triangle Girl in France* (New York: George Doran Co., 1919); Elizabeth Ashe, *Intimate Letters from France during America's First Year of War* (San Francisco: Philopolis Press, 1918); Marian Baldwin, *Canteening Overseas* (New York: Macmillan, 1920); Isabel Anderson, *Zigzagging* (Boston: Houghton Mifflin Co., 1918); Elizabeth Black, *Hospital Heroes* (New York: Charles Scribner's Sons, 1919); Amy Owen Bradley, *Back of the Front in France* (Boston: W. A. Butterfield, 1918); Carolyn Clarke, *Evacuation 114* (Boston: Hudson Printing Co., 1919); Mary Dexter, *In the Soldiers' Service* (Boston: Houghton Mifflin Co., 1918); Alice Fitzgerald, *The Edith Cavell Nurse from Massachusetts: A Record of One Year's Personal Service with the B.E.F.* (Boston: W. A. Butterfield, 1917); Katharine Foote, *88 bis and V. I. H.: Letters from Two Hospitals by an American V.A.D.* (Boston: American Monthly Press, 1919); Esther Lovejoy, *The House of the Good Neighbor* (New York: The Macmillan Co., 1919); *"Mademoiselle Miss": Letters from an American Girl Serving with the Rank of Lieutenant in a French Army Hospital at the Front* (Boston: W. A. Butterfield, 1916); Katherine Mayo, *That Damn "Y"* (Boston: Houghton Mifflin Co., 1920); Elizabeth Cabot Putnam, *On Duty and Off* (Cambridge, Mass.: Riverside Press, 1919).

6. For various expressions of the theme, see "Heiress Scrubs Tubs," *Stars and Stripes*, 1: 3 (22 Feb. 1918), and "When I Opened the Shutter," *Ladies Home Journal*, 34 (Aug. 1917); Alice B. Emerson's Ruth Fielding books, a popular series for girls published by Cupples and Leon; and the film *The Little American*.

7. David Kennedy, *Over Here: The First World War and American Society* (Oxford: Oxford University Press, 1980), pp. 217, 284; Frank Freidel, *Over There* (Boston: Little, Brown and Co, 1964), pp. 257–70, 293–313; and Schneider and Schneider, *Into the Breach*, all emphasize elite women who volunteered with U.S. and Allied forces. A significant exception is a recent study, Lettie Gavin, *American Women in World War I: They Also Served* (Niwot, Colo.: University Press of Colorado, 1997), which includes chapters on nurses, telephone operators, and a groundbreaking chapter on "reconstruction aides" (physical therapists).

8. Arnaldo Testi, "The Gender of Reform Politics: Theodore Roosevelt and the Culture of Masculinity," *Journal of American History* 81 (March 1995): 1509–33.

9. Sara Ruddick, *Maternal Thinking* (New York: Ballantine Books, 1990); Jean Bethke Elshtain, *Women and War* (New York: Basic Books, 1987); Margaret Randolph Higonnet, Jane Jenson, Sonya Michel, and Margaret Collins Weitz, eds., *Behind the Lines: Gender and the Two World Wars* (New Haven: Yale University Press, 1987); Claire M. Tylee, *The Great War and Women's Consciousness* (Iowa City: University of Iowa Press, 1990); Cynthia Enloe, *Does Khaki Become You? The Militarization of Women's Lives* (Boston: South End Press, 1983); Jane Marcus, "The Asylums of Antaeus," in *The Differences Within: Feminism and Critical Theory*, ed. Elizabeth Meese and Alice Parker (Amsterdam: J. Benjamins, 1989); Sharon Macdonald, Pat Holden, and Shirley Ardener, eds., *Images of Women in Peace and War: Cross-cultural and Historical Perspectives* (Madison: University of Wisconsin Press, 1987); Anne Summers, *Angels and Citizens: British Women as Military Nurses, 1854–1914* (London: Routledge and Kegan Paul, 1988); Miriam Cooke and Angela Woollacott, eds., *Gendering War Talk* (Princeton, N.J.: Princeton University Press, 1993); Helen M. Cooper, Adrienne Auslander Munich, and Susan Merrill Squier, eds., *Arms and the Woman: War, Gender and Literary Representation* (Chapel Hill: University of North Carolina Press, 1989); Elizabeth D. Leonard, *Yankee Women: Gender Battles in the Civil War* (New York: W. W. Norton, 1994).

Notes

10. Higonnet et al., *Behind the Lines*, p. 4.

11. Cooper et al., *Arms and the Woman*, p. xv. Also see Ruddick, *Maternal Thinking*, p. 143; Elshtain, *Women and War*.

12. Peter Filene, *Him/Her Self: Sex Roles in Modern America* (Baltimore, Md.: Johns Hopkins University Press, 1986); Elizabeth H. Pleck and Joseph H. Pleck, eds., *The American Man* (Englewood Cliffs, N.J.:Prentice-Hall, 1980); David I. Macleod, *Building Character in the American Boy: The Boy Scouts, YMCA, and Their Forerunners, 1870–1920* (Madison: University of Wisconsin Press, 1983).

13. Harriet Hyman Alonso, *Peace as a Women's Issue* (Syracuse, N.Y.: Syracuse University Press, 1993), pp. 56–66; Jane Addams, *Peace and Bread in Time of War* (1922; reprint Silver Springs, Md.: National Association of Social Workers, 1983); Linda K. Schott, *Reconstructing Women's Thoughts: The Women's International League for Peace and Freedom Before World War II* (Stanford, Calif.: Stanford University Press, 1987), makes the case that Addams, Catt, and others in the Woman's Peace Party viewed material peacefulness as socialized, not innate, pp. 40–54.

14. Nancy Cott, *The Grounding of Modern Feminism* (New Haven, Conn.: Yale University Press, 1987), chap. 1.

15. Higonnet et al., *Behind the Lines*, p. 17.

16. Margaret Randolph Higonnet and Patrice L.-R. Higonnet, "The Double Helix," in Higonnet et al., *Behind the Lines*, pp. 31–47.

17. Louise M. Newman, "Critical Theory and the History of Women: What's at Stake in Deconstructing Women's History," *Journal of Women's History* 2 (Winter 1991): 58–68; Joan Wallach Scott, *Gender and the Politics of History* (New York: Columbia University Press, 1988); Bell Chevigny, Myra Jehlen, and Judith Walkowitz, "Patrolling the Borders: Feminist Historiography and the New Historicism," *Radical History Review* 43 (Winter 1989): 23–43; Mary Poovey, "Feminism and Deconstruction," *Feminist Studies* 14 (Spring 1988): 51–65.

18. Marcus, "The Asylums of Antaeus," pp. 49–81; D'Ann Campbell, *Women at War with America* (Cambridge, Mass.: Harvard University Press, 1984).

19. Bertha Dann to Harry Cutler, 8 Sept. 1918, Jewish Welfare Board-Army Navy Papers, Box 330 (Folder: "D Misc."), American Jewish Historical Society, Waltham, Mass.

20. Maurine Greenwald, *Women, War and Work* (Westport, Conn.: Greenwood Press, 1980); Valerie Jean Conner, *The National War Labor Board* (Chapel Hill: University of North Carolina Press, 1983); Ruth Milkman, *Gender at Work: The Dynamics of Job Segregation during World War Two* (Urbana: University of Illinois Press, 1987); Nancy Gabin, *Feminism in the Labor Movement: Women and the United Auto Workers, 1935–1975* (Ithaca, N.Y.: Cornell University Press, 1990); Nelson Lichtenstein, *Labor's War at Home: The C. I. O. in World War Two* (Cambridge, UK: Cambridge University Press, 1982).

21. My analysis of workers' culture and the power relations behind daily practices in army offices and hospital wards is indebted to many practitioners of the "new labor history," especially David Montgomery, *Workers' Control in America* (Cambridge, UK: Cambridge University Press, 1979); Barbara Melosh, *"The Physician's Hand": Work, Culture, and Conflict in American Nursing* (Philadelphia: Temple University Press, 1982); Susan Porter Benson, *Counter Cultures: Saleswomen, Managers and Customers in American Department Stores, 1890–1940* (Urbana: University of Illinois Press, 1986); and Patricia Cooper, *Once a Cigar Maker: Men, Women, and Work Culture in American Cigar Factories, 1900–1919* (Urbana: University of Illinois Press, 1987).

22. Susan Ware, *Partner and I: Molly Dewson, Feminism, and New Deal Politics* (New Haven, Conn.: Yale University Press, 1987), p. 76.

23. Alma Gray Bloom, oral history, 31 March 1988, Soldier's Home, Chelsea, Mass.

24. Nancy Schrom Dye, *As Equals and as Sisters: Feminism, the Labor Movement, and the Women's Trade Union League of New York* (Columbia, Mo.: University of Missouri Press, 1980);

Ellen Carol DuBois, "Working Women, Class Relations, and Suffrage Militance: Harriot Stanton Blatch and the New York Woman Suffrage Movement, 1894–1909, *Journal of American History* 74 (June 1987): 34–58; Maurine Weiner Greenwald, "Working-Class Feminism and the Family Wage Ideal: The Seattle Debate on Married Women's Right to Work, 1914–1920," *Journal of American History* 76 (June 1989): 118–49; Meredith Tax, *The Rising of the Women* (New York: Monthly Review Press, 1980).

25. DuBois, "Working Women," 41–44, and Dubois, *Harriet Stanton Blatch and the Winning of Woman Suffrage* (New Haven: Yale University Press, 1997).

26. Harriot Stanton Blatch, *Mobilizing Woman-Power* (New York: The Woman's Press, 1918); Susan Armeny, "Organized Nurses, Women Philanthropists, and the Intellectual Bases for Cooperation Among Women, 1898–1920," in *Nursing History: New Perspectives, New Possibilities*, ed. Ellen Condliffe Lagemann (New York: Teachers College Press, 1983).

1 Mobilizing Women for War

1. Julia Stimson to Dr. R. Tait McKenzie, 2 Feb. 1932, Office of the Surgeon General, RG 112, Entry 103, Historical Data File of the Army Nurse Corps, Box 5 (Folder: "Jane A. Delano Memorial"), National Archives, Washington, D.C.

2. Jean Bethke Elshtain, *Women and War* (New York: Basic Books, 1987); Sharon Macdonald, Pat Holden, and Shirley Ardener, eds., *Images of Women in Peace and War: Cross-cultural and Historical Perspectives* (Madison: University of Wisconsin Press, 1987); Anne Hudson Jones, ed., *Images of Nurses: Perspectives from History, Art and Literature* (Philadelphia: University of Pennsylvania Press, 1988); Susan Reverby, *Ordered to Care: The Dilemma of American Nursing, 1850–1945* (Cambridge, U.K.: Cambridge University Press, 1987), chap. 3.

3. John Whiteclay Chambers, *To Raise an Army: The Draft Comes to Modern America* (New York: Free Press, 1987), p. 177.

4. Quoted in "American Women's Vast War-Work as Revealed by an Official Report," *The Literary Digest* 66 (21 Aug. 1917) 54–7; see Susan Zeiger, "She Didn't Raise Her Boy to Be a Slacker: Motherhood, Conscription, and the Culture of the First World War," *Feminist Studies* 22 (Spring 1996): 7–39.

5. Larry Wayne Ward, *The Motion Picture Goes to War: The U.S. Government Film Effort during World War I* (Ann Arbor: UMI Research Press, 1985), p. 54. For an example of popular cartoons that played on the theme of personal transformation through military service, see "Then and Now—War Makes an Awful Difference," *Stars & Stripes*, 1:1 (8 Feb. 1918).

6. Newton D. Baker, "Welfare Work for the Army" (18 Oct. 1919), mimeograph copy of speech, papers of the Jewish Welfare Board, Army Navy Division, WWI, Box 343 (Folder: "War Department 1919"), American Jewish Historical Society, Waltham, Mass.; Newton Baker, *The War and the Colleges* (New York: American Association for International Conciliation, 1917).

7. "When I Opened the Shutter," *Ladies Home Journal* 34 (Aug. 1917).

8. William Breen, *Uncle Sam at Home: Civilian Mobilization and the Council of National Defense* (Westport, Conn.: Greenwood Press, 1984).

9. Herbert Hoover, testimony before the Senate Committee on Agriculture, June 19, 1917, quoted in David M. Kennedy, *Over Here: The First World War and American Society* (New York: Oxford University Press, 1980), p. 118, and in William Clinton Mullendore, *History of the United States Food Administration, 1917–1919* (Stanford: Stanford University Press, 1941), pp. 52–53.

10. Breen, *Uncle Sam at Home*, pp. 122–23, 125; Barbara J. Steinson, *American Women's Activism in World War I* (New York: Garland Publishing Co., 1982), pp. 311–13, 330–40.

Notes

11. Blanche Wiesen Cook, ed., *Toward the Great Change: Writings of Crystal and Max Eastman* (New York: Garland Publishing Co., 1976), pp. 280–84; also see Blanche Weisen Cook, Introduction to *Crystal Eastman on Women and Revolution* (Oxford: Oxford University Press, 1978).

12. Shaw letters quoted in Steinson, *American Women's Activism,* p. 313.

13. Breen, *Uncle Sam at Home,* p. 135.

14. See Cook, *Toward the Great Change,* p. 284.

15. Ronald Schaffer, *America in the Great War: The Rise of the War Welfare State* (New York, Oxford University Press, 1991), chaps. 6, 7; Steinson, *American Women's Activism,* chap. 7; Breen, *Uncle Sam at Home,* pp. 127–29.

16. Emily Newell Blair, *The Woman's Committee of the Council of National Defense: An Interpretive History* (Washington, D.C.: Government Printing Office, 1920), p. 21.

17. Mattie E. Treadwell, *The Women's Army Corps* (Washington, D.C.: Office of the Chief of Military History, Department of the Army, 1954).

18. Maurine Weiner Greenwald, *Women, War and Work: The Impact of World War I on Women Workers in the United States* (Westport, Conn.: Greenwood Press, 1980), chap. 1.

19. Jean Ebbert and Marie-Beth Hall, *Crossed Currents: Navy Women from World War I to Tailhook* (Washington, D.C.: Brassey's, 1993), p. 8.

20. Edward Hungerford, "She Tackles the Job," *Everybody's Magazine* (Oct. 1917) 430–437.

21. The insight about the suffrage movement comes from an anonymous reviewer for Cornell University Press. *The Anti-Suffrage Review,* July 1910, quoted in Jenny Gould, "Women's Military Services in First World War Britain," in *Behind the Lines: Gender and the Two World Wars,* ed. Margaret Higonnet, Jane Jenson, Sonya Michel, and Margaret Collins Weitz (New Haven, Conn.: Yale University Press, 1987), pp. 114–25.

22. "War Openings for Women," *The Woman Citizen* (11 Aug. 1917) 184.

23. Quoted in "The Woman's Plattsburg," *The Woman Citizen* (16 March 1918), 314.

24. There are numerous articles and brief reports in *The Woman Citizen* about the Women's Overseas Hospital and the plight of women physicians. The situation of female doctors in relation to the military is discussed in Dorothy Schneider and Carl Schneider, *Into the Breach: American Women Overseas in World War I* (New York: Viking, 1991), pp. 89–94.

25. Robert V. Piemonte and Cindy Gurney, eds., *Highlights in the History of the Army Nurse Corps* (Washington, D.C.: U.S. Army Center of Military History, 1987), pp. 11–14. Even nursing histories that downplay the role of the Army Nurse Corps and underscore that of the American Red Cross acknowledge the success of Army Nurse Corps superintendents in developing important male supporters within the Office of the Surgeon General and the Army Medical Corps; see Portia Kernodle, *The Red Cross Nurse in Action* (New York: Harper Brothers, 1949), pp. 109, 124.

26. Kernodle, *Red Cross Nurse,* pp. 125–26, 133, 141–42.

27. Treadwell, *The Women's Army Corps,* pp. 5–6. Yeoman(F)s and marine(F)s received equal pay, officer rank, and veterans' benefits.

28. Linda L. Hewitt, *Women Marines in World War I* (Washington, D.C.: History and Museums Division, U.S. Marine Corps, 1974); Eunice C. Dessez, *The First Enlisted Women, 1917–1918* (Philadelphia: Dorrance and Co., 1955).

29. Joseph L. Morrison, *Josephus Daniels, the Small-d Democrat* (Chapel Hill: University of North Carolina Press, 1966), presents Secretary Daniels in this light, although he mentions the enlistment of women only in passing; Daniels himself makes much more of the episode in his book, *Our Navy at War* (New York: George Doran Co., 1922), chap. 31. For Daniels's advocacy on behalf of woman suffrage, see David E. Cronon, ed., *The Cabinet Diaries of Josephus Daniels* (Lincoln: University of Nebraska Press, 1963), pp. 257, 303, 370.

30. Quoted in Treadwell, *Women's Army Corps,* pp. 8–10.

31. Ibid., pp. 7–8.

32. Daniel Beaver, *Newton D. Baker and the American War Effort, 1917–1919* (Lincoln: University of Nebraska Press, 1966), pp. 218–24, contains a helpful discussion of Baker and the CTCA. Raymond B. Fosdick, *Chronicle of a Generation* (New York: Harper and Brothers, 1958), chap. 8; Edward Coffman, *The War to End All Wars: The American Military Experience in World War One* (New York: Oxford University Press, 1968), pp. 76–81.

33. Jewish Welfare Board, *First Annual Report* (New York: Jewish Welfare Board, 1919), p. 15.

2 Getting over There: A Social Analysis of Women's Enlistment

1. Anna Snyder to Col. Cheney, [date obscured], AEF Papers, RG 120, Entry 2006, Box 2, National Archives, Washington, D.C. (hereafter National Archives).

2. Demographic data on auxiliary workers has been obtained from the archives of three auxiliary organizations: the archives of the Y.M.C.A. of the U.S.A., in St. Paul, Minn.; the archives of the Y.W.C.A. National Board in New York City; and the papers of the JWB in the American Jewish Historical Society, Waltham, Mass. The largest and most complete of the three is the YMCA collection, which includes a file of keypunch cards for all twenty-six thousand "Y" secretaries, male and female, stateside and overseas, during the First World War. Of that group, 3,198 are women workers posted overseas. Each card contains the subject's name, date of birth, address, religion, marital status, ability to speak a foreign language, occupation, and level of education. The keypunch cards are arranged alphabetically in twenty-four file drawers. I selected a random sample of women who served overseas by taking the first seventeen keypunch cards for overseas women in each drawer; these 408 women composed a 12 percent sample. Data from each card were coded and entered onto computer files. The analysis was performed using the SAS statistical package. The personnel files of YWCA secretaries covered a narrower range of items, although they provided more detail on educational and employment history. I sampled 50 of 260, or 20 percent. The JWB data came in a unique form: visa application letters that contained name, year of birth, place of birth, occupation, city of residence, and father's and mother's places of birth and citizenship. I used all twenty-four extant letters, which constituted 30 percent of the JWB's women workers overseas. All three collections have important limitations: they say nothing of parents' occupations, family income, or household structure. For this information I reconstructed household structure and family occupations using city directories for the fifty YMCA workers from the large sample who lived in Massachusetts. No comparably comprehensive data are available on Army Nurse Corps or Army Nurse Corps Reserve nurses because a fire in St. Louis, Mo., destroyed the federal service records from World War I. Published histories of base hospital units usually provide a roster of nurses' names, sometimes with their places of residence and training. Using this data in conjunction with city directories, I have compiled household information for two groups of nurses, Base Hospital No. 5 from Boston and Base Hospital No. 19 from Rochester, N.Y.

3. See the chapter by Alice Dunbar-Nelson, "Negro Women in War Work," and the letter by Ralph Tyler, in Emmett J. Scott, *The American Negro in the World War* (Chicago: Homewood Press, 1919), pp. 374–97 and 405–7; Charles Williams, *Sidelights on Negro Soldiers* (Boston: B. J. Brimmer Co., 1923), pp. 105, 243–44, 248; John Hope Franklin, *From Slavery to Freedom* (New York: Alfred A. Knopf, 1967), pp. 470–76; Darlene Clark Hine, *Black Women in White: Racial Conflict and Cooperation in the Nursing Profession, 1890–1950* (Bloomington: Indiana University Press, 1989), pp. 94, 104–7; Mary Elizabeth Carnegie, *The Path We Tread* (Philadelphia, Pa.: J. B. Lippincott Co., 1986); Mabel Staupers, *No Time for Prejudice: A Story of the Integration of Negroes in Nursing in the United States* (New York: Macmillan,

Notes

1961); Adah Thoms, *Pathfinders: A History of the Progress of Colored Graduate Nurses* (New York: McKay, 1929).

4. Addie D. Hunton and Kathryn M. Johnson, *Two Colored Women with the American Expeditionary Forces* (Brooklyn, N.Y.: Brooklyn Eagle Press, 1920). Scott, *American Negro*, pp. 399–407; Hine, *Black Women in White*, p. 103. One of the African-American nurses, Aileen Cole Stewart, left a slim but very interesting collection of clippings and interviews to the U.S. Army Military History Institute in Carlisle Barracks, Pa. (hereafter USAMHI); Aileen Cole Stewart, WWI Survey, USAMHI; Arthur E. Barbeau and Florette Henri, *The Unknown Soldiers: Black American Troops in World War I* (Philadelphia, Pa.: Temple University Press, 1974).

5. Scott, *American Negro*, pp. 448–51; Hine, *Black Women in White*, pp. 102–4.

6. Raymond Fosdick, *Chronicle of a Generation* (New York: Harper and Brothers, 1958), pp. 148–50; "Women's Overseas Service," pamphlet, n.d., YMCA–AS 26, YMCA of the USA Archives, St. Paul, Minn. (hereafter YMCA Archives). Since the YMCA personnel data had only one category for "Lutherans & Others," including Catholics, Christian Scientists, Quakers, and Jews, specific figures are impossible to obtain; 12.3 percent of the women in the YMCA sample were categorized as "Lutheran/Other." Jewish Welfare Board, *Annual Report* (1919); Lee Levinger, *A Jewish Chaplain in France* (New York: Macmillan Co., 1921). There was no formal ban on the enlistment of Jewish women in the Army Nurse Corps, and surnames that are likely to be Jewish do appear on base hospital rosters.

7. John Higham, *Strangers in the Land* (New Brunswick, N.J.: Rutgers University Press, 1955); Frederick Luebke, *Bonds of Loyalty: German-Americans and World War I* (DeKalb: Northern Illinois University Press, 1974); Lee Levinger, *Anti-Semitism in the United States; Its History and Causes* (New York: Bloch, 1925); John Higham, *Send These to Me: Immigrants in Urban America*, rev. ed. (Baltimore, Md.: Johns Hopkins University Press, 1984); Michael Dobkowski, *The Tarnished Dream: The Basis of American Anti-Semitism* (Westport, Conn.: Greenwood Press, 1979).

8. Letter from M. Churchill, Military Intelligence Branch, War Department, to Harry Cutler, chairman of the JWB, 11 June 1918, Jewish Welfare Board–Army Navy Papers, I 180, Box 343 (Folder: "War Department"), American Jewish Historical Society, Waltham, Mass. (hereafter JWB Papers, AJHS).

9. Letter from C. J. Teller to Harry Cutler, 20 June 1918, JWB Papers, Box 341 (Folder: "Teller"), AJHS.

10. In early November 1918, the French embassy determined that nativity would "not hereafter be a bar against" the granting of visas to representatives of the JWB; Harry Cutler to Cyrus Adler, 7 Nov. 1918, JWB Papers, Box 335 (Folder: "Overseas 1918–19"), AJHS.

11. Bertha Dann to Harry Cutler, 8 Sept. 1918, JWB Papers, Box 330 (Folder: "D Misc."), AJHS.

12. Higham, *Strangers in the Land*, chaps. 8, 9, 10.

13. On the problems of using social class to analyze the experience of people in the middle strata, see Stuart M. Blumin, "The Hypothesis of Middle-Class Formation in Nineteenth Century America: A Critique and Some Proposals," *American Historical Review* 90 (April 1985): 299–338, and Arnold J. Mayer, "The Lower Middle Class as Historical Problem," *Journal of Modern History* 47 (September 1975): 409–36. I follow Mayer's description of the lower middle class encompassing two groupings, an older strata of "independent producers" (e.g., retailers and craftsmen) and a newer grouping of "dependent" employees (e.g., clerks, technicians, and lower professionals).

14. Margery Davies, *Woman's Place Is at the Typewriter* (Philadelphia, Pa.: Temple University Press, 1982).

15. Occupational data on the families of servicewomen from Massachusetts (AEF nurses and YMCA canteen workers) was obtained from various city and town directories available at the Boston Public Library.

16. James R. Green, *The World of the Worker: Labor in Twentieth-Century America* (New York: Hill and Wang, 1980), p. 5; C. Wright Mills, *White Collar: The American Middle Classes* (London: Oxford University Press, 1951), pp. 74–75.

17. Lt. Col. Ezra Davis to Major R. E. Shannon, copy of confidential memo, 23 Aug. 1918, RG 120, Entry 2017, Office of Chief Quartermaster, Box 211, National Archives.

18. The roster of nurses is printed in *A History of United States Base Hospital No. 19* (Rochester, N.Y.: Wegman-Walsh Press, n.d. [c. 1923]); only eleven of the thirty-two women who could be located in the city directories lived in a household with other family members.

19. See women's requests for transfer or discharge to the Office of the Chief Ordnance Officer, AEF Papers, RG 120, Entry 2006, Box 2, National Archives. One army hospital chief nurse wrote that her efforts to raise a full unit of nurses were eroded by "illness and domestic complications"; *History of U. S. Army Base Hospital No. 45 in the Great War* (Richmond, Va.: William Byrd Press, 1924), p. 179.

20. Lynn Weiner, *From Working Girl to Working Mother* (Chapel Hill: University of North Carolina Press, 1978), p. 13; Joanne J. Meyerowitz, *Women Adrift: Independent Wage Earners in Chicago, 1880–1930* (Chicago: University of Chicago Press, 1988).

21. *History of Base Hospital No. 19; The Story of U. S. Army Base Hospital No. 5, by a Member of the Unit* (Cambridge, Mass.: The University Press, 1919); Weiner, *From Working Girl*, pp. 19–20.

22. *Thirteenth Census of the United States, 1910*, vol. 1, "Population" (Washington, D.C.: Government Printing Office, 1913), p. 79.

23. In the YWCA sample, thirty-four of fifty women workers (68 percent) reported moving at least once. So did ten of nineteen women workers (52 percent) in the JWB sample; four others were born in Russia or Poland.

24. Personnel case files from the YWCA sample, Archives of the Young Women's Christian Association–National Board (hereafter YWCA Archives).

25. Susan Reverby, *Ordered to Care: The Dilemma of American Nursing* (Cambridge, U.K.: Cambridge University Press, 1987), pp. 77–79.

26. Alma Gray Bloom, oral history, Soldiers' Home, Chelsea, Mass., 31 March 1988.

27. Figures for the YMCA come from the YMCA sample. It is likely that widows were included in the married category, making the proportion of women without husbands even higher.

28. Maurine Weiner Greenwald, *Women, War and Work: The Impact of World War I on Women Workers in the United States* (Westport, Conn.: Greenwood Press, 1980), points out that the war accelerated preexisting patterns of women's employment rather than changing them; very few first-time women workers joined the labor force. More recently, however, Greenwald has suggested that the war may have been a factor in the slight upward trend of married women's employment; certainly awareness of and controversy about this phenomenon was heightened during the war years. Maurine Weiner Greenwald, "Working-Class Feminism and the Family Wage Ideal: The Seattle Debate on Married Women's Right to Work, 1914–1920," *Journal of American History* 76 (June 1989): 118–49. According to an official YMCA report, "few of the women sent over had dependents, but in several cases home allowances varying from $10 to $100 a month were given"; Helen Ives Gilchrist, "AEF YMCA: Women's Work in the World War", p. 50, YMCA–AS 26, YMCA Archives.

29. Labor force participation rates for married women were 6 percent in 1900 and 11 percent in 1910; Weiner, *From Working Girl*, p. 6.

30. I follow Barbara Solomon in using the term "singlehood" to denote the marital state of unmarried women; Solomon, *In the Company of Educated Women* (New Haven, Conn.: Yale University Press, 1985).

31. The median age at first marriage in 1900 was 21.9 years for women and 25.9 for men;

Notes

Ellen K. Rothman, *Hands and Hearts: A History of Courtship in America* (New York: Basic Books, 1984), p. 287.

32. Until the armistice, women under age twenty-five were generally barred from canteen work, although age limits were less strenuously enforced for auxiliary workers than they were for nurses. The YMCA technically had an upper age limit of forty, but exceptions were regularly made; in the YMCA sample, 14 percent of the women were older than forty. Information on years of previous work experience, available in half of YWCA personnel files, show than YWCA workers averaged 7.8 years of work experience before enlistment.

33. Figures on age at enlistment of Army Nurse Corps women are derived from the World War I service records of Army Nurse Corps nurses from the state of Maine; see "Maine Roster of WWI Service, 1917–1919," Maine State Library, Augusta.

34. Marian Baldwin, *Canteening Overseas* (New York: Macmillan, 1920), p. 1.

35. Gilchrist, "AEF YMCA," pp. 44–45.

36. Solomon, *Educated Women*, pp. 115–22; Barbara Harris, *Beyond Her Sphere: Women and the Professions in American History* (Westport, Conn.: Greenwood Press, 1978), pp. 100–3; Roberta Frankfort, *Collegiate Women: Domesticity and Career in Turn-of-the-century America* (New York: New York University Press, 1977); Lillian Faderman, *Surpassing the Love of Men: Romantic Friendship and Love Between Women from the Renaissance to the Present* (New York: Morrow, 1981); John D'Emilio and Estelle Freedman, *Intimate Matters* (New York: Harper and Row, 1988). Rothman states that, in the cohort of women born between 1860 and 1880, 11 percent never married, "the highest proportion in American history"; Rothman, *Hands and Hearts*, pp. 249, 283.

37. Mabel Newcomer, *A Century of Higher Education for American Women* (New York: Harper and Brothers, 1959), Table 2, p. 46; Margaret Lambie, *Verdun Experiences* (reprinted from *Vassar Quarterly*, 1919; 1945); Susan Ware, *Partner and I: Molly Dewson, Feminism and New Deal Politics* (New Haven, Conn.: Yale University Press, 1987); A. Lincoln Lavine, *Circuits of Victory* (Garden City, N.Y.: Doubleday, Page and Co., 1921), p. 273; Michelle Christides, "Women Veterans of the Great War," *Minerva*, 3 (Summer 1985): 103–27; Grace Banker, WWI Survey, USAMHI.

38. Meyerowitz, *Women Adrift*, p. 95; Agnes Von Kurowsky, *Hemingway in Love and War: the Lost Diary of Agnes Von Kurowsky*, ed. Henry Serrano Villard and James Nagel (Boston: Northeastern University Press, 1989), pp. 28, 36, 45; Christides, "Women Veterans of the Great War," 103–27.

39. Stephen Norwood, *Labor's Flaming Youth: Telephone Operators and Worker Militancy, 1878–1923* (Urbana: University of Illinois Press, 1990), pp. 47–48; Davies, *Woman's Place Is at the Typewriter*, chap. 4; Alice Kessler-Harris, *Out To Work: A History of Wage-Earning Women in the United States* (New York: Oxford University Press, 1982), esp. chaps. 5, 6. Weiner, *From Working Girl*, Table 2, p. 6.

40. The eight women in academics, not surprisingly, were almost exclusively on the faculty of women's colleges or held positions as foreign-language instructors.

41. Gilchrist, "AEF YMCA," p. 45.

42. JWB data sample, AJHS; Charlotte Baum, Paula Hyman, and Sonya Michel, *The Jewish Woman in America* (New York: The Dial Press, 1975), pp. 46–53, 125; YWCA sample, YWCA, National Board Archives; Scott, *The American Negro*, pp. 382–83.

43. Virginia Scharff, *Taking the Wheel: Women and the Coming of the Motor Age* (New York: Free Press, 1991), pp. 90–93; Ware, *Partner and I*, p. 81.

44. "How Overseas Canteen Workers Are Selected," *The Index*, 17 Aug. 1918, and "Women Canteen Workers Enlist" (unidentified newspaper, n.d.), contained in a scrapbook; Cornelia Cree, WWI Survey, USAMHI. See also Caroline Slade to Elsie Mead, 25 Sept. 1918, 19 Sept. 1918, and Slade to Mead, 5 Nov. 1918, YMCA–AS 26.

45. *New York Times*, 25 March 1917.

46. Gilchrist, "AEF YMCA," pp. 49–50.

47. Minutes of the Executive Committee meetings (Overseas), 20 March 1918, 8 Aug. 1918, 29 Oct. 1918, AS-13, YMCA Archives.

48. *The Medical Department of the United States Army in the World War* (Washington, D.C.: Government Printing Office, 1927), vol. 13, "Army Nurse Corps," p. 300. Julia Stimson argued that nurses at the time were earning $35 to $40 per *week* in private duty and that the minimum wage for general duty in hospitals was $75 per month; *Medical Department in the World War*, vol. 13, p. 300; *The American Journal of Nursing*, 18 (May 1918): 599, applauded the Canadian government for recognizing that "nurses are a wage-earning professional group and that the great majority of them have obligations from which they cannot easily be released."

49. Testimony of Mrs. Harriet Blaine Beale, Committee to Secure Rank for Nurses, and Helen Hoy Greeley, U.S. Congress, House, Committee on Military Affairs, *Hearings Before the House Committee on Military Affairs on Proposed Legislation Affecting the Medical Corps of the U.S. Army*, 65th Congress (2d session), 1918.

50. Clara Noyes to Julia Stimson, 5 Aug. 1918, American Red Cross Papers, RG 200, Box 850 (Folder: "Bureau of Nursing"), National Archives.

51. Carrie Hall Papers, Schlesinger Library, Cambridge, Mass.

52. Grace Williams Major, WWI Survey, USAMHI.

53. Julia Stimson, "History of Nursing Activities, A.E.F., on the Western Front during War Period, 1917–1919," unpublished report, National American Red Cross Papers, RG 200, Box 850 (File: Bureau of Nursing), National Archives.

54. Gilchrist, "AEF YMCA," p. 41.

55. Snyder to Col. Cheney, [date obscured], AEF Papers, RG 120, Entry 2006, Box 2, National Archives; Cornelia Cree, scrapbook, WWI Survey, USAMHI; Booth Papers, Illinois State Historical Society.

56. Lavine, *Circuits of Victory*, pp. 272–75.

57. Isabel Anderson, a Red Cross worker, named her war memoir *Zigzagging* (Boston: Houghton Mifflin Co., 1918); it is indicative of how widely used the expression was that Anderson nowhere explains it in her narrative. "Word Sketches, 1939 Members, W.O.S.L.," typed ms., Papers of Women's Overseas Service League, St. Paul Unit, Minnesota Historical Society, St. Paul; also see World War I nurses' questionnaires in USAMHI collection; Letters from and about female clerks, Office of the Chief Ordnance Officer, AEF Papers, RG 120, Entry 2006, Box 2, National Archives; Josephine Davis Gray, World War I Survey, USAMHI; and Gray, oral history, Miami, Fla, 3 Feb. 1991; Anderson, *Zigzagging*, p. 1; Alice B. Emerson, Ruth Fielding series (New York: Cupples and Leon Co., 1918 and 1919); "Report of the National War Work Council of the Y.W.C.A. of the U.S.A., 1917–1919" (microfilm Reel 155, "War Work Council"), Records Files Collection, YWCA, National Board Archives.

58. Charlotte Chilson, clippings, WWI Survey, USAMHI; Lavine, *Circuits of Victory*, pp. 272–76; Grace Banker, memoir, WWI Survey, USAMHI; Record Book of Conferences of the Women's Section of Overseas Workers of the YMCA, AS 23, YMCA Archives.

59. Anderson, *Zigzagging*, p. 2; *New York Times*, 4, 5, and 6 Oct., 1917; Grace Banker, WWI Survey, USAMHI.

60. Grace Williams, WWI Survey, USAMHI; Oleda Joure Christides, WWI Survey, USAMHI.

61. Washington, D.C., National Archives, Office of Surgeon General, RG 112, Entry 104, Case Files of Army Nurse Corps, Box 523; Christides, "Women Veterans of the Great War," 103–27.

62. Memoir of Eleanor Barnes, in Helene Sillia, *Women's Overseas Service League History* (WOSL, 1978), p. 236; Alma Gray Bloom, oral history, 30 March 1988, Chelsea Soldiers'

Notes

Home, Chelsea, Mass.; Elizabeth Black, *Hospital Heroes* (New York: C. Scribners Sons, 1919), frontispiece. The "brother/sister rule" barring from the AEF all women with close male relatives in the service overseas, which was a major barrier to recruitment for the welfare agencies, also applied to the Army Nurse Corps; however, so many nurses had brothers in France that the rule must frequently have been overlooked in the pressure to recruit nurses. See Gilchrist, "AEF YMCA," p. 21; Josephine Davis Gray, questionnaire and clippings, WWI Survey, USAMHI; Josephine Gray, oral history, 3 Feb. 1991, Miami, Fla. In my interview with Mrs. Gray, she dismissed the story of her brother, which I had found in a newspaper article, explaining with a mischievous smile that "that was just something I told that reporter." Vera Brittain, *Testament of Youth* (New York: Macmillan Co., 1935).

63. Mabel DeNyse Faulds, WWI Survey, USAMHI; Ethel Pierce, oral history, Holyoke Soldiers' Home, Holyoke, Mass., 29 May 1990; Private correspondence between the woman's daughter and author, Jan. 1989; Margaret Deland, "Amazing Exodus of American Girls," undated clipping in scrapbook, Cornelia Cree, WWI Survey, USAMHI.

64. The argument that wartime service represented a continuity with rather than a break from private and domestic roles is made most fully by D'Ann Campbell in *Women at War with America: Private Lives in a Patriotic Era* (Cambridge, Mass.: Harvard University Press, 1984), esp. pp. 3–6. On "seeing the world," see David M. Kennedy, *Over Here: The First World War and American Society* (Oxford: Oxford University Press, 1980), pp. 205–9; Telephone conversation with Jean Kenny, daughter of Lydia Warren, 13 Oct. 1990.

3 Serving Doughnuts to the Doughboys: Auxiliary Workers in France

1. Bertha Laurie, Letters From Women Workers in France, typed copies, Y.M.C.A.–Armed Services, WWI, AS 26, Archives of the Young Men's Christian Association of the U.S.A., St. Paul, Minn. (hereafter YMCA Archives).

2. Cynthia Enloe, *Does Khaki Become You? The Militarization of Women's Lives* (Boston: South End Press, 1983), p. 7.

3. Figures are derived from organizational reports: YWCA, *Report of the Overseas Committee of the War Work Council, 1917–1920* (New York: YWCA, c. 1921); National Jewish Welfare Board, *First Annual Report* (New York, 1919); American National Red Cross, *Annual Report* (n. p., 1919); *Summary of World War Work of the American YMCA* (YMCA, 1920).

4. Helen Ives Gilchrist, "AEF–YMCA Women's Work in the World War," unpublished report, p. 4, AS 26, YMCA Archives.

5. Raymond B. Fosdick, *Chronicle of a Generation* (New York: Harper and Bros., 1958), pp. 135–41.

6. John Whiteclay Chambers, *To Raise an Army: The Draft Comes to Modern America* (New York: Free Press, 1987), p.167; Fosdick, *Chronicle of a Generation*, pp. 144–45; letters to the Commission on Training Camp Activities, War Department General and Special Staffs, Record Group 165, National Archives, Washington, D.C.

7. Nancy K. Bristow, *Making Men Moral: Social Engineering during the Great War* (New York: New York University Press, 1996); Paul Boyer, *Urban Masses and Moral Order in America, 1820–1920* (Cambridge, Mass.: Harvard University Press, 1978), esp. chap. 13. Boyer describes "positive environmentalism" as "not repression but a more subtle and complex process of influencing behavior and molding character through a transformed, consciously planned urban environment" (p. 221).

8. Fosdick, *Chronicle of a Generation*, pp. 68–78; YMCA, *Service with Fighting Men* (New York: Association Press, 1922).

9. Emmett J. Scott, *The American Negro in the World War* (Chicago: Homewood Press,

1919), p. 404. See also Martha Candler, "Home Life for Soldiers and Sailors," *American Leader* 13 (June 1918): 748–51; Mary Alden Hopkins, "The Army's Skirts," *Collier's Weekly* (June 29, 1918), 22–23.

10. Fosdick, *Chronicle of a Generation*, pp. 150, 152; Chambers, *To Raise an Army*, p. 167.

11. YMCA, *Service With Fighting Men*, vol. 1, pp. 103–5.

12. A. A. Silberberg to Col. Harry Cutler, 16 Oct. 1918, Box 340 (Cutler Correspondence, Folder: "Silberberg"), Jewish Welfare Board–Army-Navy Division, American Jewish Historical Society, Waltham, Mass. (hereafter JWB Papers, AJHS).

13. Ruth Rosen, *The Lost Sisterhood: Prostitution in America, 1900–1918* (Baltimore, Md.: Johns Hopkins University Press, 1982), pp. 33–37; Reports and memos on venereal disease, AEF Papers, RG 120, Series 29, Box 3786 (Folder: "Venereal disease"), National Archives, Washington, D.C.; David Kennedy, *Over Here: The First World War and American Society* (Oxford: Oxford University Press, 1980), pp. 186–87; Judith Walkowitz, *Prostitution and Victorian Society: Women, Class and the State* (Cambridge, U.K.: Cambridge University Press, 1980); Enloe, *Does Khaki Become You?*, pp. 18–45; Minutes of the Overseas Executive Committee, 28 July 1917, 3 Aug. 1917, AS 13, YMCA Archives; Allan M. Brandt, *No Magic Bullet: A Social History of Venereal Disease in the United States Since 1880* (New York: Oxford University Press, 1985), chap. 3.

14. Newton Baker, "Welfare Work for the Army," 18 Oct. 1919, mimeographed copy of speech, Box 343 (Folder: "War Department 1919"), JWB Papers, AJHS; Jewish Welfare Board, *First Annual Report* (New York, 1919), pp. 13–14.

15. Correspondence of Mrs. Alexander Kohut and Mrs. Abraham Simon with Harry Cutler, Box 334 (Cutler Correspondence, Folder: "Kohut") and Box 335 (Cutler Correspondence, Folder: "Simon"), JWB Papers, AJHS. Elsie Mead, "A Woman's War," typed manuscript, vol. 1, pp. 3–4, AS 29, YMCA Archives. Only the Knights of Columbus decided against employing women workers in France; Maurice Francis Egan and John Kennedy, *The Knights of Columbus in Peace and War* (New Haven, Conn.: Knights of Columbus, 1920), pp. 368, 374–75.

16. See Folder: "Women's Work, General Correspondence," AS 26, and Marguerite Cockett, "Criticism of the Y.M.C.A.," Papers of Marguerite Cockett, Biographical File A, both YMCA Archives. See also memo to Col. Cutler, 12 Sept. 1918, Box 329 (Cutler Correspondence, Folder: "Misc."), and Mortimer Schiff to Cutler, 8 Jan. 1919, Box 335 (Cutler Correspondence, Folder: "Schiff"), JWB papers, AJHS.

17. Evangeline Booth, *The War Romance of the Salvation Army* (Philadelphia: J. B. Lippincott Co., 1919), p. 78.

18. Evangeline Booth, "Pies and Doughnuts in the Trenches," *Ladies Home Journal* 35 (Sept. 1918): 21. Also see Hopkins, "Army's Skirts," 23; John R. Mott, "The Y.M.C.A. in War—Keeping Alive Home Influence," *Ladies Home Journal* 34 (July 1917): 3.

19. Editorial, "The Ladies—Bless 'Em," *Stars and Stripes* 1:4 (1 March 1918) (hereafter *S&S*). See also "Women, Two Varieties," *S&S* 1:2 (15 Feb. 1918); "Salutes and Blushes for Sergeant Chloe," *S&S* 1:7 (22 March 1918); "Pies and Donuts for Men Up Front," *S&S* 1:8 (29 March 1918); "Home is Where the Heart Is," *S&S* 1:12 (26 April 1918); "Substitute Home Now on Program for Men of A.E.F.," *S&S* 1:32 (13 Sept. 1918).

20. Paul Fussell, *The Great War and Modern Memory* (London: Oxford University Press, 1975. Robert Westbrook's concept of "political obligation" in World War II strongly influenced my understanding of the war effort in World War I; Robert Westbrook, "'I Want a Girl Just Like the Girl That Married Harry James': American Women and the Problem of Political Obligation in WWII," *American Quarterly* 42 (Dec. 1990): 587–614.

21. Paula Baker, "The Domestication of Politics: Women and American Political Society, 1780–1920," *American Historical Review* 89 (June 1984): 620–47; Marlene Stein Wortman,

Notes

"Domesticating the Nineteenth-Century American City," *Prospects* 3 (1977): 531–72; Karen Blair, *The Clubwoman as Feminist* (New York: Holmes and Meier, 1980)

22. George Creel, *How We Advertised America* (New York: Harper & Bros., 1920).

23. Jane Marcus, "The Asylums of Antaeus," in *The Differences Within: Feminism and Critical Theory*, ed. Elizabeth Meese and Alice Parker (Amsterdam: John Benjamins, 1989); Jean Bethke Elshtain, *Women and War* (New York: Basic Books, 1987), pp. 58–59, 92–120, 191–93.

24. Denise Riley, "Some Peculiarities of Social Policy concerning Women in Wartime and Postwar Britain," in *Behind the Lines: Gender and the Two World Wars*, ed. Margaret Randolph Higonnet, Jane Jenson, Sonya Michel, and Margaret Collins Weitz (New Haven, Conn.: Yale University Press, 1987), pp. 260–71.

25. Copy of letter, R. Fosdick to E. Mead, 27 Feb. 1919, in folder of commendations, "Women's Work, General Correspondence," AS 26, YMCA.

26. See Susan Gubar, "'This Is My Rifle, This Is My Gun': World War II and the Blitz on Women," in *Behind the Lines*, ed. Higonnet et al., pp. 227–59; Enloe, *Does Khaki Become You?*; Westbrook, "'I Want a Girl"; Claire Culleton, "Gender-Charged Munitions: The Language of World War I Munitions Reports," *Women's Studies International Forum* 11 (1988): 109–16; Claus Thewelheit, *Male Fantasies*, vol. 1, trans. Stephen Conway (Minneapolis: University of Minnesota Press, 1987); Leila Rupp, *Mobilizing Women for War: German and American Propaganda, 1939–1945* (Princeton, N.J.: Princeton University Press, 1978).

27. Anonymous, *Red Triangle Girl in France* (New York: George Doran Co., 1918); Margaret Deland, "Amazing Exodus of American Girls," undated clipping in scrapbook, Cornelia Cree, WWI Survey, USAMHI.

28. Lucy Lester, Marian Watts, and Bertha Laurie, Women's Letters, AS 26, YMCA Archives; Margaret Hall Papers, Massachusetts Historical Society, Boston (hereafter MHS).

29. Marian Baldwin, *Canteening Overseas* (New York: Macmillan, 1920), p. 101; Isabel Anderson, *Zigzagging* (Boston: Houghton Mifflin Co., 1918), p. viii; "Report on the General Federation of Women's Clubs Unit," AS 26, YMCA Archives; *Uncensored Letters of a Canteen Girl* (New York: Henry Holt and Co., 1920), p. 6; *Red Triangle Girl*, p. 67; Baldwin, *Canteening Overseas*, p. 105.

30. Examples in Baldwin, *Canteening Overseas*, pp. 104–5, 108; *Red Triangle Girl*, p. 124; *Uncensored Letters of Canteen Girl*, pp. 10–14; Anne Frances Hardon, *43 bis: War Letters of an American V.A.D.* (New York: priv. printed, 1927), p. 318.

31. Letters of commendation from enlisted men and officers, in folder "Women's Work, General Correspondence," AS 26, YMCA Archives; Charles Williams, *Sidelights on Negro Soldiers* (Boston: B. J. Brimmer Co., 1923), p. 243; Letter from Mary Kibben, Aug. 1918, YWCA Report, Reel 154; Katherine Mayo, *That Damn "Y"* (Boston: Houghton Mifflin Co., 1920), pp. 3–4; Violet Bennett letter in Women's Letters, AS 26, YMCA Archives.

32. "Report of the YMCA Investigation," RG 120, Entry 445, Box 3462, National Archives. For soldiers' attitudes toward canteen services, see letters in Margaret Sheldon Papers, RG 20. 3, Salvation Army Archives and Research Center, New York), and Men's Letters, AS 26, YMCA Archives. On black soldiers and welfare workers, see Williams, *Sidelights*, pp. 108–10. Auxilliary agencies had no formal written policies on racial segregation in the canteens. The Knights of Columbus and Salvation Army appeared to serve all, irrespective of race or religion. The YMCA, according to anecdotal evidence, let individual canteen directors set policy.

33. Clipping from *San Antonio Light*, 20 Oct. 1918, Papers of Marguerite Cockett, Biographical File A, YMCA Archives; Men's Letters, AS 26, YMCA Archives.

34. Letters from soldiers in papers of Florence Turkington, RG 20.1, SAARC. For an example of a woman who joked with soldiers, see "Her Hair Was Red and They Liked It," *S&S* 1:18 (7 June 1918).

35. Kathy Peiss, *Cheap Amusements: Working Women and Leisure in Turn-of-the-century New York* (Philadelphia: Temple University Press, 1986).

36. "Report from Mary Louise Kibben," Hostess Houses, WWI Overseas Commission, Records Files Collection, Reel 154, National Board Archives, YWCA, New York.

37. Series 763 (General Correspondence, Office of Commander of First Army) and Series 1687 (General Correspondence, General Staff, G-1), RG 120, National Archives.

38. Elizabeth Putnam, *On Duty and Off* (Cambridge, Mass.: Riverside Press, 1919), p. 35; Katharine Grinnell Prest, *One of 9000* (Boston: Marshall Jones Co., 1934), pp. 28–29.

39. Newspaper clipping, "WWI file No. 4," SAARC; Marian Watts, Women's Letters, AS 26, YMCA Archives; Helen King, "Women's Work in the Paris Region," typed report, Jan.–April 1919, AS 26, YMCA Archives; Helene M. Sillia, *A History of the Women's Overseas Service League* (n.p.: Women's Overseas Service League, 1978), p. 223.

40. Laurie, Women's Letters, AS26, YMCA Archives. See also relationship of Molly Dewson and Polly Porter, in Susan Ware, *Partner and I: Molly Dewson, Feminism and New Deal Politics* (New Haven, Conn.: Yale University Press, 1987), chap. 6. The extent to which possibilities for explicitly gay and lesbian experience emerged during World War I are still being explored; see Lillian Faderman, *Odd Girls and Twilight Lovers: a History of Lesbian Life in Twentieth-Century America* (New York: Columbia University Press, 1991), pp. 63–64, and George Chauncey, Jr., "Christian Brotherhood or Sexual Perversion? Homosexual Identities and the Construction of Sexual Boundaries in the World War I Era," *Journal of Social History* 9 (Winter 1985): 189–211.

41. Watts, Women's Letters, AS 26, YMCA Archives; YWCA, *Report of the Overseas Committee*, pp. 20–29. See also *S&S* 1:26 (2 Aug. 1918), which suggested that the YWCA recreation center for women at Tours be named "No Man's Land."

42. *Red Triangle Girl*, p. 70; "YMCA Investigation," vol. 2, p. 267, RG 120, National Archives.

43. Elsie Janis, *The Big Show* (New York: Cosmopolitan Books, 1919).

44. "Report on the GFWC Unit," AS 26, YMCA; Hall Papers, MHS; *Those War Women, by One of Them* (New York: Coward McCann, 1929); *War Nurse* (New York: Cosmopolitan Books, 1930); Mary Josephine Booth, letters, Illinois State Historical Society, Springfield (hereafter ISHS).

45. Caroline Slade to Elsie Mead, 5 Nov. 1918, Slade-Mead correspondence, AS 26, YMCA Archives. Also see "Report on the GFWC Unit," AS 26, YMCA Archives.

46. "YMCA Investigation," vol. 2, p. 268, RG 120, National Archives.

47. Ibid.

48. For one version, see the typescript copy in Folder: "Women's Work, General Correspondence," AS 25, YMCA Archives.

49. Women's Letters, AS 26, YMCA Archives; Diary entries, Papers of Florence Turkington, RG 20.1, SAARC.

50. Booth Papers, ISHS; Hall Papers, MHS.

51. Quoted in Gilchrist, "Women's Work," pp. 1–2.

52. YMCA, *Service With Fighting Men*, vol. 1, pp. 259–60, 481.

53. "Report on women personnel," ARC papers, National Archives.

54. The majority of YMCA employees were listed as canteen workers, but 63 women in the sample (15.5 percent) were given specialized or supervisory placements. Supervisors were far more educated: 62 percent graduated from college compared with 37 percent of nonsupervisors; only 19 percent of supervisors ended their education at high school or below, whereas 38 percent of nonsupervisors did so.

55. "How Overseas Canteen Workers Are Selected," *The Index*, 17 Aug. 1918, and "Women Canteen Workers Enlist," (unidentified newspaper, n. d.); clippings in scrapbook, Cornelia Cree, WWI Survey, USAMHI.

56. Booth Papers, ISHS; "Report on the GFWC Unit," AS 26, YMCA Archives; Mary

Notes

Gertrude Ronayne to Mrs. Robert Mead, 4 Oct. 1918, Slade-Mead Correspondence, AS 26, YMCA Archives; Anderson, *Zigzagging*, p. xi.

57. Gilchrist, "Women's Work," p. 48, YMCA Archives.

58. Letter from "Sara," Easter (1918), contained in scrapbook, Cornelia Cree, WWI Survey, USAMHI.

59. Mary Lee to mother, 3 Oct. 1918, Mary Lee Papers, Box 3, Folder 23, Schlesinger Library, Cambridge, Mass; Women's Letters, AS 26, YMCA Archives.

60. "YMCA Investigation," vol. 3, pp. 584–87, RG 120, AEF Papers, National Archives.

61. Cockett Papers, Biographical File A, YMCA Archives; "YMCA Investigation" and "Report of the Investigation of Other Welfare Agencies in France," RG 120, Entry 445, Box 3462. See also *Uncensored Letters of a Canteen Girl*, pp. 182–84.

62. Gilchrist, "Women's Work," pp. 88, 90, 91, YMCA Archives; Minutes of Exec. Comm., 29 Aug. 1918, AS 13, YMCA Archives; Erma Clair Jones to Mrs. William Watson Smith, 5 Dec. 1919, copy in scrapbook, Cornelia Cree, WWI Survey, USAMHI; Minutes of Cabinet Meetings, 26 March 1919, 9 April 1919, AS 13, YMCA Archives.

63. Minutes of the Overseas Executive Committee, 28 July 1917, 3 Aug. 1917, AS 13, YMCA Archives; Gilchrist, "Women's Work," p. 95, YMCA Archives; Faith Jayne Hinckley, *Forgotten Fires* (Lewiston, Me.: Lewiston Journal Co., 1923), p. 86; Baldwin, *Canteening Overseas*, pp. 87–88.

64. Kennedy, *Over Here*, pp. 186–87; reports and memos on venereal disease, AEF Papers, RG 120, Series 29, Box 3786 (Folder: "Venereal disease"), National Archives.

65. Gilchrist, "Women's Work," p. 97, YMCA Archives.

66. Margaret Hall Papers, MHS; Baldwin, *Canteening Overseas*, pp. 96, 114.

67. Baldwin, *Canteening Overseas*, pp. 133, 127. Trench service was an area where auxiliary men had distinguished themselves; as Evangeline Booth put it in *War Romance*: "The Salvation Army men who worked among the soldiers in advanced positions from which all women are barred are among the heroes of the war" (p. 100).

68. Booth, *War Romance*, pp. 106, 130, 205–6; Baldwin, *Canteening Overseas*, pp. 135–41.

69. Putnam, *On Duty and Off*, pp. 44–45.

4 "The Stenographers Will Win the War": Army Office Workers and Telephone Operators

1. Elizabeth Putnam, *On Duty and Off* (Cambridge, Mass.: Riverside Press, 1919), pp. 78–80.

2. Helen Ives Gilchrist, "Women's Work in the World War," unpublished manuscript, p. 56, AS-26, YMCA of the U.S. Archives, St. Paul, Minn. (hereafter YMCA Archives). The administrator, Martha McCook, was referring in part to the dozens of office workers brought to France by the YMCA to staff its own offices.

3. "Work place culture" or "work culture" is defined by Barbara Melosh and Susan Porter Benson as the set of understandings, practices, lore, and social rules that allows for "adaptations or resistance to constraints imposed by managers, employers, or the work itself." This definition appears in Melosh, *"The Physician's Hand": Work, Culture and Conflict in American Nursing* (Philadelphia: Temple University Press, 1982), pp. 5–6, and in Benson, *Counter Cultures: Saleswomen, Managers and Customers in American Department Stores, 1890–1940* (Urbana: University of Illinois Press, 1986), p. 228.

4. *Stars and Stripes* (hereafter *S&S*), 1:48 (3 Jan. 1919); James G. Harbord, *Leaves from a War Diary* (New York: Dodd, Mead and Co., 1925), p. 349; see also Harbord's tribute to Dawes, pp. 353–56; Edward Coffman, *The War to End All Wars: The American Military Experience in World War I* (New York: Oxford University Press, 1968), pp. 34–35, 129; Michael Knapp,

"World War I Service Records," *Prologue* 22 (Fall 1990): 300–4, points out that modern personnel records were also introduced during World War I. On the Bell System, see A. Lincoln Lavine, *Circuits of Victory* (Garden City, N.Y.: Doubleday, Page and Co., 1921); Walter S. Gifford, "The Activities of the Bell System during the World War," provided courtesy of AT&T Archives, Bell Laboratories, Warren, N.J. (hereafter AT&T Archives); Robert W. Garnet, *The Telephone Enterprise: The Evolution of the Bell System's Horizontal Structure, 1876–1909* (Baltimore, Md.: Johns Hopkins University Press, 1985); Neil Wasserman, *From Invention to Innovation: Long-Distance Telephone Transmission at the Turn of the Century* (Baltimore, Md.: Johns Hopkins University Press, 1985).

5. An important precursor to the use of women in army clerical work was the federal government's employment of female clerks in nonmilitary offices during the Civil War; Cindy S. Aron, "To Barter Their Souls for Gold: Female Clerks in Federal Government Offices, 1862–1890," *Journal of American History* 67 (March 1981): 835–53.

6. "250 WAACS Here to Relieve Men From S.O.S. Duty," *S&S* 1: (2 Aug. 1918); see also Lavine, *Circuits of Victory*, pp. 271–72, and *Telephone Review*, Sept. 1918, AT&T Archives. Cartoon reprinted in Captain Linda L Hewitt, U.S. Marine Corps, *Women Marines in World War One* (Washington, D.C.: History and Museums Division, U.S. Marine Corps, 1974), p. 13.

7. Joseph A. Hill, *Women in Gainful Occupations, 1870–1920* (Washington, D.C.: Government Printing Office, 1929), p. 56, Table 41; Joseph L. Morrison, *Josephus Daniels, the Small-d Democrat* (Chapel Hill: University of North Carolina Press, 1966), p. 97; *New York Times*, 21 March 1917. Chief Signal Officer, "Annual Report," 1919; quoted in press release, US Army Signal Center and School, 1972, AT&T Archives. See also numerous memos to the Office of the Chief Signal Corps Officer, AEF, RG 120, Entry 2040, Office of Chief Signal Officer, Boxes 100, 101, National Archives.

8. Raymond Aron, *The Century of Total War* (Garden City, N.Y.: Doubleday and Co., 1954), pp. 19–22.

9. See requests and letters of complaint from the fall of 1917 and winter of 1918, RG 120, Entry 2040, Office of Chief Signal Officer, Box 101 (Folder: "Tel. Ops."), National Archives; Chief Signal Officer, "Annual Report," 1919, quoted in press release, US Army Signal Center, AT&T Archives.

10. The appropriation of canteen workers for office jobs prompted a formal complaint from the Chief of the American Red Cross Service; memo, C. in C., A. S. General Staff to Chief of Air Service, 7 Dec. 1917, RG 120, Entry 2040, Box 101 (File: "Tel. ops."); Mattie Treadwell, *The Women's Army Corps* (Washington, D.C.: Office of the Chief of Military History, Department of the Army, 1954), pp. 6–10; *S&S*, 1:34 (27 Sept. 1918). Copy of Confidential Cable no. 1284 from General Pershing, 12 June 1918, to Adjutant General, Washington, D.C.; AEF Papers, RG 120, Office of the Chief Quartermaster, Entry 2017, Box 211.

11. The exact manner of women's enlistment in the Signal Corps continues to be a point of contention between women veterans and the army. As recently as April 1968, the Department of the Army issued a report on the status of Signal Corps women in the First World War that denied that the women were ever sworn in as members of the armed services; a copy of this report can be found in the papers of Merle Egan Anderson, private collection of Mark Hough, Seattle, Wash. Women veterans of the Signal Corps continue to insist that this swearing-in did take place. See Karen Hillerich, "Black Jack's Girls," *Army* (December 1982): 48; interview with Josephine Davis Gray, oral history, Miami, Fla, 3 Feb. 1991; and Michelle Christides, "Women Veterans of the Great War," *Minerva* 3 (Summer 1985): 121–22. On military drill, see First Lieut. Eugene D. Hill to Chief Signal Officer, 27 Sept. 1918, AEF Papers, RG 120, Entry 2040, Box 99.

12. My estimate that 500 U.S. clerical and telephone workers were employed in France by the military is based on the following: 223 U.S. telephone operators; 120 U.S. women in

Notes

Quartermaster Corps units; and at least 150 other women office workers in Ordnance, Signal Corps, Medical Corps, and other army offices.

13. Susan Hartmann estimates that by the end of World War II, only one-third of army personnel were assigned to strictly military occupations and more than 10 percent were in clerical positions, necessitating the creation of the women's military corps. Susan M. Hartmann, *The Homefront and Beyond: American Women in the 1940s* (Boston: Twayne Publishers, 1982), p. 34. See also D'Ann Campbell, *Women at War with America: Private Lives in a Patriotic Era* (Cambridge, Mass.: Harvard University Press, 1984), p. 19.

14. Editorial in *S&S*, 1:48 (3 Jan. 1919).

15. Eric J. Leed, *No Man's Land: Combat and Identity in World War I* (Cambridge, U.K.: Cambridge University Press, 1979); cf. Gerald Linderman, *Embattled Courage: The Experience of Combat in the American Civil War* (New York: Free Press, 1987); *S&S*, 1:14 (10 May 1918); Letter from male field clerk to *S&S*, 1:18 (7 June 1918); See also *S&S*, 1:14 (10 May 1918), 1:17 (31 May 1918), and 1:52 (31 Jan. 1919). A group of Quartermaster corpsmen, for example, had to suffer through a round of "Mother, Pull Down Your Service Flag, Your Son's in the S.O.S.," performed by a barber shop quartet of U.S. army aviators; letter to *S&S*, 1:50 (17 Jan. 1919); Faith Jayne Hinckley, *Forgotten Fires* (Lewiston, Me.: Lewiston Journal Co., 1923), pp. 56–57.

16. "Heroic S.O.S. Acts Recorded in G.O.," *S&S*, 1:48 (3 Jan. 1919). "Everybody Safe: No, Not Exactly, But Holding On," *S&S*, 1:29 (23 Aug. 1918).

17. "Six Hello Girls Help First Army," *S&S*, 1:35 (4 Oct. 1918).

18. Alfred Chandler, *The Visible Hand: The Managerial Revolution in American Business* (Cambridge, Mass.: Belknap Press, 1977); George Gordon, *The Communications Revolution: A History of Mass Media in the United States* (New York: Hastings House Publishers, 1977). Carolyn Marvin, *When Old Technologies Were New: Thinking about Electric Communication in the Late Nineteenth Century* (New York: Oxford University Press, 1988), pp. 22–32. See also Margery Davies, *Woman's Place Is at the Typewriter: Office Work and Office Workers, 1870–1930* (Philadelphia: Temple University Press, 1982), pp. 80–89.

19. Mary Synon, "Wheat's UP!," *Good Housekeeping* (March 1917): 14; also see Catherine Lynch, "Out of College into Business: How One Girl Did It," *Ladies Home Journal* (June 1917): 96.

20. On women in World War I–era spy films, see Michael Isenberg, *War on Film: The American Cinema in World War I* (London and Toronto: Associated University Presses, 1981); *Ladies Home Journal* (Aug. 1917): 18; Joseph Gollomb, *Spies* (New York: Macmillan Co., 1928), p. x. For the emergence of modern intelligence and the interconnections between military and civilian intelligence during World War I, see Joan M. Jensen, *The Price of Vigilance* (Chicago: Rand McNally and Co., 1968), pp. 9–16; also see Marc B. Powe, *The Emergence of the War Department Intelligence Agency, 1885–1918* (Manhattan, Kan.: Military Affairs, 1975); Ernest May, *Knowing One's Enemies: Intelligence Assessment before the Two World Wars* (Princeton, N.J.: Princeton University Press, 1984); and Walter C. Sweeney, *Military Intelligence: A New Weapon in War* (New York: Frederick A. Stokes, 1924).

21. Anna Snyder to Col. Cheney, AEF Papers, RG 120, Entry 2006, Box 2; Oleda Joure Christides, WWI Survey, U.S. Army Military History Institute, Carlisle Barracks, Pa. (hereafter USAMHI); Isabel E. Belt to Col. Norton, 14 Sept. 1918, RG 120, Entry 2006, Personnel Division, Ordnance Dept., Box 2.

22. Davies, *Woman's Place Is at the Typewriter*, chap. 4; Stephen Norwood, *Labor's Flaming Youth: Telephone Operators and Worker Militancy, 1878–1923* (Urbana: University of Illinois Press, 1990), pp. 47–48; Barbara Solomon, *In the Company of Educated Women* (New Haven, Conn.: Yale University Press, 1985), p. 130; Grace Banker, memoir, WWI survey, USAMHI.

23. Papers in RG 120, Entry 2017, Office of Chief Quartermaster Corps, Box 211, National Archives; Lavine, *Circuits of Victory*, chap. 25.

24. *Telephone Review*, Sept. 1918; Grace Banker, memoir, WWI Survey, USAMHI; *Telephone Review*, July 1918, AT&T Archives. For a description of the equipment and organization of a typical telephone office in this period, see John Schacht, *The Making of Telephone Unionism* (New Brunswick, N.J.: Rutgers University Press, 1985), pp. 30–33.

25. Putnam, *On Duty*, pp. 83, 99–101, 156–58; Mary Lee, *"It's a Great War!"* (New York: Houghton Mifflin Co., 1929), pp. 112, 142–45.

26. Adele Hoppock, WWI Survey, USAMHI.

27. Banker, memoir, WWI Survey, USAMHI; telephone operator quoted in Lavine, *Circuits of Victory*, p. 278–79.

28. Helen Scriver Papers, Minnesota Historical Society, St. Paul, Minn. Mary Lee to her mother, n. d., Mary Lee Papers, Folder 121, Schlesinger Library, Cambridge, Mass. Various rosters of civilian employees, RG 120, Entry 2017, Office of the Chief Quartermaster, Box 211 (Folder: "American Women for Overseas Service").

29. *S&S*, 1:8 (29 March 1918).

30. In contrast to World War I, Campbell, *Women at War with America*, pp. 36–44, and Hartmann, *The Homefront and Beyond*, p. 39.

31. Christides, "Women Veterans," 113.

32. Quotation attributed to Harry A. Williams of the *Los Angeles Times*, 14 May 1918; quoted in Lavine, *Circuits of Victory*, p. 271. *S&S* 1:8 (29 March 1918). See also Lavine, *Circuits of Victory*, p. 280.

33. *Report of the Overseas Committee of the War Work Council, Young Women's Christian Association* (New York: National Board, YWCA, 1920).

34. Ibid., pp. 29–30.

35. See Joanne J. Meyerowitz, *Women Adrift: Independent Wage Earners in Chicago, 1880–1930* (Chicago: University of Chicago Press, 1988), pp. 78–89; Adele Hoppock, WWI Survey, USAMHI.

36. Hoppock, WWI Survey, USAMHI. Christides, WWI Survey, USAMHI.

37. Hoppock, WWI Survey, USAMHI; Josephine Davis Gray, oral history, Miami, Fla, 3 Feb. 1991; Oleda Joure Christides, WWI Survey, USAMHI.

38. Jensen, *Price of Vigilance*, pp. 177–87; "Procedure for Handling Investigations of Civil Employees," AEF Papers, RG 120, Series 1705, Box 448; "X-92 Suspect Files," AEF Papers, RG 120, Series 1705, Boxes 449–55. It seems suspicious that in the thousands of case files I reviewed, no one was rejected and only one woman was investigated for pro-German sentiments. This raises the possibility that a separate file of rejected applicants was kept and later destroyed or that it is contained in a different set of papers. I found one vague reference to a separate file among the discussions of military intelligence procedures: "Procedure for Handling Investigations of Civil Employees," AEF Papers, RG 120, Series 1705, Box 448, refers to a "separate dossier for our files . . . for the person whose employment is disapproved," in contrast to the "general file (X-92) and index" for approved applicants.

39. "Memorandum for Chief, Intelligence Section, L. of C. Regarding the Proposed Control of Nantes and St. Nazaire," AEF Papers, RG 120, Series 1705, Box 446. Lavine, *Circuits of Victory*, pp. 327–30, 398–405; "Report of the Chief Signal Corps Officer," *War Department Annual Reports, 1919* (Washington, D.C.: Government Printing Office, 1920), esp. p. 1211.

40. Christides, "Women Veterans," 113; Putnam, *On Duty*, p. 102; Lee, *It's a Great War*, p. 208; Lavine, *Circuits of Victory*, pp. 327–28; Banker, WWI Survey, USAMHI.

41. Banker, WWI Survey, USAMHI.

42. Harry Braverman, *Labor and Monopoly Capital* (New York: Monthly Review Press, 1974); David Montgomery, *Workers' Control in America* (Cambridge, U.K.: Cambridge University Press, 1979); Maurine Weiner Greenwald, *Women, War and Work: The Impact of World War I on Women Workers in the United States* (Westport, Conn.: Greenwood Press, 1980), p. 185. See also Greenwald, chap. 5, and Norwood, *Labor's Flaming Youth*, pp. 33–40.

Notes

43. Office of Commander in Chief, AEF to Henrietta Roelofs, 21 June 1918, RG 120, Entry 2017, Office of Chief Quartermaster, Box 211.

44. Greenwald, *Women, War and Work*, p. 199.

45. "What's a Peg Count?," *195 Bulletin* (Aug. 1949), AT&T Archives.

46. Louise Barbour Papers, Schlesinger Library, Cambridge, Mass.

47. Office Regulation No. 28, 30 May 1918, and Office Regulation No. 48, 16 October 1918, RG 120, Entry 2040, Office of the Chief Signal Corps Officer, Box 101. Headquarters Commandant to Chief Ordnance Officer, 26 Dec. 1918, AEF Papers, RG 120, Entry 2006, Box 2.

48. Greenwald, *Women, War and Work*; Norwood, *Labor's Flaming Youth*.

49. *Telephone Review*, Sept. 1918, AT&T Archives; see also Lee, *It's a Great War*, pp. 208–11. Telephone operator quoted in Lavine, *Circuits of Victory*, p. 279. *Telephone Review*, May 1918, AT&T Archives. Christides, "Women Veterans," 110. Louise Barbour to "Darling Mother," 24 Nov. 1918, Louise Barbour Papers, Schlesinger Library.

50. Lee, *It's a Great War*, pp. 208–9. *Telephone Review*, July 1918, AT&T Archives. Louise Barbour to "Darling Mother," 24 Nov. 1918, Barbour Papers; Christides, "Women Veterans," 113–14.

51. Mary Lee to her mother, 1 March 1918; Lee to Guy, 14 March 1916 [incorrectly dated by author], Lee Papers, Folder 121, Schlesinger Library.

52. Memo from U.S. stenographers, 27 Sept. 1917, RG 200, National American Red Cross Papers, Commission to France, Box 852 (Folder: "Health & Welfare"). Beatrice Campbell to Col. Ames, 18 May 1919, AEF Papers, RG 120, Entry 2006, Box 2.

53. Banker, WWI Survey, USAMHI; Putnam, *On Duty*, pp. 81, 84. Also see Lee, *It's a Great War*, p. 208.

54. Helen Scriver Papers, Minnesota State Historical Society, St. Paul, Minn; Lee to father, 1 March 1918, Lee Papers, folder 121, Schlesinger Library.

55. Lee, *It's a Great War*, pp. 14–15, 20, 40, 71–72; scene with nuns, 54–56.

56. Grace Banker, WWI Survey, USAMHI.

57. "Memento of the Telephone Operating Units, Christmas 1918," gift booklet published by Army Signal Corps; *CITE* AT&T Archives. Many of the women telephone operators preserved this booklet: Barbour Papers, and Mark Hough's personal collection, Seattle, Wash.

58. Louise Barbour to Helen Carey, 19 Jan. 1939, Barbour Papers, folder 6.

5 "Compassionate Sympathizers and Active Combatants": Army Nurses in France

1. Letter quoted in National American Red Cross, *History of American Red Cross Nursing* (New York: Macmillan Co., 1922), p. 646.

2. Mary Lee, *"It's a Great War!"* (Boston: Houghton Mifflin Co., 1929), pp. 76, 80.

3. Julia Stimson, *Finding Themselves, The Letters of an American Army Chief Nurse in a British Hospital in France* (New York: Macmillan Co., 1927), p. 3.

4. Margaret H. Darrow, "French Volunteer Nursing and the Myth of War Experience in World War I," *American Historical Review* 101 (February 1996): 80–106.

5. See Burton Bledstein, *The Culture of Professionalism: The Middle Class and the Development of Higher Education* (New York: Norton, 1976).

6. Paul Starr, *The Social Transformation of American Medicine* (New York: Basic Books, 1983); Judith Leavitt and Ronald L. Numbers, eds., *Sickness and Health in America: Readings in the History of Medicine and Public Health* (Madison: University of Wisconsin Press, 1978); Susan Reverby and David Rosner, eds., *Health Care in America: Essays in Social History* (Philadel-

phia: Temple University Press, 1979); Morris J. Vogel and Charles E. Rosenberg, eds., *The Therapeutic Revolution: Essays in the Social History of American Medicine* (Philadelphia: University of Pennsylvania Press, 1979); Morris J. Vogel, *The Invention of the Modern Hospital* (Chicago: University of Chicago Press, 1980).

7. Classic studies include Lavinia Dock, *A Short History of Nursing*, 3rd ed. (New York: G. P. Putnam's Sons, 1931); Vern Bullough and Bonnie Bullough, *The Care of the Sick, the Emergence of Modern Nursing* (New York: Prodist, 1978); Philip A. Kalisch and Beatrice J. Kalisch, *The Advance of American Nursing* (Boston: Little, Brown and Co., 1978); Mary Roberts, *American Nursing: History and Interpretation* (New York: Macmillan Co., 1955). Recent contributions include Ellen Condliffe Lagemann, ed., *Nursing History: New Perspectives, New Possibilities* (New York: Teachers College Press, 1983); Susan Reverby, *Ordered to Care: The Dilemma of American Nursing, 1850–1945* (Cambridge: Cambridge University Press, 1987); Barbara Melosh, *"The Physician's Hand": Work, Culture and Conflict in American Nursing* (Philadelphia: Temple University Press, 1982); Darlene Clark Hine, *Black Women in White: Racial Conflict and Cooperation in the Nursing Profession, 1890–1950* (Bloomington: Indiana University Press, 1989).

8. Amitai Etzioni, ed., *The Semi-Professions and Their Organization* (New York: Free Press, 1969); Melosh, *The Physician's Hand*, chap. 1.

9. Roberts, *American Nursing*, pp. 137–41; *Notable American Women, 1607–1950*, Edward T. James, ed., vol. 2 (Cambridge, Mass.: Belknap Press, 1971), s. v. "Nutting, Mary Adelaide," by Virginia M. Dunbar.

10. Susan Armeny, "Organized Nurses, Women Philanthropists, and the Intellectual Bases for Cooperation among Women, 1898–1920," in *Nursing History*, ed. Lagemann, pp. 13–45; Robert Piemonte and Cindy Gurney, eds., *Highlights in the History of the Army Nurse Corps* (Washington, D.C.: U.S. Army Center of Military History, 1986). The Navy Nurse Corps was founded in 1908. See also Anne Summers, *Angels and Citizens: British Women as Military Nurses, 1854–1914* (London: Routledge and Kegan Paul, 1988).

11. On Anita McGee, see Gloria Moldow, *Women Doctors in Gilded-Age Washington* (Urbana: University of Illinois Press, 1987); *Notable American Women*, vol. 2, s. v. "McGee, Anita," by Mary R. Dearing. *Notable American Women*, vol. 1, s. v. "Delano, Jane," by Jeanette Nichols. Portia Kernodle, *The Red Cross Nurse in Action* (New York: Harper and Brothers, 1949), pp. 38–52.

12. Piemonte and Gurney, *Highlights in the History of the ANC*, pp. 14–16; *The Medical Department of the United States Army in the World War* (Washington, D.C.: Government Printing Office, 1927), vol. 13, "Army Nurse Corps," 351.

13. "Army Nurse Corps," 303–6.

14. The Treasury Department argued that nurses would technically not be on duty if they were captured, as they would be unable to carry out their nursing responsibilities; *New York Times* (hereafter *NYT*), 6 Oct. 1918; Philip A. Kalisch and Margaret Scobey, "Female Nurses in American Wars: Helplessness Suspended for the Duration," *Armed Forces in Society* 9:2 (Winter 1983): 220. Nurses were also excluded from retirement benefits, although they were entitled to the discharge bonus and discount furlough fares and were eligible for victory medals; "Army Nurse Corps," 300.

15. The regulation was borrowed from the British, but the parenthetical phrase was added to the U.S. version. U.S. Congress, House Committee on Military Affairs, *Hearings Before the House Committee on Military Affairs on Proposed Legislation Affecting the Medical Corps of the U.S. Army*, 65th Congress, 2d session, 1918 (hereafter *House Hearings on Medical Corps*). The amendments specified the areas of authority only for the chief nurse in relation to enlisted men; nurse leaders feared this limited clarification would further undermine the position of the ward nurse, since her areas of authority were not specified.

Notes

16. Under a relative rank system, nurses did not have commissions, equal pay and allowances for the equivalent rank, or "the power of command" over male officers of lower rank; "the highest officer of the Nurse Corps ranks below the lowest officer of the Medical Corps," Helen Greeley explained. Relative rank granted nurses only the name of the rank, the right to wear its insignia, and military authority to carry out their duties as delineated by law. *House Hearings on Medical Corps.* See Armeny, "Organized Nurses," 29–34, and Philip A. Kalisch, "How Army Nurses Became Officers," *Nursing Research* 25:3 (May-June 1976): 164–77.

17. Ellen DuBois, "Working Women, Class Relations, and Suffrage Militance: Harriet Stanton Blatch and the New York Woman Suffrage Movement, 1894–1909," *Journal of American History* 74 (June 1987): 34–58.

18. Testimony of Gen. Gorgas and Major W. J. Mayo, *House Hearings on Medical Corps.*

19. Reverby, *Ordered to Care,* pp. 160–64; Roberts, *American Nursing,* pp. 130–43.

20. Daniel Beaver, *Newton D. Baker and the American War Effort, 1917–1919* (Lincoln: University of Nebraska Press, 1966), pp. 88–91.

21. Adelaide Nutting's plan was probably sound, given the high rate of prewar unemployment among private-duty nurses and the huge pool of experienced, untrained nurses available for civilian work.

22. African-American nurses were finally called into service because of the influenza epidemic; Hine, *Black Women in White,* pp. 94–107.

23. *NYT,* 4 April 1918; letters to the editor: Mary Campbell Preston, 8 April 1918; from G. K. Dickinson, chair of the New Jersey State Committee on Hospital Standardization, 9 April 1918; from "A VICTIM," 12 April 1918; from Dr. F. H. Edsall, M.D., 18 May 1918. See also article quoting excerpts of a letter by Dr. Charles Grimshaw, superintendent of Roosevelt Hospital, to the acting head of the Academy of Medicine, urging short courses and practical nurse training, *NYT,* 4 April 1918.

24. *NYT,* letters to the editor from Dr. Charles Grimshaw, 4 April 1918; from G. K. Dickinson, 9 April 1918; editorials, 4 and 5 April 1918; letter to the editor from John Cabot, M.D., 4 May 1918. Letter of 28 May 1918, quoted by Kernodle, *Red Cross Nurse,* p. 139.

25. Natalie Boymel Kampen, "Before Florence Nightingale: A Prehistory of Nursing in Painting and Sculpture," in *Images of Nurses,* ed. Anne Hudson Jones (Philadelphia: University of Pennsylvania Press, 1988), pp. 6–39.

26. In *Readers' Guide to Periodical Literature* for 1914–1918, the category "European War—Women and the War" contains 118 listings; of those, approximately 32 are about U.S. women as auxiliary workers, and only one is specifically about nurses. Under the heading "nurses," only a handful of articles appear, almost exclusively related to the administrative problems of recruitment.

27. Rumors are documented in dozens of letters written to the American Red Cross Bureau of Nursing by women responsible for nurse recruitment and by concerned citizens. The letters document 43 separate rumors, only one of which made any reference to canteen workers. Rumors about nurses were sufficiently widespread that in November 1921 Senator Watson of Georgia called for an investigation. National American Red Cross Papers (hereafter NARC Papers), RG 200, Box 95 (Folders: "Nurses—Brutal Treatment of by Germans" and "Nurses Charged with Immorality"), National Archives, Washington, D.C. See also Lee, *It's a Great War,* p. 70.

28. NARC Papers, RG 200, Box 85 (Folder: "Nurses—Brutal Treatment"). See Kathy Peiss, *Cheap Amusements: Working Women and Leisure in Turn-of-the-century New York* (Philadelphia: Temple University Press, 1986), pp. 50, 163–84.

29. NARC Papers, RG 200, Box 85 (Folder: "Nurses—Brutal Treatment").

30. NARC Papers, RG 200, Box 85 (Folder: "Nurses—Brutal Treatment"). James Morgan

Read's classic study, *Atrocity Propaganda, 1914–1919* (New Haven, Conn.: Yale University Press, 1941), indicates that such atrocity tales were not espionage but homegrown propaganda generated by the warring nations to discredit the enemy. The nurse rumors circulated in the United States were closely linked in theme and tone to the anti-German propaganda produced in abundance by the Allies from the first months of the war; for example, the mutilation stories are clearly descendants of French, British, and Belgian propaganda about the enemy "Hun" chopping off the hands of children or the breasts of women during the "rape" of Belgium. Read discusses two other incidents that are possible sources for these rumors in the United States: British press reports on the capture, mutilation, and execution by the Germans of nurse Grace Humet, which turned out to be a hoax, and the actual execution of Edith Cavell, a British nurse who helped French and English soldiers escape from Belgium. It is interesting to note that, at least during the war, Cavell's death was cast as a "mutilated nurse story" and not as a tale of female courage, ingenuity, martyrdom, or humanitarianism. See also Arthur Ponsonby, *Falsehood in War-Time* (New York: E. P. Dutton and Co., 1928), esp. chap. 6.

31. Read, *Atrocity Propaganda*. Themes of the powerful nurse are developed in *Images of Nurses*, ed. Jones, especially Leslie A. Fiedler, "Images of the Nurse in Fiction and Popular Culture," 100–12, and Barbara Melosh, "'A Special Relationship': Nurses and Patients in Twentieth Century Short Stories," 128–49.

32. On rumors of sexual promiscuity in the Women's Army Corps during World War II, see D'Ann Campbell, *Women at War with America: Private Lives in a Patriotic Era* (Princeton, N.J.: Princeton University Press, 1984), p. 37; Leisa D. Meier, *Creating G.I. Jane: Sexuality and Power in the Women's Army Corps During World War II* (New York: Columbia University Press, 1996).

33. Irene Wilkinson O'Connor, World War I Survey, U.S. Army Military History Institute, Carlisle Barracks, Pa. (hereafter USAMHI).

34. *American Journal of Nursing* 18:12 (September 1918): 1182; Mildred Brown, WWI Survey, USAMHI.

35. For the concept of "work culture," see Barbara Melosh, *The Physician's Hand*, pp. 5–6; also see Susan Porter Benson, *Counter Cultures: Saleswomen, Managers, and Customers in American Department Stores, 1890–1940* (Urbana: University of Illinois Press, 1986).

36. *A History of U.S. Army Base Hospital No. 19* (Rochester), p. 25. Sophie Burns, chief nurse of Mobile Hospital No. 9, in appendix to Julia Stimson, "History of Nursing Activities, A.E.F. on the Western Front during War Period, May 8, 1917-May 31, 1919," p. 13, unpublished report, NARC Papers, RG 200, Box 850, file: Bureau of Nursing (hereafter "History of Nursing Activities, AEF"). Maude Crawford, ANC nurse with Base Hospital No. 7, in appendix to Stimson, "History of Nursing Activities, A.E.F.," p. 11. See also Clarke, *Evacuation 114*, pp. 58–59; Alice Kelley, in appendix to Stimson, "History of Nursing Activities, A.E.F.," p. 23; Elizabeth Campbell Bickford, questionnaire, WWI Survey, USAMHI.

37. The original plan for the base hospitals provided for fifty nurses and twenty-five nurses' aids. When the first base hospitals were mobilized for overseas service, the aids were eliminated and the nursing staff increased to sixty-five. Soon this was found to be inadequate and one hundred nurses became the operating figure. The 133 base hospitals, which were grouped into enormous hospital centers, constituted the backbone of AEF medical service. Mesves, the largest center, had a daily capacity of twenty-five thousand patients between November and December of 1918 and several thousand staff. On its peak day, the entire system cared for 193,026 hospitalized soldiers. *The Medical Department of the United States Army in the World War* (Washington, D.C.: Government Printing Office, 1927); vol. 2, "Administration, American Expeditionary Force," pp. 127, 473–76, 522, 629–748; vol. 13, "Army Nurse Corps," p. 333. Stimson, "History of Nursing Activities, AEF."

38. Women doctors did serve under the Red Cross and other relief organizations, and some worked as ambulance drivers or volunteer nurse's aids. Mary Roth Walsh, *Doctors Wanted, No Women Need Apply* (New Haven, Conn.: Yale University Press, 1977), pp. 218–19; Regina Morantz-Sanchez, *Sympathy and Science: Women Physicians in American Medicine* (New York: Oxford University Press, 1985), p. 291. Lettie Gavin, *American Women in World War I: They Also Served* (Niwat, Colo.: University Press of Colorado, 1997) covers this subject fully in chap. 7.

39. *Medical Department in World War*, vol. 2, p. 483.

40. *Concerning Base Hospital No. 5* (1920), Harvard Medical Archives, Countway Library, Boston, Mass. This memento for the unit, written by enlisted men, contained a brief, often humorous entry for each of the nurses, enlisted men, and officers; nurses' nicknames are given with their entries; see pp. 65–80. Oral histories of World War I nurses confirm this picture of informality and joking among nurses and enlisted men; Ethel Pierce, oral history, Holyoke Soldiers' Home, Holyoke, Mass., May 1990; Alma Bloom, oral history, Soldiers' Home, Chelsea, Mass., May 1989. See also Frederick A. Pottle, *Stretchers* (New Haven, Conn.: Yale University Press, 1929), a first-hand account of war service by a Sanitary corpsman. *History of the Pennsylvania Hospital Unit in the Great War* (New York: Paul B. Hoeber, 1921), pp. 111–22.

41. Carrie Hall to family, 7 Nov. 1917, Carrie Hall Papers, Schlesinger Library, Cambridge, Mass. Ultimately Hall found that a forceful male administrative head was the only solution to this problem at her hospital; see her letters to George Hall, 24 Mar. 1918, and Sara Parsons, 24 Aug. 1917. Helen Hoy Greeley, "Rank for Nurses," *Annual Report of the National League of Nursing Education* (1918), p. 300.

42. *House Hearings on Medical Corps*. See also Grace E. Allison, "What the War Has Taught Us About Nursing Education," *American Journal of Nursing* 19 (August 1919): 835.

43. Sara E. Parsons, "Impressions and Conclusions Based on Experience Abroad by Overseas Nurses," *American Journal of Nursing* 19 (August 1919): 832–33. See also Helen Hoy Greeley, "Rank for Nurses," *American Journal of Nursing* 19 (August 1919): 843; Stimson, *Finding Themselves*, p. 60.

44. Both quotations are from a camp magazine published irregularly by the corpsmen of Base Hospital No. 5: *The Vanguard*, Christmas 1917, p. 24; *The Vanguard* 11:1, p. 149; in Carrie Hall Papers, *Concerning Base Hospital No. 5*, pp. 65–80.

45. *House Hearings on Medical Corps*.

46. Pottle, *Stretchers*, pp. 122–23.

47. Sara Parsons, quoted in Greeley, "Rank for Nurses," 851. For doctors' praise of nurses' valor, see W. M. L. Coplin, quoted in *American Red Cross Base Hospital No. 38 in the World War* (Philadelphia: E. A. Wright, 1923), pp. 88–99. Carrie Hall to Annie J. Hall, 2 Oct. 1917. Hall evidently carried a feud with Dr. Harvey Cushing from the Peter Bent Brigham Hospital to their base hospital in France; see her letters to Lilla, 2 Dec. 1917 and n.d. (1918?); to Sara Parsons, 15 Oct. 1917. Pierce, oral history.

48. Greeley, "Rank for Nurses," 851–52, includes testimony on this topic by Sara E. Parsons, Grace E. Allison, and Amy M. Hilliard. See also Julia Stimson, "Report of Trip Taken by the Chief Nurse of A.R.C. on September 12, 13 and 14th, 1918," NARC Papers, RG 200, Box 850, "A.R.C. Commission to France." On officers' disregard for nurses, see Lee, *It's a Great War*, pp. 39, 63, 64, 68, 82. *House Hearings on Medical Corps*.

49. Nola B. Uttley, WWI Survey, USAMHI.

50. Shirley Millard, *I Saw Them Die* (New York: Harcourt, Brace and Co., 1936), pp. 36–39; Pierce, oral history. See also Lee, *It's a Great War*, pp. 117, 145–46, for references to sexual harassment of women at the front.

51. Catherine MacKinnon, *Sexual Harassment of Working Women* (New Haven, Conn.:

Yale University Press, 1978); L. Farley, *Sexual Shakedown* (New York: McGraw-Hill, 1978); Elizabeth A. Stanko, "Keeping Women In and Out of Line: Sexual Harassment and Occupational Segregation," in *Gender Segregation at Work*, ed. Sylvia Walby (Milton Keynes, U.K.: Open University Press, 1988), pp. 91–99.

52. *Concerning Base Hospital No. 5*, pp. 65–80. In this roster of nurses, fifty-six of the women have nicknames listed; of those, thirty-four are men's names or unisex names. Millard, *I Saw Them Die*, p. 56; Marion Adams, questionnaire, WWI Survey, USAMHI; Stimson, *Finding Themselves*, p. 74.

53. Florence Blanchfield Papers, Box 1, Folder 7, Nursing Archives, Mugar Memorial Library, Boston University, Boston, Mass.

54. Marion Adams, Grace Williams, Annette Munro, Emma Peterson, questionnaires, WWI Survey, USAMHI.

55. Reverby, *Ordered to Care*, pp. 60–65; see also Melosh, *The Physician's Hand*, pp. 47–67.

56. Annette Munro, questionnaire, WWI Survey, USAMHI; Stimson, *Finding Themselves*, p. 86.

57. Florence Blanchfield papers, Nursing Archives. Blanchfield was later promoted to colonel in the U.S. Army, and served as chief of the Army Nurse Corps during World War II, 1943–47. Carrie Hall to family, 6 June 1917, and Carrie Hall to Sara E. P[arsons?], 14 Sept. 1917, Hall Papers.

58. Some women also asked that nurses be eligible for promotion in the postwar military. *House Hearings on Medical Corps.*

59. DuBois, "Working Women, Class Relations"; Nancy Cott, *The Grounding of Modern Feminism* (New Haven, Conn.: Yale University Press, 1987), esp. chap. 1.

60. In "Female Nurses in American Wars," Kalisch and Scobey argue that "large-scale combat engenders many dangers other than enemy-inflicted wounds" and that "combat situations" should be defined to include disease, deprivation, psychological and physical strain, and exposure to bombing and gas; p. 216.

61. See Elizabeth Campbell Bickford, questionnaire, WWI Survey, USAMHI; Maude Crawford and Alice Kelley, appendix to Stimson, "History of Nursing Activities, A.E.F.," pp. 11, 23; Millard, *I Saw Them Die*, p. 21; Carolyn W. Clarke, *Evacuation 114* (Boston: Hudson Printing Co., 1919), p. 28, in Carolyn Clarke Goodsell Papers, Petersham Historical Society, Petersham, Mass.

62. *Carry On*, 10:1 (Feb. 1931); Marjorie Reynolds, clippings from WWI scrapbook, Rare Books Collection, Countway Medical Library, Boston, Mass.; *NYT*, 17 Sept. 1917; Sigrid Jorgensen, report included in appendix to Stimson, "History of Nursing Activities, A.E.F.," pp. 20–21; Julia Stimson to Clara Noyes, 19 July 1918, NARC Papers, Box 850, File: "Bureau of Nursing, Reports."

63. AEF deaths were 116,516: more than sixty-two thousand from disease and more than fifty thousand in battle. *Medical Department in World War*, vol. 15, p. 1183.

64. Stimson, "History of Nursing Activities, A.E.F."; Grace Williams, questionnaire, WWI Survey, USAMHI.

65. Stimson, "History of Nursing Activities, A.E.F."; NARC Papers, RG 200, Box 411 (Folder: "Nurses Who Died in War Service").

66. Alice S. Kelley, report on shock team work, included as an appendix to Stimson, "History of Nursing Activities, A.E.F.," p. 24; Millard, *I Saw Them Die*, pp. 70–71; Carrie Hall to George, 9 Sept. 1917, Carrie Hall Papers; Stimson, *Finding Themselves*, p. 86; Clarke, *Evacuation 114*, pp. 13–14.

67. Sigrid Jorgensen, appendix to Stimson, "History of Nursing Activities, A.E.F.," p. 16; Stimson, "History of Nursing Activities, A.E.F.," p. 24.

68. Elizabeth Campbell Bickford, questionnaire, WWI Survey, USAMHI.

Notes

69. Pottle, *Stretchers*, pp. 155–56.

70. Nearly thirty thousand U.S. soldiers in Europe were admitted to the hospital for neuropsychiatric disease; *Medical Department of U.S. Army*, vol. 10, "Neuropsychiatry," p. 153. See also Elaine Showalter, "Rivers and Sassoon: The Inscription of Male Gender Anxieties," in *Behind the Lines: Gender and the Two World Wars*, ed. Margaret Higonnet, Jane Jenson, Sonya Michel, and Margaret Collins Weitz (New Haven, Conn.: Yale University Press, 1987), pp. 61–69.

71. Stimson, *Finding Themselves*, p. 41; Pottle, *Stretchers*, pp. 117–18; Theresa Muller to Aunt Rose, 20 July 1918; Muller to her sister, 27 Nov. 1918; Muller Papers, Nursing Archives, Boston University.

72. Stimson, "History of Nursing Activities, A.E.F.," pp. 8–9; Pierce, oral history.

73. Millard, *I Saw Them Die*; Stimson, *Finding Themselves*; Roberta Love Tayloe, *Combat Nurse: A Journal of World War Two* (Santa Barbara, Calif.: Fithian Press, 1988); Lynda Van Devanter, *Home Before Morning* (New York: Warner Books, 1984); Kathryn Marshall, *In the Combat Zone: An Oral History of American Women in Vietnam, 1966–1975* (Boston: Little Brown, 1987).

74. Clarke, *Evacuation 114*, p. 30; Maude Crawford, appendix to Stimson, "History of Nursing Activities, A.E.F.," p. 11; Millard, *I Saw Them Die*, pp. 79, 80; Stimson, *Finding Themselves*, pp. 78, 81, 210; see also Carrie Hall to brother, 14 Oct. 1917, Hall Papers. Lee, *It's a Great War*, p. 191; Millard, *I Saw Them Die*, p. 12.

75. Stimson, *Finding Themselves*, pp. 43, 156–57, 216, 217; Jorgensen, quoted in Stimson, "History of Nursing Activities, A.E.F.," p. 17.

76. Clarke, *Evacuation 114*, p. 30; Maude Crawford, in appendix to Stimson, "History of Nursing Activities, A.E.F.," p. 12.

77. Elizabeth Campbell Bickford, questionnaire, WWI Survey, USAMHI. Paul Fussell argues that "the inadequacy of language itself to convey the facts about trench warfare is one of the motifs of all who wrote about the war," although Fussell only analyzes the writing of male military personnel; Paul Fussell, The *Great War and Modern Memory (New York: Oxford University Press, 1975),* p. 170.

78. For a provocative discussion of the role of memory and literary convention in war nurses' portrayal of caring for soldiers, see Alice Fahs, "The Civil War and the Construction of the Meaning of Work: Northern Civil War Nurses' Reminiscences," paper presented at the Berkshire Conference on the History of Women, June 1990.

79. Ethel Pierce, oral history; Millard, *I Saw Them Die*, p. 15; Lee, *It's a Great War*, p. 192; *War Nurse: The True Story of a Woman Who Lived, Loved and Suffered on the Western Front* (New York: Cosmopolitan Books, 1930), pp. 46, 58–59.

80. Compare with Elaine Scarry, *The Body in Pain* (New York: Oxford University Press, 1985).

81. Ethel Pierce, oral history; Stimson, *Finding Themselves*, p. 93; Millard, *I Saw Them Die*, p. 14.

82. Stimson, *Finding Themselves*, p. 152; Carrie Hall to "my dear people" (family), 6 June 1917, Hall Papers.

83. Alice Kelley, in Stimson, "History of Nursing Activities, A.E.F.," p. 24.

84. Millard, *I Saw Them Die*, pp. 30–31; Sophie Jevne Winton, Ruth Bennett Carr, and Elizabeth Bickford Campbell, questionnaires, WWI Survey, USAMHI.

85. In "The Double Helix," Margaret Higonnet and Patrice Higonnet argue that the experience of war "precedes and long outlasts formal hostilities"; see *Behind the Lines*, ed. Higonnet et al., pp. 45–47. See also Sherna Berger Gluck, *Rosie the Riveter Revisited: Women, the War and Social Change* (Boston: Twayne Publishers, 1987).

86. Ethel Pierce, oral history; Millard, *I Saw Them Die*, p. 110.

6 Serving Uncle Sam: The Meaning of Women's Wartime Service

1. Address of U.S. President on Woman Suffrage, Senate Document 284, 65th Congress, 2d session, 1918 (Washington, D.C.: Government Printing Office, 1918).

2. Josephine Daskam Bacon, "Uncle Sam's Niece—and Yours!", *Colliers Magazine* 61 (18 May 1918): 11; Charlotte Light Chilson and Ruth Anna Riddle White, questionnaires, World War I Survey, U.S. Army Military History Institute, Carlisle Barracks, Pa. (hereafter USAMHI).

3. Emily N. Blair, quoted in "American Women's Vast War Work as Revealed by an Official Report," *Literary Digest* 66 (21 Aug. 1920): 54–55.

4. *The United States Army in the World War, 1917–1919*, vol. 12, "Reports of the Commander-in-Chief, Staff Sections and Services" (Washington, D.C.: Center of Military History, U.S. Army, 1991), p. 70. Speech of Major General Helmick, n. d. (c. 1919), Y.M.C.A. Armed Services, World War I, AS 26, Archives of the Young Men's Christian Association of the United States, Saint Paul, Minn. (hereafter YMCA Archives).

5. War Department Annual Reports, 1919, vol. 1, pt. 1, "Report of Chief Signal Corps Officer" (Washington, D.C.: Government Printing Office, 1920), pp. 1245, 1421. Letter from Merritte Ireland quoted in *History of American Red Cross Nursing* (New York: Macmillan Co., 1922), p. 984. Also see War Department Annual Reports, 1919, vol. 1, pt. 3, "Report of the Surgeon General" (Washington, D.C.: Government Printing Office, 1920), pp. 3013–6; "Report of the YMCA Investigation," RG 120, Entry 445, Box 3462, National Archives, Washington, D.C.

6. Speech of Major General Helmick, n. d. (c. 1919), AS 26, YMCA Archives. Theodore Roosevelt made this point in similar terms: "In this new world women are to stand on an equal footing with men, in ways and to an extent never hitherto dreamed of." But he hastened to add, "equality of right does not mean identity of function." Theodore Roosevelt, foreword to Harriot Stanton Blatch, *Mobilizing Woman-Power* (New York: The Woman's Press, 1917), pp. 5–10.

7. Elaine Tyler May introduces the term "gender containment" to describe a convergence of family policy and foreign policy during the Cold War, which served conservative, patriarchal interests; May, *Homeward Bound: American Families in the Cold War Era* (New York: Basic Books, 1988), pp. 13–14.

8. YMCA, *Service With Fighting Men* (New York: Association Press, 1922), vol. 1, pp. 103–5; Helen Ives Gilchrist, "AEF YMCA Women's Work in the World War," unpublished report, p. 44, AS 26, YMCA Archives; Newton D. Baker, "Invisible Armor," speech to the National Conference of War Camps Community Service, 23 Oct. 1917, reprinted in Baker, *Frontiers of Freedom* (New York: George H. Doran, 1918), pp. 94–95; Nancy Bristow, *Making Men Moral: Social Engineering During the Great War* (New York: New York University Press, 1996), chap. 1.

9. Helen Ives Gilchrist, "Women's Work in the World War," unpublished manuscript, p. 110, and "Reports, clippings, women's work," AS 26, YMCA Archives.

10. Leisa D. Meyer, *Creating GI Jane: Sexuality and Power in the Women's Army Corps During World War II* (New York: Columbia University Press, 1996), chap. 2; D'Ann Campbell, *Women at War with America:Private Lives in a Patriotic Era* (Cambridge, Mass.: Harvard University Press, 1984), chap. 1.

11. Klaus Theweleit, *Male Fantasies*, vol. 1, trans. Stephen Conway (Minneapolis: University of Minnesota Press, 1987); Cynthia Enloe, *Does Khaki Become You: The Militarisation of Women's Lives* (Boston,: South End Press, 1983); Leila Rupp, *Mobilizing Women for War: German and American Propaganda, 1939–1945* (Princeton, N.J.: Princeton University Press, 1978); Jean Bethke Elshtain, *Women and War* (New York: Basic Books, 1987).

Notes

12. Memo from Intelligence Officer to Soldiers and Officers of Base Section No. 7, n. d., AEF Papers, RG 120, Series 1705, Box 447, National Archives, Washington, D.C.

13. Evangeline Booth and Grace Hill, *The War Romance of the Salvation Army* (Philadelphia: J. B. Lippincott, 1919), pp. 174–77; see also p. 79.

14. *Stars and Stripes* 1:5 (8 March 1918) (hereafter *S&S*); poem by 1st Lieut. Fairfax Downey.

15. Elshtain, *Women and War*, pp. 56–75.

16. Margarethe Cammermeyer, with Chris Fisher, *Serving in Silence* (New York: Viking Press, 1994), p. 77.

17. *History of American Red Cross Nursing*, pp. 310–11.

18. Ibid., pp. 984–88.

19. Sandra M. Gilbert, "Soldier's Heart: Literary Men, Literary Women, and the Great War," in *Behind the Lines: Gender and the Two World Wars*, ed. Margaret Randolph Higonnet, Jane Jenson, Sonya Michel, and Margaret Collins Weitz (New Haven, Conn.: Yale University Press, 1987), pp. 197–226.

20. Philip Kalisch, "How Army Nurses Became Officers," *Nursing Research* 25 (May-June 1976): 164–77; Susan Armeny, "Organized Nurses, Women Philanthropists, and the Intellectual Bases for Cooperation Among Women, 1898–1920," in *Nursing History: New Perspectives, New Possibilities*, ed. Ellen Condliffe Lagemann (New York: Teachers College Press, 1983), pp. 13–45; and *History of Red Cross Nursing*, pp. 1064–76.

21. "Report of the YMCA Investigation," RG 120, Entry 445, Box 3462, National Archives; Memo of Marguerite Cockett, Biographical File A, YMCA Archives. Gilchrist, "Women's Work in the World War," p. 110, and Clippings, "Reports, Clippings, Women's Work," AS 26, YMCA Archives. Mortimer Schiff to Col. Cutler, 8 Jan. 1919, Box 335 (Cutler correspondence, folder: "Schiff"), and (anonymous) Memo to Col. Cutler, 12 Sept. 1918, Box 329 (Cutler Correspondence, folder "misc."), Jewish Welfare Board—Army-Navy Division, American Jewish Historical Society, Waltham, Mass.

22. "A Home Room in the 'Y'," typed manuscript (no author, n. d.), "Reports, Clippings, Women's Work," AS 26, YMCA Archives; see also "Equal Status of Men and Women Secretaries," in Gilchrist, "Women's Work," p. 48. "C. Howard Hopkins, *History of the Y.M.C.A. in North America* (New York: Association Press, 1951), pp. 720–22; *YMCA Yearbook and Official Rosters, 1962* (New York: Association Press, 1962), pp. 7–8; also Gilchrist, "Women's Work," p. 68.

23. Jewish Welfare Board, *First Annual Report* (New York: n.p., 1919), pp. 14–15.

24. Shirley Millard, *I Saw Them Die* (New York: Harcourt, Brace and Co., 1936), pp. 4–5; Elizabeth Walker Black, *Hospital Heroes* (New York: Charles Scribner's Sons, 1919), p. 19.

25. *A Red Triangle Girl in France* (New York: George Doran Co., 1918), pp. v, viii, 93, 70.

26. Mildred Byers, questionnaire and letter, WWI Survey, USAMHI.

27. Campbell, *Women at War with America*; Anne Summers, *Angels and Citizens: British Women as Military Nurses, 1854–1914* (London: Routledge and Kegan Paul, 1988).

28. Baldwin, *Canteening Overseas*, p. 17; Poem by Nina Macdonald, quoted in Sandra Gilbert, "Soldier's Heart: Literary Men, Literary Women, and the Great War," *Signs* 8 (Spring 1983): 425; Diaries of Florence Turkington, Turkington Papers, and Margaret Sheldon, 13 Sept. 1917, RG 20.3, Salvation Army Archives, New York.

29. *Uncensored Letters of a Canteen Girl* (New York: Henry Holt and Co., 1920), pp. 262–63. YMCA; women's letters; Salvation Army Archives. Millard, *I Saw Them Die*. Katherine Grinnell Prest, *One of 9000* (Boston: Marshall Jones Co., 1934), pp. 28–9; for another story of "unskirting," see Ona M. Rounds, *Buck Privates on Parnassus* (Boston: Meader Publishing Co., 1933), p. 212. "Report on GFWC Unit," AS 26, YMCA Archives. Wearing pants at the front was pioneered by Dr. Mary Livermore; see Elizabeth D. Leonard, *Yankee*

Women: Gender Battles in the Civil War (New York: Norton, 1994). Black, *Hospital Heroes*, pp. 19–22.

30. Eleanor Kilham, *Letters from France, 1915–1919* (Salem, Mass.: privately printed, 1941), and Baldwin, *Canteeing Overseas*, pp. 43, 61.

31. Elsie Janis, *The Big Show: My Six Months with the American Expeditionary Forces* (New York: Cosmopolitan Books, 1919), pp. 72–73.

32. *Uncensored Letters of a Canteen Girl*, p. 261. Margaret Hall, typescript journal, p. 178, Margaret Hall Papers, Massachusetts Historical Society, Boston (hereafter MHS).

33. For examples in twentieth-century warfare, see John Dower, *War without Mercy* (New York: Pantheon Books, 1986), pp. 63–66, and Christian Appy, *Working-Class War: American Combat Soldiers and Vietnam* (Chapel Hill: University of North Carolina Press, 1993), pp. 265–7.

34. Isabel Anderson, *Zigzagging* (Boston: Houghton Mifflin, 1918), p. xi.

35. Claire M. Tylee, *The Great War and Women's Consciousness, Images of Militarism and Womanhood in Women's Writings, 1914–64* (Iowa City: University of Iowa Press, 1990), pp. 93–102; Ellen LaMotte, *The Backwash of War*, 2nd ed. (London: Puttnam, 1934). I am grateful to an anonymous reviewer for Cornell University Press for pointing out the relevance of LaMotte to this discussion.

36. Hall Papers, MHS. "Report of the American Women's Club, July-Sept. 1920," YWCA Records Files Collection, Reel 154, WWI Overseas Commission, National Board Archives, YWCA, New York.

37. Tylee, *Great War*.

38. Record Book of Conferences of the Women's Section of Overseas Workers of the Y.M.C.A., AS 23, YMCA Archives.

39. Black, *Hospital Heroes*, p. 15; Mary Josephine Booth Papers, Illinois State Historical Society.

40. Deland, "Amazing Exodus," clipping, Cornelia Cree, WWI Survey, USAMHI.

41. Arthur Barbeau and Floreete Henri, *The Unknown Soldiers: Black American Troops in World War I* (Philadelphia: Temple University Press, 1974).

42. Rounds, *Buck Privates*, pp. 209–10, 212. On the ambivalent relationship of women veterans of the Vietnam war with male Vietnam veterans, see Kathryn Marshall, *In the Combat Zone: An Oral History of American Women in Vietnam, 1966–1975* (Boston: Little, Brown Co., 1987); Linda Van Devanter, *Home Before Morning* (New York: Beaufort Books, 1983); Keith Walker, *A Piece of My Heart: The Stories of Twenty-Six Women Who Served in Vietnam* (New York: Ballantine Books, 1987).

43. Ellis Hawley, *The Great War and the Search for a Modern Order: A History of the American People and Their Institutions, 1917–1933* (New York: St. Martin's Press, 1979), pp. 80–99. See also John Kenneth Galbraith, *The Great Crash*, 3rd ed. (Boston: Houghton Mifflin, 1972); Albert Romasco, *The Poverty of Abundance: Hoover, the Nation, the Depression* (London: Oxford University Press, 1965). But cf. Frank Stricker, "Affluence for Whom?—Another Look at Prosperity and the Working Classes in the 1920s," *Labor History* 24 (Winter 1983): 5–33, and in *The Labor History Reader*, ed. Daniel Leab (Urbana: University of Illinois Press, 1985), pp. 288–316.

44. Lydia Oden Linge, questionnaire, WWI Survey, USAMHI.

45. For "typical cases" of servicewomen aided by the WOSL and the results of the League's disability survey, see *Carry On* 9 (August 1930): 50, and 10 (November 1931): 3–6.

46. Helene M. Sillia, *A History of the Women's Overseas Service League* (n.p.: WOSL, 1978), p. 8; this figure includes both AEF nurses and nurses who served stateside.

47. U.S. Veterans' Bureau, *Annual Report of the Director* (Washington, D.C.: Government Printing Office, 1930), p. 10; *Carry On* 12 (November 1933): 13.

48. Reverby, *Ordered to Care*, pp. 110, 176–77; Barbara Melosh, *"The Physician's Hand"*:

Notes

Work, Culture and Conflict in American Nursing (Philadelphia: Temple University Press, 1982), pp. 77–79, 87.

49. American Medical Association, "Hospital Service in the U.S., 1929," reprinted from the *Journal of the American Medical Association* 92 (30 March 1929): 1043–54. Gustavus A. Weber and Laurence F. Schmeckebier, *The Veterans' Administration: Its History, Activities and Organization* (Washington, D.C.: The Brookings Institution, 1934). U.S. Veterans' Bureau, *Annual Report of the Director* (Washington, D.C.: Government Printing Office, 1925), p. 359; *Annual Report*, 1930, p. 15.

50. Bickford, questionnaire, letters and newsletter, and Nola Uttley, questionnaire and clippings, WWI Survey, USAMHI. Letter from Clara Bouwhuis to Congresswoman Edith Nourse Rogers, 7 Feb. 1945, Box 1, Folder 16, Edith Nourse Rogers Papers, Schlesinger Library, Cambridge, Mass. Robert Piemonte and Cindy Gurney, eds., *Highlights in the History of the Army Nurse Corps* (Washington, D.C.: U.S. Army Center of Military History, 1987), p. 11. U.S. Veterans' Bureau, *Annual Report*, 1925, p. 359. Reverby, *Ordered to Care*, p. 105. See for example hiring and referral patterns among one group of nurse-veteran friends; papers of the Women's Overseas Service League—St. Paul Unit, Minnesota State Historical Society, Saint Paul (hereafter St. Paul WOSL, MSHS). Nurse veteran quoted in Melosh, *Physician's Hand*, p. 86.

51. Barbara Melosh, *Physician's Hand*, "Public Health Nurses and the 'Gospel of Health,' 1920–1955," pp. 113–57. See also M. Louise Fitzpatrick, *The National Organization for Public Health Nursing, 1912–1952: Development of a Practice Field* (New York: National League for Nursing History, 1975).

52. *Carry On* 10 (May 1931): 63. Munro, WWI Survey, USAMHI; Sillia, *WOSL History*, p. 12. For information on postwar employment of nurse-veterans, see rosters and clippings in papers on St. Paul WOSL, MSHS.

53. The Bell system had 192,000 employees in 1917, 358,500 in 1929, and 244,800 in 1933; *Bell System Statistical Manual* (1946), p. 701, AT&T Archives. Similar figures are given in John N. Schacht, *The Making of Telephone Unionism, 1920–1947* (New Brunswick, N.J.: Rutgers University Press, 1985), p. 37.

54. Kathleen Hyatt McKee, questionnaire, WWI Survey, USAMHI. On the elaboration of management structure in the Bell system after the war, see Schacht, *Making of Telephone Unionism*, pp. 28–36. For the disparity between the white-collar status of telephone work and its blue-collar working conditions, see Stephen Norwood, *Labor's Flaming Youth: Telephone Operators and Worker Militancy, 1878–1923* (Urbana: University of Illinois Press, 1990), pp. 47–48. Laura M. Smith, "Opportunities for Women in the Bell System," *Bell Telephone Quarterly* 11 (January 1932): 34–49. *Bell System Statistical Manual* (1946), p. 706; according to the "Distribution of Employees by Principal Occupational Groups," 14 percent of the female work force held managerial positions in 1928. About half of Signal Corps veterans had advanced into supervisory posts, however. Of approximately seventy-five telephone veterans who responded to a questionnaire sent out by AT&T in 1929, thirty-six worked outside the home and nineteen were employed by the telecommunications industry; nine veterans worked as rank-and-file telephone operators, while ten had attained supervisory or managerial positions; Louise Barbour Papers, Schlesinger Library, Cambridge, Mass.

55. *Carry On* 10 (February 1931). The survey of Signal Corps veterans revealed a similar pattern. In addition to the 19 Bell system employees, 17 women reported an occupation outside of the telephone industry. Two went into male-dominated, professional fields. The rest were in female semiprofessions or service jobs: four teachers, three clerical workers, three saleswomen in retail, two dressmakers, and three miscellaneous; Barbour Papers.

56. Robert O'Brien to Mary Lee, 14 June and 26 June, 1929; Lee to Robert O'Brien, 23 June 1929, Mary Lee papers, unprocessed collection, Box 11, Folder 377, Schlesinger Library. *Carry On* 10 (February 1931).

57. *Carry On* 7 (May 1928): 24; *Carry On* 7 (August 1928): 10; *Carry On* 8 (August 1979): 40; *Carry On* 11 (May 1932): 58; *Carry On*, 14 (November 1935); *Carry On* 10 (August 1931): 25–26.

58. Helen Hoy Greeley, "Rank for Nurses," *American Journal of Nursing* 19 (August 1919): 840, 845–46.

59. Mattie E. Treadwell, *The Women's Army Corps* (Washington, D.C.: Office of the Chief of Military History, Department of the Army, 1954), pp. 1–9.

60. Jean Ebbert and Marie-Beth Hall, *Crossed Currents: Navy Women from World War I to Tailhook* (Washington, D.C.: Brassey's, 1993), pp. 16–21.

61. Bristow, *Making Men Moral*, chap. 6. War Department, *Report of the Conference on Moral and Religious Work in the Army* (Washington, D.C.: Government Printing Office, 1923), pp. 1–2.

62. Sillia, *WOSL History*, p. 8; *Carry On* 7 (May 1928): 60.

63. Sillia, *WOSL History*, pp. 219–21.

64. Ibid., pp. 15–16.

65. *Carry On* 12 (November 1933).

66. Nancy Cott, *The Grounding of Modern Feminism* (New Haven, Conn.: Yale University Press, 1987), esp. pp. 97–99 on the Women's Joint Congressional Committee.

67. *Carry On* 13 (February 1934), 11 (May 1932). When navy women attempted to form an organization called Women Veterans of World War I during the 1930s, the WOSL challenged their legitimacy and pressured General Pershing to disavow his initial endorsement of the new group.

68. Patrick J. Kelly, *Creating a National Home: Building the Veteran's Welfare State, 1860–1900* (Cambridge, Mass.: Harvard University Press, 1997), esp. definition of "martial citizenship" on p. 2. Carol Pateman, "The Patriarchal Welfare State," in *Democracy and the Welfare State*, ed. Amy Gutman (Princeton, N.J.: Princeton University Press, 1988), pp. 231–60.

69. Unpublished typescript of radio address, St. Paul WOSL, MSHS.

70. Helen Carey to Louise Barbour, n. d. (1938), Barbour Papers.

71. See the collection of papers gathered by Merle Egan Anderson, a Signal Corps veteran of World War I who led the campaign for military status, and left to Mark Hough, an attorney in Seattle, Wash., who provided invaluable assistance to the Signal Corps veterans.

72. U.S. Congress, House Committee on Armed Services, Hearing before the Military Personnel Subcommittee . . . on Women in the Military, 96th Congress, 1st and 2nd sessions, 1980.

Index

Page references followed by f indicate illustrations. References followed by t or n indicate tables or endnotes, respectively.

Auxiliary workers (*continued*)
51–76; investigation of, 67–68, Jewish, 30–31; level of education, 36–37, 37t; living in cities, 33–34, 34t; number of, 52–53; placement patterns, 70; postwar, 166–67; praise for, 140–41; recruitment of, 43–45; relations with soldiers, 61–68; urbanization of, 33–34, 34t. *See also* voluntary agencies; entries for *specific types of workers*

Baker, Newton, 12, 53, 81, 112
Baldwin, Marian, 61, 73–75
Barbour, Louise, 96–97, 103, 172
Barnard College, 39, 47, 161–62
Barton, Clara, 48
Battle, 158–59
Belgian refugees, 23
Bell Telephone System, 45, 78–79, 81, 96, 166, 203nn54–55
Belmont, Alva, 55
Black, Elizabeth, 158
Blacks. *See* African-Americans
Blair, Emily Newell, 16, 138–39
Blanchfield, Florence, 126
Blatch, Harriet Stanton, 9–10, 110, 126, 151
Bloom, Alma, 9. *See also* Alma Gray
"Blue Circle" nurses, 28
Booth, Mary Josephine, 45, 69–70, 162
Boston Herald, 1–2
Boston marriages, 36
British Red Cross, 149
Brittain, Vera, 48
brother/sister rule, 58, 146, 185n62
Bryn Mawr, 39
Bureau of Investigation, 94
Bureaucracy, 78–79
Business of war, 134–35
Business women, 79

Cammermeyer, Margarethe, 147
Camp followers, 58
Canadian army, 110
Canteen workers, 6, 60–68, 63f, 68–76, 157; compared with army office workers, 85; prewar employment, 38–40; *Red Triangle Girl in France, A*, 2, 155
Canteening Overseas, 2
Canteens; at front, 74–75; "homey," 57; mobile, 59f
Caring labor, 91, 140
Carry On, 167, 171
Catholic French, 32
Catholics, 14, 29, 32
Catt, Carrie Chapman, 5, 19
Cavell, Edith, 196n30

Charity girls, 53
Christian-American women, 30
Christy, Howard Chandler, 27
Circle for Negro War Relief, 28
Citizenship, 5, 137–39, 171–72, 173–174
Civil War, 48, 190n5
Clarke, Carolyn, 129
Clerical workers, 88, 101–03; in Civil War, 190n5; enlistment of, 85–86; in France, 32, 190n12; French, 89; postwar, 166–67; qualifications, 96; security clearance system, 94. *See also* office workers
Clothing, 42, 65, 109, 157, 163; "mannish," 157–58
Cockett, Marguerite, 63–64, 72
Combat situations, 104–36, 198n60; canteens at the front, 74–75; nurses in, 127–36
Commission on Training Camp Activities (CTCA), 23, 43, 53–55, 169
Committee on Women's Defense Work (Council of National Defense) (Woman's Committee), 13–16
Compassionate sympathizers, 104–36
Competence, female, 156
Contagious Diseases Act, 56
Council of Jewish Women, 57
Council of National Defense, 13–16, 112
Crib prostitution, 53
CTCA. *See* Commission on Training Camp Activities
Cutler, Harry, 57

Dancing problem: for canteen workers, 72–73, 76; for nurses, 125
Daniels, Josephus, 15, 169
Danville Soldiers' Home, 170
Daughters of the American Revolution, 107
Davis, Josephine, 48, 93
Dawes, Charles G., 79
Deland, Margaret, 49, 60, 162–63
Delano, Jane A., 48, 106–07, 108f, 110–11, 151–52
Dennis, Faustine, 170–71
Dewson, Molly, 9, 188n40
Dock, Lavinia, 106
Doctors, 19, 112–13, 117, 122–25, 197n38. *See also* physicians
Domestic caring labor, 140
Domestication: of war, 6, 25, 57–59; of women's service, 140
Doughboy French, 89
Doughboy humor, 143, 145
Doughnut girls, 51–76, 143–45, 144f
Doughnuts, 60–61
Drunkenness, 53, 152

Index

Index

Index